DIARY OF THE
9th (Q.R.) LANCERS
DURING THE
SOUTH AFRICAN
CAMPAIGN, 1899 to 1902

Major Capt. Capt. Lieut. &
Capt. Wilberforce, 2nd Capt. Capt. Bde.-Maj., Skeffington Capt. Lieut. Qr.-Mstr. Lall Khan,
Major Forrest, A.D.O. Lieut. Ellison. Colvin. Stanley. K.D.G's Smyth. Lund. Cavendish. Laing. Khitmutgar.
Follett. R.A.M.O. Fiennes. Q. Bays. Wynn.

Capt. Lieut. Lieut. Capt. Lord Colonel General Lieut. Sadleir-
Campbell, Theobald. Brooke. D. Compton. Little, Gordon, Jackson.
A.D.C., 7th Hrs. Comdg. 3rd Cav.
Brigade.
Lieut. J. S. Duckett. Lieut. Lord F. Blackwood. 2nd Lieut. Trower. Lieut. Allhusen. Lieut. Durand.

GROUP OF OFFICERS, 9TH LANCERS
By kind permission of Mr. DEALE, Bloemfontein.

Diary of the 9th (Q.R.) Lancers

DURING THE

South African Campaign,

1899 to 1902

BY

BT.-LIEUT.-COLONEL F. F. COLVIN

AND

CAPTAIN E. R. GORDON

CECIL ROY

4, Bank Buildings, Gloucester Road, South Kensington

1904

Dedicated

TO OUR COMRADES

LIST OF SUBSCRIBERS.

The following Officers have kindly subscribed towards the publication of this Diary in order to present a copy to every N.C.O. and man who served with the Regiment during the War, as a memento of the Campaign :

Maj.-Gen. H. A. BUSHMAN, C.B.

Lieut.-Col. B. GOUGH.

Bt.-Col. M. O. LITTLE.

Bt.-Lieut.-Col. S. W. FOLLETT.

Bt.-Lieut.-Col. F. F. COLVIN.

Maj. Hon. C. H. WILLOUGHBY.

Bt.-Lieut.-Col. F. T. LUND.

Maj. Lord D. COMPTON.

Capt. H. E. FIENNES.

Capt. E. R. GORDON.

Bt.-Maj. D. G. M. CAMPBELL.

Capt. F. H. ALLHUSEN.

Bt.-Maj. Lord C. BENTINCK.

Capt. D. BEALE-BROWNE.

Capt. E. BELL.

Capt. V. R. BROOKE, D.S.O.

Capt. G. H. SKEFFINGTON SMYTH, D.S.O.

Capt. T. M. KINCAID-SMITH.

Capt. H. M. DURAND, D.S.O.

Lieut. Hon. D. M. CARLETON.

Lieut. E. H. ABADIE, D.S.O.

Lieut. Lord F. H. T. BLACKWOOD, D.S.O.

Lieut. F. W. CAVENDISH.

Lieut. J. S. DUCKETT.

Lieut. L. W. SADLEIR-JACKSON.

Lieut. R. V. WYNN.

Lieut. A. S. TROWER.

Lieut. Earl of LEITRIM.

Lieut. R. S. CHADWICK.

Lieut. D. K. L. TOOTH.

2nd Lieut. G. M. NEILSON.

2nd Lieut. R. H. BROCKLEBANK.

2nd Lieut. H. F. WOOD.

2nd Lieut. Earl of ROCKSAVAGE.

2nd Lieut. Hon. R. B. COLE.

INTRODUCTION.

THE following pages have been compiled from our private diaries, assisted by other officers of the Regiment, and only have for their aim a short and simple record of the work done by the Regiment during the war in South Africa. They have been written in diary form as a book of easy reference.

There are no doubt many incidents which have not been recorded. We much regret this, but trust that the Diary, incomplete as it is, may help to recall the stirring times passed by our old comrades during those two and a-half years, and be of some interest to past and present 9th Lancers.

It was hoped to add to this diary a summary of the doings of the "C" Squadron, while detached from the Regiment, but owing to lack of notes and information this has been found impracticable.

Our thanks are due to Capt. J. V. Forrest, R.A.M.C., *The Illustrated London News, With the Flag to Pretoria, The King and Navy and Army*, and Mr. Deale, for their kindness in allowing us to reproduce the photographs.

The accompanying map is compiled from the I. D. Maps No. 1367, by kind permission of the War Office.

We would also testify to the great assistance rendered by Mr. A. J. Hoare in the compilation of the Diary.

The status of the Uitlanders in the Transvaal had come to such a pass owing to their treatment by the Dutch Government that they were forced to bring forward their grievances, the chief ones being :—

(1.) Heavy taxation without representation.

(2.) No voice in the choice or payment of the officials.

(3.) No control over education.

(4.) No power of municipal government.

(5.) Despotic government as regards press and public meetings.

(6.) Disqualified from serving on a jury.

(7.) Annoying legislation as regards the mining interest, such as the dynamite monopoly, etc. The President—Mr. Kruger — would not, however, listen to them, and so they appealed to the British Government. Representations were made to the Dutch Republic by the Government, but without avail, Mr. Kruger finally demanding the withdrawal of the troops from the Natal frontier, etc., and then sending an outrageous ultimatum to the effect that if this was not done within a certain time (by 5 p.m. on October 11th, 1899), his commandos would cross the frontier. We were fortunate in having such an able statesman as Sir Alfred Milner as Governor, who thoroughly understood the Boers and their motives, and who commanded the implicit confidence of all Loyalists in South Africa.

Such demands as Mr. Kruger made of the British Government could only have one result, and matters were brought to a climax by the Boers invading British territory on the Natal side and also capturing an armoured train at Kraaipan, 40 miles south of Mafeking.

LIST OF ILLUSTRATIONS.

CONTENTS.

DIARY OF THE 9TH LANCERS

DURING

THE SOUTH AFRICAN CAMPAIGN,

1899 to 1902.

——◆——

ABOUT 7 in the morning the Acting-Adjutant, Capt. E. R. Gordon, received a telegram from Simla for the C.O., ordering the Regiment to mobilize and prepare for active service in the event of its being required in South Africa. Naturally excitement reigned supreme, and all officers and men on leave and detachment were recalled at once.

1899.
SEPT.
Fri. 8th
Muttra.

Maj. Little returned from Simla and assumed command, Col. Gough being on sick leave in England. The whole day was occupied in the necessary preparations for active service.

Sat. 9th

Received definite orders for service in South Africa.

Mon. 11th

Up to Sunday, the 17th, the work of mobilization was unceasingly carried out, during which time nearly all those away had rejoined.

Sun. 17th

Started entraining the baggage, as it was thought probable that we might leave the following day.

1899.
SEPT.
Mon. 18th

Received the Bombay "Concentration Programme," which arranged for our arrival at Deolali at daybreak on the 23rd, halting at Jhansi, Hoshangabad and Deolali *en route*, and sailing on the 24th. This necessitated leaving Muttra on Wednesday, the 20th, at an early hour. A telegram was received from home saying that all officers in England were to rejoin in Natal, including Col. Gough and 2nd Lieut. P. Brassey, who had just been gazetted, and that the strength of the Regiment as regards officers was to be made up accordingly, and that any extra in the several ranks were to be left behind at the depôt at Muttra.

This resulted in Capt. Stanley, 2nd Lieut. Cobden, and Riding-Master Baxter, together with R.Q.M.S. Gibbs, S.Q.M.S. Hemingway and R.R.S.S.M. Lewis being the unfortunate officers and N.C.O.'s left behind.

Tues. 19th   By evening everything was ready for the departure next morning.

Wed. 20th   The Regiment, consisting of 16 officers * (including the medical officer, Capt. Forrest, R.A.M.C.), 475 rank and file, and 518 horses and chargers, 36 mules and one transport-sergeant with 29 natives (bakery establishment, etc.), paraded at daybreak to entrain.

The first train left about 7.30 a.m., the next following in half-an-hour, these being occupied by the "C" Squadron, men and horses ; "D" Squadron following

* Majors : M. O. Little, S. W. Follett ; Captains : F. T. Lund, H. Fiennes, E. R. Gordon ; Lieutenants : F. H. Allhusen, H. M. Durand, R. H. Abadie, Hon. D. P. Carleton ; Second Lieutenants : S. Theobald, S. H. Cavendish, Lord F. Blackwood, J. S. Duckett, L. Sadleir-Jackson ; Lieutenant and Quartermaster D. Laing ; Captain R. V. Forrest, R.A.M.C.

1899.
SEPT.

three-quarters of an hour later in the next two trains and " A " Squadron entraining three-quarters of an hour after " D " Squadron. It was, of course, a very quiet departure owing to the smallness of the place, and being still the hot season. However, it was described in the local Press as follows : " The 9th Lancers left Muttra this morning amidst the cheers and good wishes of a large and enthusiastic crowd of friends and spectators " ! !

On reaching Agra, where we had to detrain from the narrow gauge and entrain into the broad gauge carriages, we found the I. M. Railway arrangements disgraceful. There were not sufficient carriages for the men nor trucks for the horses, and only one lamp for the trucks. Most of the horses had to be jumped into the trucks in order to save time.   The heat was terribly trying, and what we should have done but for the hospitality of the York and Lancaster Regiment it is hard to say. They had arranged breakfast for the whole Regiment, and un-limited mineral waters throughout the day. The whole day was occupied in detraining and entraining, the last squadron not finishing until after dark. The first train reached Jhansi about 8 p.m. ; the last, not until 5 a.m., the morning of Thursday, the 21st.

Went on again in the afternoon, the first train leaving at 4 p.m., the others at one hour's interval. Watered and fed at Bina, and reached Hoshangabad early on Friday, the 22nd.

Thur. 21st
Jhansi.

Watered and fed and took in cooked rations and forage, then had breakfast, and resumed the journey about 8.30 a.m.

Fri. 22nd
Hoshanga-bad.

Arrived at Deolali about 7.30 a.m. Here we received the detailed instructions for the transports. The Regiment had to be re-arranged in six trains again, so as to negotiate the Ghauts ; but, thanks to the I. M. Railway, everything had got so muddled up that all the rosters had to be altered, and the shunting required to get the right carriages on to the right trains took nearly the whole afternoon. The first train got away at 8.30 p.m., and arrived at Prince's Dock, Bombay, at 5.30 a.m.

The " C " Squadron, under Capt. Lund, which occupied the first two trains, was to embark in the *Wardha.* The arrangements at Bombay were excellent ; the men of each train detrained at once with their arms, etc. ; were told off into messes, marched straight on board, got into fatigue dress, and then came back to the dock and had tea. The saddles were then unloaded and carried to the ship's side by coolies, after which the horses were unboxed and inspected by a veterinary officer and taken over to their ship, those for the upper deck being walked on board and those for below " slung on." After this, saddles, stores, etc., were shipped. The two transports had to be out of dock before 1.30 p.m. on account of the tide. The *Wardha* got off at 10.30 a.m., and the *Nowshera*, with " D " Squadron and regimental head quarter staff, cast off about 12.30 p.m., and by 1 p.m. both ships were in the Bay.

The short notice and the extreme heat rendered the duties entailed by the mobilization, entraining and embarkation of the Regiment excessively severe, and nothing could have been better than the splendid behaviour and example set by all ranks in carrying them so cheer- fully and successfully through.

As the *Nowshera* left the harbour three cheers were given for the " Ladies of Bombay," who had most kindly sent the troops boxes of games and books.

The *Nairung*, with the " A " Squadron on board, leaves to-morrow.

The voyage to Durban was fairly calm until the night of Sunday, October 8th, when we ran into a gale, being then about 400 miles from Durban. The *Nowshera* anchored off the harbour about 4.30 p.m. on Tuesday, October 10th, having gone too far north owing to dense fog, although in reality she was quite close to Durban at 6.30 a.m.

The *Wardha* arrived at Durban on Monday, October 9th, and went on to Cape Town that evening, while the *Nairung* arrived on Tuesday, October 10th, and left again on the morning of Wednesday, October 11th, followed by the *Nowshera* in the afternoon. Orders had been received from England for the Regiment to proceed to Cape Town, but the native establishments and reserve stores and forage had to be landed. In the town there was great excitement, as Kruger had issued an ultimatum to the British Government, " that if the troops were not withdrawn from the frontier by 5 p.m. on Wednesday, October 11th, he would commence opera- tions." A transport with a squadron of the 5th Dragoon Guards arrived at Durban soon after the *Nowshera* got into the harbour.

During the afternoon a heavy gale sprang up, which

the *Wardha* encountered, having left Durban in the morning, and the experiences of those on board cannot be better described than by the account given in a letter of Lieut. Lord F. Blackwood's to his father.

(Copy of a letter from Lord F. Blackwood to his father) :

" S.S. *Wardha,*
" October 12th, 1899.

" I do not really know where to begin this letter, such exciting and horrible things have happened since I last wrote to you. We got to Durban safe and sound and as happy as larks on Monday, October 9th, expecting to disembark, and go up to the front immediately. To our disgust, however, we were told not to land, but to go off at once to the Cape. Accordingly, at 5 p.m. that night, we started off again. Next morning the sea seemed fairly calm, and we were all laughing and joking at the way we were rolling about. You must understand that one troop of horses was in wooden stalls on the upper deck. This was my troop, consisting of 38 horses, together with my own chargers, and 12 mules. All the other troops and their horses were down below between decks. 'Stables' were at 11 a.m., when it had begun to get rather rough. However, we still smiled, but the rolling got worse and worse, and my horses on the upper deck began to fall down, and we smiled no more. Every man was told to hang on to his horse so as to keep its chest away from the front board when the animal was thrown forward by the roll. At last the rolling became terrific and the seas enormous. All my troop were drenched over and over again. One man, a corporal, got washed off his feet, and was thrown with great violence four times up and down the deck. The extraordinary thing was that he did not break anything. At last the wooden framework of the stabling began to crack, and I expected every minute to see the whole thing collapse and all my men killed. I then went to Lund (our squadron leader), and told him that I thought that it was getting dangerous for my men to stay on any longer, and he gave the order for No. 1 troop horses to be abandoned. Five minutes after that one entire side of the woodwork gave way. Two of my chargers and four others were at once washed overboard. Now came the most horrible scene I have ever witnessed. The deck was covered with one struggling mass of horses and mules, mixed up with the broken woodwork of the stables, the whole being hurled first to one side of the deck and then the other. All were horribly wounded, most with broken legs and some with eyes torn out. My first charger (the one you gave me, and the nicest horse I am ever likely to have) was amongst them, but I managed to get a shot at her with my revolver from a hatchway, and so I am glad to say that none of my three suffered the torments of Hell like the others. To make a long story short, out of 50 horses and mules on my deck, only three were saved—two horses, whose stalls remained intact, and one mule, which had a most mira- culous escape, having been washed down the hatchway into the hold below, and being absolutely unhurt. Things were hardly better between decks. On one deck a huge watertank broke loose and went hurtling about, killing two horses. On this account this deck had to be abandoned by the men. It was a horrible thing having to jump this way and that to avoid the horses that kept hurtling up and down, kicking and screaming. The arms-rack gave way, and I was sent to try and collect the carbines. We had managed to collect most of them when an enormous roll came and down they all went, rushing from one side to the other. Luckily we were all able to jump on tables, except one man, who fell among the wreckage, cutting his head open and laying him out. All the men down below remained with the horses until 6 p.m., when they were ordered up and lay huddled in the passages and in the engine-room, shivering and chattering all night with the cold. All my men had been long since drenched to the skin, and not a man got a bite of food except what we could give them in the shape of a few biscuits. I wish you could have seen the way the men behaved. It was really magnificent. They never thought of letting go their horses until they were absolutely ordered to, although they did not know when the wooden frame might not give way. All this time, as the captain told us, the ship was not under control and would not steer. He thought at the time that it was because they had taken out a lot of cargo at Durban and so lightened her. The next morning, however, when the sea went down, and she still would not answer her helm, he had the rudder examined and found it broken and useless. It was not very pleasant when the dear old skipper came down and informed us that we were rudderless, and that if an easterly gale sprang up we should go ashore. I did my best, but I did not eat much breakfast that morning. However, things turned out better than we expected, and we are now going five knots an hour with a jury rudder, and are getting in the track of ships again, when we hope to get towed in somewhere. We are nearing Durban again. Last night we saw a ship and sent up five rockets, but the brute took no notice. If we go ashore that ship will have a lot to answer for. Night is now coming on and if we get through that we shall be all right. We are about six miles from land, and so the danger is over unless the jury rudder breaks and we are washed ashore. It is quite impossible to get moody about it with all the men in such good spirits. The day of the 11th was not pleasant, as we had to hoist all the dead horses up and shove them overboard. A good many were still alive and out of 150 horses we have lost 92 horses and mules. The Captain, who has been over 30 years at sea, says he never saw such huge waves. I have an extract from his log which may interest you. I cannot write more, but all I can say is that Tuesday, October 10th, 1899, will never be forgotten by the " C " Squadron, 9th Lancers, not if we live to be Methuselahs ! "

(Copy of the Official Log).

Transport No. 16, S.S. *Wardha.*

10 a.m. Working up into a S.W. gale, put vessel on starboard tack to edge away from the land.

12 noon. Gale and sea increasing rapidly. Vessel

lying in the trough of the sea and quite unmanage-able.

About 1 p.m. unbent starboard cable and paid out 120 fathoms to try and bring the vessel up to the sea, but with little or no effect.   Unbent port cable and paid out 90 fathoms.   Engines working ahead and helm hard-a-port.   Gale rapidly increasing with tremendous seas, vessel still lying helplessly in the trough of the sea.

About 2.30 p.m. shipped a heavy sea over the after deck, washing several officers' chargers, troop horses and mules out of their stalls, several horses being swept overboard.

About 3 p.m. blowing a hurricane, with fearful seas, vessel still lying helplessly in the trough of the sea and rolling very violently.   The whole of the stalls on the port side of the main deck collapsed, every animal being killed or rolled overboard, with the exception of one mule, which was pitched down No. 3 hold and two others which survived.   The same sea carried away the mail boat out of the davits, smashed the rails and gangways and one bridge ladder, washed two hen coops overboard, smashed ventilators on after deck and damaged the water tanks for the horses on that deck.

About the same time the arms-rack in No. 1 'tween decks also collapsed, the whole of the carbines rolling the 'tween decks.

A cask of rum for the use of the troops broke adrift and was smashed.

Besides we anticipate a large amount of damage to the other stores for the use of the troops.

A large number of horses were pitched clean out of their stalls through the front and side pieces giving way, both on the upper deck and 'tween decks, and were either killed clean outright or died from their wounds subsequently.

All the officers and men of the 9th Lancers stood by their horses till the stables gave way, and there was absolute risk of loss of life ; even then the horses were attended to as much as possible.

From 6 p.m. the gale gradually abated.

0.30 a.m. of 11th inst. Commenced heaving in starboard cable.

After it was hove in we tried for two hours to get in the port cable, but found it impossible, and eventually it had to be slipped.

In trying to heave it in it ran out to 120 fathom shackle, the whole of which had to be shipped.

At 6 a.m. tried to get the vessel on her course, but finding she would not steer, examined the rudder, and found the rudder head broken inside the rudder trunk.

Rove off wire rudder ropes and made for Port Natal, steering by the winches.

We considered it more advisable with a broken rudder to make for Port Natal, as, if we were caught in a S.E. gale on the S. coast, we would be on a lee shore and quite helpless.

The morning after the gale (11th) it was found that no less than 92 horses and mules had either been killed or washed overboard during the gale.

1899.
OCTOBER.

The loss included :—

Officers' chargers	12
Troop horses	71
Bullocks	1
Mules	9

(Signed) E. Y. WATSON.   (Signed) J. ANDERSON.
Mate.   Master.

Sat. 14th   The *Nairung* arrived at Cape Town on Saturday, October 14th, and the work of disembarking and entraining at the quay for De Aar began at once.

[Reproduced by permission of The Amalgamated Press, Limited
(London), from *With the Flag to Pretoria.*]

Sun. 15th   The *Nowshera* arrived at 6 a.m. on Sunday morning, when "D" Squadron disembarked and followed the

CAMP—ORANGE RIVER (RIGHT).

CAMP—ORANGE RIVER (CENTRE).

1899.   " A " Squadron, each squadron going up in two trains.
Col. Gough and Capts. Hon. C. H. Willoughby, Lord D.
Compton and Lieuts. E. Bell and V. Brooke were awaiting the arrival of the Regiment at Cape Town.   Capt.
Campbell and Lieut. Stirling had been sent to Stellenbosch in order to get together the regimental transport
and take it up country, while Lord D. Compton remained

CAMP—ORANGE RIVER (LEFT).

at Cape Town as regimental disembarkation officer.
Here Lieut. E. F. Bell resumed his duties as adjutant.
The mishap to the " C " Squadron was most unfortunate,
as the Regiment would otherwise have made the voyage
with the loss of only one horse per ship.

" A " Squadron went straight on to Orange River
Station, and the " D " Squadron, after detraining at De
Aar and pitching camp on Tuesday morning, October

17th, received orders to entrain for Orange River Station, which was reached that night at 7 p.m.

Detrained and pitched camp south of the river on the west side of the railway. After getting the camp squared up, everyone who was free indulged in a bathe in the river, which was rather muddy, but cool and refreshing to those who had been travelling since Sunday.

Patrols were sent out at daybreak, the remainder standing to arms until their return. Expect to remain here some little time, as it is absolutely necessary for us to hold the railway bridge until more troops come up. At 11.45 a.m. received orders for one troop to proceed to Hopetown to prevent a reported party of Boers crossing the river to the south. Capt. Gordon, with Lieut. Carleton's troop, went off at once, and returned late in the afternoon having seen no signs of the enemy. Hopetown was some 10 miles down the river, and west of camp, and the bridge there had been already destroyed by our engineers. Part of the " C " Squadron turned up to-day.

The force here at present consists of

> 9th Lancers.
> 1st Batt. Northumberland Fusiliers.
> ½ Batt. Munster Fusiliers.
> ½ Batt. Loyal North Lancashire.
> 4 Cos. Mounted Infantry.

List of officers present :

> Lieut.-Col. B. Gough.
> Maj. Little.

1899.
OCTOBER.
Wed. 18th
*Orange
River
Station.*

Thur. 19th

Maj. Follett, commanding " A " Squadron.

Capt. Hon. C. Willoughby, commanding " D " Squadron.

Capt. Lund, commanding " C " Squadron.

Capt. Lord D. Compton, " A " Squadron.

Capt. Fiennes, " C " Squadron.

Capt. Ellison, " D " Squadron.

Capt. Gordon, " D " Squadron.

Capt. Campbell, " A " Squadron.

Lieut. Bell (adjutant).

Lieut. Allhusen, Maxim gun.

Lieut. Brooke, " C " Squadron.

Lieut. Skeffington Smyth, " D " Squadron.

Lieut. Stirling, " C " Squadron.

Lieut. Durand, " A " Squadron.

Lieut. Abadie, " A " Squadron.

Lieut. Hon. D. Carleton, " D " Squadron.

Lieut. Theobald, " D " Squadron.

2nd Lieut. Cavendish, " A " Squadron.

2nd Lieut. Lord F. Blackwood, " C " Squadron.

2nd Lieut. Duckett, " C " Squadron.

2nd Lieut. Sadleir-Jackson, " D " Squadron.

Lieut. & Q.M. D. Laing.

. *Senior N.C.O.'s.*

Regt. S.M. W. Grant.

	S.S.M.'s.	*S.Q.M.S.'s.*
" A " Squadron ..	A. Bateman.	D. Ankers.
" C " Squadron ..	R. Gidden.	L. Bell.

"D" Squadron .. A. Pollock. W. Letts. 1899.
also S.S.M.'s C. Wardell, J. Praeger (O.R.S.), S.I.F. OCTOBER.
A. Beck, F.Q.M.S. H. Whittaker.

Sergeants.

C. Smith, T. Connor, T. Shute, F. Spittle, G.
Knight, W. Odell, S. Coope, T. Smith, R. Ford,
W. Nice, G. Drury, F. Andrews, H. Grey, J.
Broad, J. Gratton, M. Flannery, J. Johnson,
E. Ketley, G. Casebow, R. Mason, J. Gentry,
G. Grupie, F. Draper, J. Mercer, T. Langford,
C. Atkins, W. Anderson, T. Dandy, F. Beckett,
C. Ambrose, W. Herrick.

Had a quiet day. Got news yesterday of a big fight at Sat. 21st
Glencoe, which was the opening battle of the war, between
Gen. Penn Symons and Gen. Lucas Meyer, on Talana Hill.
Everyone felt rather disappointed at our enforced in-
activity while so much was going on in Natal. How-
ever, our horses needed a rest and required to be got fit.
Capt. Fiennes arrived in camp with remounts to com-
plete the loss suffered by the gale.

Capt. Gordon was sent out to make a sketch of camp Sun. 22nd
and surrounding positions as far as Signal Hill, four miles
to the east, where we have a daily officer's picquet.
Capt. Campbell and one sergeant were sent out to find
and report upon the ford supposed to be near Signal
Hill. In their endeavours to locate the ford both Capt.
Campbell and Sergt. Westman got into deep and heavy
water and were nearly drowned.

1899.
OCTOBER.
Mon. 23rd
Received the details of the fight at Elandslaagte, which took place on Saturday, October 21st, under Gen. French, in which Col. Scott Chisholme, commanding the Imperial Light Horse (late Major in the 9th Lancers), fell at the head of his regiment.

Tues. 24th
Usual squadron parades. Heard that Lieut. Lord Charles Bentinck had been slightly wounded at Mafeking, where he is serving with the Defence Force, having gone out there in July as a special service officer.

2nd Lieut. Brassey joined the Regiment from England.

Wed. 25th
The Royal Engineers are flooring the railway bridge, so that wheeled transport can utilise it. Lieut. Brooke, who was in charge of the picquet at Signal Hill, had a chase after a couple of Boers, who were supposed to have come from a commando of 800 Boers reported to be a few miles off on the Free State side of the river.

Thur. 26th
Soon after turning out at 4.30 a.m. it began to rain, and continued off and on all day. Lieut. Gordon Stirling caught some Cape boys at the farm near the picquet, who were brought into camp and questioned, and corroborated the rumour that there is a commando of some 700 Boers on the opposite side of the river from Zout Pans Drift.

Fri. 27th
A battery and a half arrived here from home.

Sat. 28th
During the earlier part of the night we were washed out of camp by a terrific thunderstorm, and this was no sooner over than we were turned out for a false alarm,

raised by an infantry picquet at the station camp, and
had to " stand to " for nearly three hours. The alarm
turned out to have been caused by an ostrich which
refused to answer the challenge !

The afternoon was spent in cleaning up and drying
one's kit, which had been soaked through and through.
Fortunately, the soil was sandy, and by evening stables
one would scarcely have known there had been a storm
at all.

Col. the Hon. G. Gough arrived to-day, and took over
the command of the troops.

One troop under Capt. Gordon and Lieut. Carleton
started at 4.30 a.m. on a reconnaissance over the river
in a westerly direction until the main road from Hopetown to Belmont was struck, whence to proceed to
Fincham's Farm and Witteputs Station, about 7½ miles
from Belmont, with the object of reporting on the
suitability of the road for wheeled transport, together
with a road sketch. This was a long round of from
25 to 30 miles, the party returning to camp about
4.30 p.m.

The " A " Squadron and some M. I. were sent out in
a S.E. direction on a three days' reconnaissance.
Dalton's Pont was reached the first day and Petrusville
on the second, and on the third day a return to Orange
River Station, viâ Leeuwfontein, was made, about 100
miles being covered in the three days.

Capt. Gordon was sent out at 3.45 a.m. with a
troop of 18 men to Suffolk Farm, east of Wigtown
Siding, where a Boer patrol were supposed to have

1899.   bivouacked the night before. This party, however,
Nov.   saw no signs of the enemy, and returned to camp at
8.30 a.m.

Wed. 8th   Just before lunch orders came to say we were to be
ready by 3 p.m. to take part in a three days' reconnaissance towards Belmont, the force to be composed of
" C " and " D " Squadrons, 9th Lancers ; 100 M. I.,
under Maj. Milton, and three guns, together with our
Maxim. We crossed the river so as to be ready to start
the following morning.

Thur. 9th Started at 5 a.m. and reached Fincham's Farm at
9 a.m., where we watered and fed, and went on at 11.30
a.m. to Belmont, getting there about 3 p.m. Returned
to bivouac at Fincham's Farm, having seen nothing.
Lord D. Compton took a patrol of three men up the railway to Fincham's Farm, and having got information
and a guide, proceeded out to the open country eastwards
towards Luipers Kop. After a short halt there he was
fired at and pursued back to Fincham's Farm by 15 Boers
without being able to ascertain the position of the Boer
laager.

Fri. 10th Started at 5 a.m., " D " Squadron in advance, moving
in an easterly direction. After proceeding some miles,
the direction was changed northwards, when " C "
Squadron went on in advance, and some two miles
further on Boers were reported about 500 strong to our
front on a horse-shoe shaped range of hills, of which they
were holding the eastern half or Luipers Kop. Having
reached the south-west corner a man galloped in
from the east, saying that Lieut. Brooke, who

was out sketching, had been fired on, and his horse shot under him. Maj. Little ordered two troops of the " D " Squadron to go to his assistance, and accompanied them himself, but returned soon afterwards for reinforcements. Capt. Gordon, with the remaining two troops of the squadron, reinforced Capt. Willoughby, and just before joining him came under shell fire.

The remainder of the column then came up in support, and " D " Squadron advanced in column of half squadrons in extended order until within about 1,200 yards of the position, when the squadron formed line and dismounted, and at once came under heavy rifle fire from Luipers Kop. " C " Squadron were in echelon of troops on the left rear. The object of the reconnaissance had now been accomplished as the Boer position was plainly revealed, but the M. I. having pushed home their feint more than was intended, were now heavily engaged on the right flank. The Regiment received orders to cover the retirement of the M. I., who had several casualties. On the ambulance going up to the M. I. all firing ceased on both sides ; the Boers could be seen standing up all along the ridge while the medical officers were attending to and collecting the casualties, and curiously enough the Boers allowed the retirement to be carried out without firing another shot.

Col. Keith Falconer and Lieut. Wood, both of the Northumberland Fusiliers, were killed and mortally wounded respectively, and two other subalterns and two men were wounded.

S.-Sergt.-Maj. Gidden was the only man we had touched, having his heel bruised by a bullet ; several horses were killed, wounded and died of exhaustion. Returned to Fincham's Farm at 4.30 p.m., having covered about 25 miles besides the fighting. This was the first time the Regiment had been under fire.

Lieut. Brooke had a narrow escape while sketching, his horse being killed and a bullet put through his helmet. He managed to escape by running for a wire fence which delayed the Boers, and by the timely appearance of a patrol under Sergt. Atkins, who mounted him on his horse, and got him within sight of the reinforcements.

Lieut. Durand's report on his reconnaissance to Honeynest Kloof :—

At Fincham's Farm.

" On the evening of November 9th Col. Gough sent for me and said he wanted me to go up the line from Belmont Station next day as far as I could towards Honeynest Kloof, and report on the damage done to the line ; he offered to let me take what men I chose. So next morning at daybreak I started, taking Pte. Salter with me. We asked the guide for details of the country near the line, but the only thing he was sure about was that we should never come back ; so much cheered we went off.

" We made a *détour* to the west from the farm, as the line runs close to Belmont position and in full view from it, the Boers being reported to be on Belmont heights, and struck the line again some three miles north of Belmont Station, where the line goes over a neck.   Here there was a ganger's hut and we had some food ; while breakfasting we heard the boom of the first gun, and shortly after several more.   I fancy every Boer within miles heard them too, and dashed off to see what was going on, for Salter and I rode up the line along the road, over the big open plain of Graspan, through the centre of what was afterwards the position of Enslin, and down the slope to Honeynest Kloof Station without seeing the sign of a Dutchman, and I firmly believe without a Dutchman seeing us.

" The station at Honeynest Kloof was wrecked and the telegraph machine destroyed, much of the line had been torn up, some culverts blown up, and numbers of telegraph poles broken down.   I climbed up the big signal pole and saw all over the Modder River plain for miles, but saw no living thing.   We made our way home as quickly as we could ;   soon after reaching Enslin we branched off to the west, giving Belmont a wide berth. We reached Fincham's to find all dark and the column returned to Orange River, and heard the story of the fight.   We slept at Fincham's, as our horses were done, and made tracks before daylight and any inquisitive Dutchmen made their appearance.

" Belmont Station to Honeynest Kloof is, I fancy, about 14 miles."

On returning to Fincham's Farm horses were watered

and fed, and we were ordered to return to Orange
River Station at 6 p.m. It was a very weary ride
after such a long day, and the last squadron did not
get in until 12.30 midnight, making the march about
40 miles.

Sat. 11th   Horse inspection. Keith Falconer and Wood were
buried in the afternoon, the latter having died during
the march back to camp.

Sun. 12th   Lord Methuen arrived this afternoon to take over command of the Division.

Mon. 13th   Lord Methuen inspected the Regiment.

Wed. 15th   Rimington's Guides arrived to-day.

Fri. 17th   Sorting and packing kits, as a forward move is expected
at any time. A battery and two battalions of Guards
and divisional details have arrived since the beginning of
the week.

Sun. 19th   One of the patrols was fired on this morning.

Mon. 20th   Soon after dinner orders came that we were to strike
camp and be ready to march at midnight. Everything
was ready by about 10 p.m. when the time of march was
changed to 3.30 a.m.

Tues. 21st   The Regiment moved off at the head of the Division,
and after reaching Fincham's Farm was ordered to proceed eastwards and reconnoitre towards Kaffir Kop,
which we found occupied in considerable force. We
then fell back on Thomas' Farm, near Belmont Station,
where we came under sharp fire from Krupp and Mausers.
We retired out of range, and Colonel Verner, I.O., personally reconnoitred the Belmont position. We returned
to bivouac at 3 p.m. after a long day. Expect to move

forward to-morrow evening and assault the position the
following morning.

Orders came for the Division to concentrate at 4 p.m.
and march as far as Belmont, preparatory to an attack
on the position.

"D" Squadron and Rimington's Guides, all under

WATERING AFTER FINDING BELMONT EVACUATED.

Maj. Rimington, were left at Witteputs for the night,
and were to work in an easterly direction, and swing
round to the south-east of the enemy's position, endeavouring to get at their laager, which was reported to be
near Ramdam.

The main body, composed of the Guards' brigade, was
on the right, supported by the 18th Batt. and Naval
Brigade ; 9th Brigade on the left, along the railway,

and the " A " and " C " Squadrons, 9th Lancers, with
two companies of M. I., to the west of railway to threaten
the Boer retreat and cut them off if possible.

The advance commenced at 3 a.m., the main body
making a frontal attack on the position. Maj. Rimington's party got round to the Boers' left rear, and from
there saw the heights carried by the Guards, and the
Boers retreating by the neck between the main position
and Luipers Kop. Rimington then moved on towards
Ramdam to try and locate the main laager, and after
going some five or six miles he halted to water the
horses ; being unable to reach Ramdam he rejoined
head-quarters at 5 p.m.

Col. Gough's force, which consisted of the " A " and
" C " Squadrons of 9th Lancers under Maj. Little, and
some M. I. under Maj. Milton, moved out at 4 a.m.
This force moved in a north-easterly direction, past
Thomas' Farm, and on to the railway, which was
crossed.

They advanced at a good hand gallop in an easterly
direction, with the object of cutting off some Boers
who, even at that early hour, it being then only a short
time after daybreak, were beginning to quit. Soon,
however, bullets began to drop among them from front
and flanks, and almost immediately afterwards a heavy
fire commenced from a kopje to their right front. Col.
Gough headed towards the kopje, thinking no doubt that
he would be able to seize the hill which was in the Boer
line of retreat. Whatever Boers were in retreat, those
on this hill most certainly were not, and the heavy fire

they poured in soon showed they were too strong to be turned out by the few troops at his disposal. He therefore wheeled the head of the column away to the right and took up a position behind a small kopje, from which he could watch the Boer movements and seize any opportunity of making an attack.

They had been informed that the Boer laager was at Ramdam, and that that place was about 10 miles east of Belmont. As there were no maps available for troops, they were in ignorance that that place was really nearly north and not east of Belmont. Information being brought that the Boers were all retiring, Col. Gough pushed forward due east, some M. I. being somewhat ahead to their left front. The Boers, however, were retiring in good order, and seeing by how few they were being followed, they quickly assumed the offensive ; so the retirement of the whole force being necessary, Col. Gough withdrew to Belmont.

Although both at Belmont and at Enslin the Boers were forced to retire, they did so in large bodies, and it would have required at least a brigade of cavalry with horse artillery to have turned their retreat into a rout.

The casualties were heavy, four officers and 71 men killed or died of wounds, 21 officers and 199 men wounded, the Grenadiers bearing the brunt.

The Regiment had the following casualties : Lance-Corp. P. Featherstone, " A " ; Pte. R. Morgan, " C " ; Pte. G. Lockett, " C " ; Pte. — Lazenby, " C."

The Boer loss was estimated at 100, besides 40 prisoners, wagons, ammunition and cattle.

Advanced towards Graspan, about seven miles north of Belmont, the Regiment being sent on to reconnoitre the position that the Boers were reported to have taken up. Having ascertained that the report was correct, the Regiment returned to camp at Swinkpan just before dark.

Here both men and horses suffered considerably from want of water, there being only one small filthy pan for all purposes.

Started at 4 a.m., " A " and " C " Squadrons, with Rimington's Guides and two companies M. I., going round enemy's left flank, while the " D " Squadron, with one company M. I. and one company N. S. Wales Lancers, went round the right flank. This party was under Maj. Milton, M.I.

The artillery and naval guns began shelling the position at an early hour, the effect of their shells being plainly visible to Maj. Milton's party, which had worked well round to the enemy's right rear.

Maj. Milton tried to effect a junction with the other squadrons, which were now seen coming round the northeast side, being too weak to act independently with any effect.   This move was, however, frustrated by about 500 Boers, together with two guns, who, evidently grasping the intention, galloped down to prevent it, and at the same time a similar force galloped out against Maj. Milton, who was compelled to retire in order to save being cut off.

With some difficulty he was able to withdraw.   The retirement was greatly facilitated by a party of N.S.W. Lancers, who got amongst some small kopjes and

checked the advance by shooting some half-dozen
Boers.

The " A " and " C " Squadrons moved out under
Maj. Little, and after covering the advance and reconnoitring the position, concentrated and worked round to
the enemy's left rear.   Col. Gough now arrived and took
over command.   We were now in a splendid position to
intercept the Boer retreat to Ramdam or Modder River.
Unfortunately the weakness of our numbers made the
excellence of our position of small avail.   All day long
our small force kept moving about in rear of the position,
movement being necessary, as the enemy kept a gun
playing on us the whole time, and we had no gun with
which to reply, and there was no cover from the Boer
fire.   In this way our casualties were very few, but it
tired out the horses, who had been on the go from before
daybreak.   About 3 o'clock the Boers began to leave
the position by the road to Modder River, but there was
no confusion about the movement at all, the whole force
retiring in large bodies, far too large for us to make any
impression upon.   The country between where we were
and the road along which the Boers were retiring was
practically level, but was intersected in all directions by
barbed wire fences.   On seeing the retirement Col. Gough
opened fire with the Maxim, and then ordered the two
squadrons to advance at the gallop in succession of
troops to try and cut off the retreat.   We were soon
checked by the wire and Boer fire, and it became evident
that a further advance could produce no good results,
and the horses were all dead beat.   Moreover, a force of

Boers with a gun had appeared on the left rear. There was nothing for it but to retire, which Col. Gough reluctantly did towards camp.

Here, again, the want of sufficient cavalry deprived Lord Methuen of the extra advantage which would have been gained by turning his victory into a rout.

The Naval Brigade made a very dashing but costly assault against their part of the position, losing four officers and nine men killed and two officers and 72 men wounded.

Our casualties were :—

Killed—Pte. W. Wilkins (" D ").

Wounded—Sergt. G. Grupie (" A "), Pte. J. Hobbs (" A "), Pte. T. Smith (" C "), Pte. A. James (" C ").

Missing—Corpl. S. S. Marriott (" A "), Pte. Pierce (" C ").

The following incident, which took place at Enslin, can best be described in Capt. Campbell's own words : " Soon after we had got round the flank of the Boer position it was reported that a force of Boers was coming from the direction of Ramdam, so Compton and I got permission to go a short way and see if we could see anything. We rode out about a mile, and were looking about us, when we saw a man riding towards us more or less from the direction in which we had come. We watched the man carefully for a time, and as he continued to ride towards us at a walk, I said, ' He must have a message,' and rode forward to meet him. As I approached he raised his hat to me and I waved my hand to show it was all right. When I got to within a hundred yards I saw him cock his leg over his pony's neck and turn the pony broadside on, and almost in the same movement covered me with his rifle over the saddle.   I turned my horse and galloped in a slanting direction to give a more difficult shot.   He fired, and the bullet blew out my horse's fore-head, and turned him over a complete somersault like a shot rabbit.   Getting up, I ran towards Compton, who was galloping towards me at a great risk to himself, as we were both only armed with revolvers, and so at the mercy of the man with the rifle.   I mounted behind Compton, but as his horse was very nervous, showed a strong desire to jump barbed wire fences, and each of us thought the other had the stirrups, the ride was far from enjoyable, and I soon got Compton to set me down whilst he fetched a patrol, accompanied by whom I returned and recovered my belongings ; but my saddle was smashed to atoms by the force of my fall.   Whether my friend mistook me for a Boer or not I do not know ; in any case, the way he dismounted and covered me was a very smart piece of work, and had it not been for Compton I should have been in a bad way.   The Boer only fired two shots ; one killed my horse stone dead, and the other went through my revolver case."

Lieut. Gordon Stirling, who went out with one of the early morning patrols, was fired on from a farm where only some women were seen, who treacherously invited him to come in and have some coffee.   The bullet broke the bone of his left fore-arm and his horse was also badly wounded, as also were the other horses of the patrol. Corpl. Green sent back information, and then sat with him for some time under fire and eventually brought him in on his own horse, holding him on while he rode Lieut. Stirling's. The Boers moved their laager and trekked towards Jacobsdal and Modder River.

The " D " Squadron left Enslin, marching to within about seven miles of Modder River, along the west side of the railway over the range of kopjes through Naauw-poort. From this elevated position a huge cloud of dust could be seen, indicating a Boer trek from the west towards Modder River, and a considerable force appeared to be holding Modder River.

The " A " and " C " Squadrons reconnoitred down the line in front of the Division, which bivouacked near Klok-fontein, some five or six miles short of Modder River railway bridge.

Maj. Little took over the command of the Regiment.

The Division marched from near Klokfontein at 4 a.m. to effect the crossing of the Modder River. The three squadrons of the Regiment covered the advance, making for the railway bridge. The first shot was fired at our patrols at 5.15 a.m. ; and while the position was being reconnoitred, the M. I. had been sent to the right front, and were now endeavouring to clear a farm-house that was held. The Regiment and two guns were sent to their assistance, under cover of which the place was taken and occupied by the M. I.

The Boers then turned a Nordenfeldt and big gun on to us, which necessitated our moving back out of range, there being no cover available.

We afterwards moved in towards the centre, where a

terrific artillery and long-range rifle fire was going on
against the village and trenches on the banks of the
river.

Again a move to the eastwards was made, but it was
impossible to do anything on this flank, which was
strongly watched ; but although we were powerless, the
fact of our being there prevented the Boers making a
flank attack on our fighting line or supports.

It was terribly hot all day, especially while halted out
in the open, and everyone was getting very drowsy when
we were rudely awakened by a shell from the Jacobsdal
ridge, pitched clean into the middle of " D " Squadron.
This was quickly followed by several others before we
got out of range, but fortunately with little loss, though
one poor fellow [Pte. E. Lloyd (" A ")] had his leg badly
shattered, necessitating amputation. The firing was
kept up with scarcely a check, but the infantry could
make little headway across the absolutely flat 1,000 yards
that lay on the south side of the river.

Once more the Regiment was sent eastwards, and then
had to cover the M. I. on withdrawing from the exposed
farm that they had held.

It was now about 5 p.m., and firing began to slacken
down, with the exception of that of the 62nd Battery,
which had made a splendid forced march, and had only
shortly before arrived on the field.   This battery pounded
away until after dark.

During this slackening in the firing, an attempt at
watering the unfortunate horses was made. This was
successfully done by the first parties, but the Boers saw

what was up and shelled the last lot, fortunately without doing any harm.

We now supported two guns which were turned on to a farm that had been bothering us all day, and soon cleared it of its occupants. Darkness was coming on, so we were ordered to bivouac where we were, and throw out outposts. It had been a very hot day, and owing to the lack of cover, neither food nor water had been able to reach the men. The infantry, and particularly the Highlanders, suffered terribly from lying in the sun all day.

The casualties were pretty heavy, amongst them being Lord Methuen himself, shot through thigh. Fortunately the Regiment got off with the one case already mentioned. Capt. F. F. Colvin arrived at camp early in the morning and was able to take part in the battle.

Wed. 29th
*Modder
River.*
The river and village were reconnoitred at daybreak, and discovered to be evacuated, the Boers having hastily made off, leaving their guns about 9 p.m. the night before, evidently fearing a bayonet charge after the shelling which continued till after dark. We heard subsequently that they returned about midnight and removed their guns. The " A " and " C " Squadrons crossed the river about 7 a.m. and the " D " Squadron remained on outposts on the south side of the river to guard against an attack from the direction of Jacobsdal. The railway bridge was broken down, and every house and shanty was riddled by shell and rifle fire. " A " and " C " Squadrons moved to the north-east, and occupied a farm for the day, leaving a guard over the Boer hospital,

where there were a good many Boer wounded and an old 1899.
Nov.
Boer doctor.

The " A " Squadron went out on reconnaissance at Thur. 30th
daybreak, and reported the kopjes at Maagersfontein
occupied by the enemy. DEC.

Spytfontein and Jacobsdal were both reported strongly Fri. 1st

FITTING PACK SADDLES ON MULES.
[Reproduced by permission of the *Illustrated London News.*]

held.   Cronje and Delarey were the chief commanders of
the Boer forces in this vicinity.

Shifted camp to the west of the railway and made our Sat. 2nd
headquarters at the wreck of Wilson's Hotel.

One squadron of the 12th Lancers, under Maj. Ralli, Sun. 3rd
came in about 10 p.m.   A heavy sand and thunderstorm
all day.

3*

1899.
DEC.
Tues. 5th
Gen. Babington and staff, consisting of Capt. Briggs, K.D.G.'s, Brig.-Maj. and Capt. Wormald, 7th Hussars, A.D.C., arrived and inspected the horses of the Regiment, and saw the ones for casting, numbering 38. Capt. Egerton Green's squadron, 12th Lancers, came in.

Wed. 6th
The remainder of the 12th Lancers came in under Col. Lord Airlie, also the Black Watch.

Thur. 7th
The Boers under Prinsloo, consisting of 1,000 men and three guns under Albrecht, attacked Enslin from Jacobsdal and destroyed the telegraph and part of the railway. Two companies of Northamptons defended the place, and the 12th Lancers and 62nd Battery and the Northumberland Fusiliers left Modder River at 6 a.m. to assist in repelling the attack. We got orders to turn out if required, but the relieving force got there in time to save the Northamptons and drove the Boers off.

Bad dust storms all day and heavy rain and thunder all night.

Fri. 8th
The 12th Lancers returned at 3.30 p.m.

Sat. 9th
We paraded at 2.30 a.m. and formed up on the north side of the railway station with the M. I., Rimington's Guides, one battery R. H. A., one battery R. F. A., and the 4.7 naval gun " Joe," to make a reconnaissance in force of the position at Maagersfontein. The naval gun opened fire at daybreak. We covered the advance with the " C " and " D " Squadrons, the " A " Squadron moving on the east of the railway. Lieut. Durand while patrolling on the right had rather a curious experience. He had been told to look out for some of Rimington's Guides, who were also in front, and when returning over

the scrubby plain he saw a party of some 50 Boers coming
on behind.   As these, however, stopped about 300 yards
off, one man only cantering on to within a few yards,
Lieut. Durand with Sergt. Mercer and another man
waited, while his patrol went on, when the following con-
versation took place.

Boer : Who are you ?

Durand : Who are you ?

Boer :   I am a Burgher—who are you ?

Durand : You had better clear out.

Boer : Are you the enemy ?

On this the Boer turned round and galloped to his
party, and Durand, who was dismounted, mounted at
once and galloped back, and by the time the Boer got
back to his own people Durand had retired to a safe
distance, when the Boers opened fire on him.

A howitzer battery and balloon section arrived to-day.

We shelled away at the kopjes, but no fire was returned, and came back to camp at 8.30 a.m.   A party of
300 Boers were seen to trek eastwards.

Lieut. Tristram, 12th Lancers, who was out on patrol
towards Jacobsdal, was cut off and badly wounded in
two places while trying to save one of his patrol.

Church parade at 9.30 a.m.   Sun. 10th

At 3 p.m. a column, consisting of 9th Lancers, " G "
Battery R. H. A., 1st Brigade Division F. A., Highland
Brigade, Yorks Light Infantry, howitzer battery, balloon
section, telegraph section and the M. I. moved out north
and north-east from the railway station.   The Regiment
covered the advance with two squadrons, the third being

in support. The advanced parties came under fire
across the whole front from the railway to the river. The
guns came into action and commenced shelling the
Maagersfontein position, while the Regiment was sent
to take up a position on the right front near Brown's
Drift on the Modder River. The Boers stopped our
advance there by fire from their trenches, and at 7 p.m.
the force was retired to bivouac about one and a half
miles back. The Boers did not reply to our guns and
kept very tight to their trenches.

Mon. 11th   As we were turning out about 3.45 a.m. after a wet
night, a terrific fusillade broke out from the position,
which we knew must be the Highland Brigade, under
Gen. Wauchope, storming the position. The morning
was very dark, and as we moved off we were ordered up
to the right flank to force our way through the scrubby
country along the right bank of the river to Brown's
Drift, which was strongly held, and we were not able to
get beyond Moss Drift, " C " Squadron coming under
heavy rifle and pom-pom fire, where Sergt. Ambrose's
horse was shot and fell, pinning him to the ground. He
lay there suffering intense agony from the extreme heat,
having his British warm coat on, which he was unable to
get off, and the Boers fired at him incessantly and finally
wounded him in the arm ; he was not released from this
terrible position until late at night when some of the
Guards found him and helped to extricate him.

Several attempts were made to force our way along the
river bank, but it was impossible to get forward, owing
to the heavy fire from the front and from across the

river where Albrecht and the Jacobsdal commando were posted. No guns could be spared to cover our advance, and so the whole Regiment was dismounted and placed in the firing line, while the 12th Lancers were in a similar position near " G " Battery R. H. A., which was within 1,000 yards of the position.

Later on the Yorkshire Light Infantry, coming up

9TH LANCERS MAXIM GUN DETACHMENT UNDER LIEUT. F. ALLHUSEN.

from Voet Pads Drift, which they had been ordered to hold, relieved the Regiment, and the Guards came up into the firing line in the centre. The behaviour of the gunners was magnificent. The Maxims of the 9th and 12th Lancers, under Lieut. F. Allhusen and Lieut. Macnaughten, also did splendid work, and remained alongside " G " Battery all day practically in the firing line.

Firing continued all day, but no further advance was accomplished, and at 6.30 p.m. we collected close to the guns, together with the transport, which formed so enormous a target, that we very soon drew the attention of the Boer guns. We retired towards the river to bivouac at dusk.

Tues. 12th   Turned out at 4 a.m. after a bitterly cold night, and the Regiment took up a position south of an old pan between the river and the guns. A mutual armistice was going on. The Boers were all outside their trenches, and both sides were busily engaged collecting the dead and wounded round the trenches. The wounded had a terrible time, many of them lying out for 24 hours exposed to a terrible fire by day and intense cold at night.

A consultation between Gen. Lord Methuen, Gen. Babington, and Col. Sir H. Colville took place to decide further operations, and a general retirement was agreed upon, owing to the scarcity of ammunition for the guns and the losses of the Highland Brigade. At 10 a.m. the naval gun " Joe " opened fire from the gangers' hut on some Boers advancing down the line, not knowing an armistice was going on, and this drew fire from the Boer gunners, who turned their attention on " G " Battery and part of the 12th Lancers. The " G " Battery stood magnificently and never moved or fired a shot, and as soon as the Long Tom could be stopped the Boers ceased fire and allowed the ambulance work to continue. At 12 noon the retirement commenced, the 9th Lancers covering it, with " A " Squadron on the right, " D " Squadron on the left. At 1.20 p.m. the infantry had

retired sufficiently far to allow the Regiment to withdraw.
While the Boers were shelling the retirement, the guns
retired to a second position, giving the ridge and position
a splendid shelling, the howitzer battery placing four
lyddite shells in a volley as a farewell shot, and completely smothering the kopje east of and next the railway.

The " D " Squadron, who formed the rear squadron,
reached Modder River camp at 4 p.m. Found our tents
had arrived. The Boers made no attempt to harass the
retirement. Capt. Briggs, K.D.G.'s, our Brigade-Major,
was wounded during the engagement.

Killed : Pte. R. Rae, " C " Squadron.
Wounded : Sergt. C. Ambrose (" C ").
Lance-Corp. W. Burton (" C ").
Pte. W. Gilchrist (" C ").
Pte. J. Clarkson (" C ").
Pte. J. Lee (" C ").
Pte. A. Reeve (" C ").
Pte. H. Whitehead (" C ").
Pte. J. Newman (" C ").
Pte. A. Fenn (" C ").
Pte. J. Moore (" A ") (died of wounds).

Two chargers and six troop horses were killed and
three chargers and 16 troop horses were wounded.

Capt. E. R. Gordon was appointed Brigade-Major to Wed. 13th
Maj.-Gen. Babington, vice Briggs, wounded. Capt. Beale-
Browne arrived, together with Capt. Brinton, 2nd L. G.,
the latter being appointed galloper to the General.

1899.
DEC.
The total casualties of the battle were 23 officers and 182 men killed, 45 officers and 645 men wounded, 76 men missing. Out of this the Highland Brigade lost 46 officers and 706 men killed and wounded.

Thur. 14th
One hundred fresh horses arrived from England. Cronje sent a doctor in for a supply of field dressing, who reported the Boer losses as very heavy !

Fri. 15th
The R. F. A., 9th Lancers, two squadrons 12th Lancers and M. I. paraded at 5 a.m. to make a demonstration in a north-westerly direction towards Brown's Farm. We advanced seven or eight miles and turned back to camp when the Boer guns opened on us, but were short in their range.

Lord Methuen inspected the horses of the Regiment, and expressed his approval of the work it had done in the late operations, and the steadiness of the men under fire.

Sat. 16th
A day of rest.

Two heavy explosions were heard some way up the line, the enemy evidently blowing up culverts on the line which passed through their position.

Sun. 17th
Church parade at 9 a.m.

Mon. 18th
Regiment paraded at 4 a.m. and made a reconnaissance as far south as Klockfontein, then turned westwards to Marais' Farm, and returned to camp at 11 a.m.

Capt. Beale-Browne was ordered to return to his staff duties at Cape Town.

Wed. 20th
Paraded at 4 a.m. to make a reconnaissance with R. H. A., M. I., and 12th Lancers westward and on south side of river to Vaal Kop ; searched Boshof's Farm, and returned to camp at 11 a.m.

Boers shelled Highland Brigade camp.

Cavalry Brigade paraded at 6 a.m., and again visited Boshof's Farm ; Boshof was arrested with several others. " C " Squadron went on to search Marais' Farm. Got back to camp at 2 p.m. Had a regimental " bonfire " and " sing-song."

1899.
DEC.
Thur. 21st
Sat. 23rd

LORD METHUEN'S HEADQUARTERS, MODDER RIVER.

Church parade 9 a.m.

Church parade 9.45 a.m. Maj. Little addressed the Regiment, and the Queen's Message read out :—" I wish you and all my brave soldiers a Happy Xmas. God bless and protect you all.—V. R. I."

This was read out to every unit at 12 noon, when the camp rang with cheers.

Sun. 24th
Mon. 25th

Bathing sports had been arranged for the men, the following being the successful competitors :—

Diving Competition : 1st, Pte. Brosker ; 2nd, Pte. Williamson ; 3rd, Pte. Bell.

Obstacle Race : 1st, Pte. Williamson ; 2nd, Pte. George ; 3rd, Pte. Claydon.

100 *yards :* 1st, Pte. Brosker ; 2nd, Pte. Jessop ; 3rd, Corp. Smith.

Tug-of-War : " D " Squadron. A splendid perform-ance as they had already had a very hard pull with the " A " Squadron.

Grey Mare Tournament : 1st, Sergt. Andrews ; 2nd, Pte. Williamson.

Tues. 26th . Paraded 5.45 a.m., with two guns R. H. A., 50 M. I., and a section of R. E., under Maj. Little, and proceeded up the right bank of the river to destroy a house that was being used by the Boers at night. The two advanced troops under Lieuts. Abadie and Durand came under fire at 7.15 a.m., and the M. I. were sent up to support them, and hold the bushy ridge while the R. E. blew up the house and kraal. While this was going on, the Boers' " Long Tom " on Maagersfontein dropped 16 shells in and around the support at a range which must have been fully 7,000 yards. Fortunately no damage was done.

Lieut. Bell swam across the river to search another farm-house, where he found an old Dutchman and a small boy, who were brought back to camp. The farm was eventually demolished and a return made to camp.

At 10.30 p.m. the Boers got a fright, and commenced

a heavy fusillade all along their trenches, which lasted about a quarter of an hour.

The Cavalry Brigade made a reconnaissance north-west on the right bank of the river, for some nine miles, and returned to camp about noon.

Boers shelled our naval guns and outpost line. Our

PONTOON BRIDGE, MODDER RIVER.

" Long Tom " tried the effect of a lyddite shell at 11 p.m., and for fully 15 minutes the Boers fired incessantly from the whole position.

Gen. Babington inspected the horses of the Regiment.

Our Xmas turkeys, ordered by the Mess President, Capt. Fiennes, arrived from Cape Town after six days in a blazing sun, and had to be promptly buried !

1899.   The Boers tried our game, firing at night, but our
Dec.   outposts were not to be " drawn."

Sat. 30th   The Cavalry Brigade paraded at 6.30 a.m. for a reconnaissance to the west on the north side of river.

Sun. 31st   Church parade 9 a.m.

Pte. Clarkson, " C " Squadron, who was wounded at
Maagersfontein in five places, returned to duty.

1900.

―――

COPY of a wire sent to friends at home by the corre-
spondent of the *Daily Telegraph,* Mr. J. Grenfell, from
Modder River, and published by that paper with many
others from other regiments:

" From 9th Lancers.—We drank your health at
Xmas. Our stay in this charming watering-place is
pleasing to the flies and inhabitants, both of whom bleed
us freely. We are living on the best of sand, washed
down by Chateau Modder. We only regret that you are
not here to share it."

The Regiment paraded at 3 a.m. with the Cavalry
Brigade and M. I., under Gen. Babington. We went as
far as Valschfontein (Vorster's Farm), some nine or ten
miles, and remained there all morning, going on some
five miles in the afternoon, but returning to bivouac.
A splendid view of all the country towards Ploysberg
and Koodoosberg was obtained from Vaal's Kop, close
by, but nothing was seen of the Boers.

The object of this move was to act as a support on the
flank to a small column of Colonials, under Col. Pilcher,

1900.   sent out from Belmont to relieve Douglas.   A squadron
JAN.   of the Greys also went out from Honeynest Kloof.

Tues. 2nd   Remained in observation all day, and in the afternoon
went on and bivouacked near Van Niekerk's Farm.
Gen. Babington heard during the afternoon that Col.
Pilcher had had a smart little fight at Sunnyside, and had
afterwards hoisted "the Jack" at Douglas.   He also
asked us to remain where we were until he had retired.
Very late getting into bivouac.

Wed. 3rd   The Brigade remained here all day, chiefly owing to
information that Cronje had sent down some 500 or
600 men from Maagersfontein to endeavour to cut off
Col. Pilcher.   They were reported to have crossed the
river and gone on to Mier Kraal, so a couple of troops of
the 12th Lancers were sent out in that direction.   The
Boers, however, changed their minds and retraced their
steps to the northern side of the river.   As this intelligence had been wired to Pilcher, he again asked us to
remain where we were for the night.

Thur. 4th   Having heard from Col. Pilcher during the night that
he was safe, the Brigade started back for Modder River
about 4.30 a.m., and got in about 9 a.m.

Fri. 5th   Heard from the Greys at Honeynest Kloof that they
had found and buried the body of Pte. Wilkins, " D "
Squadron, who was killed during the fight at Graspan or
Enslin.

Sat. 6th   Divisional sports, final day.

Maj. Little won the Modder River Cup on his b.w.h.
" Arcano," squandering a large and varied field of quad-
rupeds.

Regiment paraded with the remainder of the Cavalry
Brigade at 9 p.m. for a reconnaissance towards Ramdam,
viâ Honeynest Kloof. Had a weary march, and reached
Honeynest Kloof at 3.30 a.m., where we remained for
the night, Gen. Babington going on to Enslin during the
afternoon.

After a very wet night started at 6 a.m. for Ramdam,

RAMDAM, FIRST BIVOUAC FOR THE RELIEF OF KIMBERLEY.

and spent a wet day in reconnoitring, being joined by
the Victorian Mounted Rifles from Enslin. A party of
400 Boers were reported on the hills between Jacobsdal
and Enslin ; this we were unable to verify, no sign being
seen of them. Bivouacked at Ramdam.

Woke up soaking wet and continued our advance at
5.30 a.m. into the Orange Free State. Sighted a column

4

1900.   about 7 a.m., which turned out to be Colonel Pilcher's
Jan.   force returning from the east to Belmont.

Lubbe's (the Jacobsdal commandant) farms were
visited and searched and subsequently burnt, according
to orders from headquarters. Returned to Enslin,
getting in about 2.30 p.m. The horses were considerably
knocked up, owing to the tiring work and length of time
they were without food. This may be considered the
first entry into the Free State by any considerable force,
some 25 miles having been reconnoitred.

Thur. 11th   We had hoped to spend a day resting and grazing the
horses here, but were recalled by wire from headquarters
in the morning, and started back at 1.30 p.m., getting to
Modder River at 5.30 p.m.

Fri. 12th   A strong rumour prevails that Cronje is withdrawing
part of his force to knock out Kimberley.

Mon. 15th   Officers 9th Lancers played officers 12th Lancers at
hockey, the Regiment won by four goals to one.

Tues. 16th   The Division made a reconnaissance of the Maagersfontein position at 2.45 p.m., the Cavalry Brigade being
to the west of the railway. The demonstration failed
to make Cronje disclose his dispositions, and after shelling
the position we returned to camp at dark. The Boers
only replied with a very few shots and only one horse
was wounded.

Wed. 17th   The 12th Lancers went off to Enslin so as to rest the
horses and get the benefit of the grass there.

The siege guns shelled the Maagersfontein position.

Officers Present.

Maj. M. O. Little.
Maj. W. Follett.
Capt. F. Colvin.
Capt. Hon. C. Willoughby.
Capt. F. T. Lund.
Capt. Lord D. Compton.
Capt. H. T. W. Fiennes.
Capt. G. Ellison.
Capt. E. R. Gordon.
Capt. D. Campbell.
Lieut. E. Bell (adjutant).
Lieut. F. Allhusen.
Lieut. V. Brooke.
Lieut. Skeffington Smyth.
Lieut. H. M. Durand.
Lieut. Hon. D. P. Carleton.
Lieut. E. Abadie.
Lieut. Lord F. Blackwood.
Lieut. H. Cavendish.
Lieut. S. Theobald.
Lieut. J. Duckett.
Lieut. Sadleir-Jackson.
Lieut. P. Brassey.
Lieut. & Quar.-Mast. D. Laing.
Vet.-Lieut. Todd.
Capt. Forrest, R.A.M.C.

Maj. Little went out to Klokfontein to inspect the

4*

" A " Squadron, who were bivouacked there to rest and graze their horses.

Fri. 19th   " D " Squadron, under Capt. Willoughby, were ordered out to Vorster's Farm to hold Fraser's Drift. Had a hockey match, Officers *v.* N.C.O.'s, the former winning by four goals to two.

Sat. 20th   Very heavy thunderstorm. " D " Squadron started for Vorster's Farm at 3 p.m.

Lieut. V. Brooke took out a patrol of 15 men to reconnoitre towards Douglas along the south bank of the Riet River, Capt. Chester-Masters accompanying him with a party of Rimington's Guides. He was to bivouac at Van Niekerk's Farm and go on the next day. The M. I. were to hold Boschof's Drift, and a force from Belmont under Col. Rochfort Boyd were to follow them the next day.

Two guns R. H. A. were sent to Belmont, leaving the Cavalry Brigade with only one squadron cavalry (" C " Squadron), four guns R. H. A. and part of the M. I.

Sun. 21st   Church parade 9 a.m. Modder River bridge is very nearly reconstructed.

Mon. 22nd   The siege guns at No. 2 Redoubt tried to knock out the Boer gun on the east side of Maagersfontein. The howitzer battery went out to the front, supported by infantry, and shelled the trenches in front of the kopjes. The prevailing impression to those who witnessed the shelling was that the Boer gun was worked on a moveable platform, and changed its position after each shot. This idea was subsequently exploded when Maagersfontein was evacuated, and it was seen that the gun was cleverly placed amongst the rocks in an ordinary gun epaulment ; there were no signs of a shell having pitched into it. The Boers directed all their fire against the howitzer battery, but did no damage.

Lieut. Lord F. Blackwood came under heavy pom-pom fire and cross rifle fire from the trenches, when out

9TH LANCERS CROSSING FRASER'S DRIFT ON THE MODDER RIVER.

with his patrol watching some wagons which were evidently sent across his front to entice him on.

H. M. the Queen's New Year's gift of chocolate arrived. Tues. 23rd

Heavy dust storm and thunder. Wed. 24th

Maj. Little rode over to visit Capt. Willoughby's Thur. 25th squadron at Fraser's Drift.

Cavalry Brigade played Guards Brigade at hockey, former won by four goals to love.

1900.
JAN.

1900.
JAN.
Fri. 26th

Maj. Little rode over to Klokfontein to visit " A " Squadron. The Boers fired on our grazing party to the west, and Capt. Lund took " C " Squadron out to try and cut them off, but they had gone after rounding up some cattle.

Modder River Post Office was a seething mass of soldiers, who were all sending home their " Queen's chocolate boxes," and as they all had to be registered, it took a very long time. No gift was ever more appreciated.

Sat. 27th

" C " Squadron went out and lay in the bushes beyond " One Tree Hill " for stray Boers, and returned at 1.30 p.m.

" D " Squadron returned from Fraser's Drift.

Sun. 28th

Church parade 9.15 a.m.

Two troops of " C " Squadron, under Capt. Fiennes, went out to escort 150 head of cattle to Klokfontein and bring back 66 mules. Had a false alarm of a party of Boers beyond " Rosmead " and " One Tree Hill," where we had a patrol under Lieut. Carleton, who saw nothing of them.

Lieut. Bell placed on the sick list with enteric.

Capt. F. F. Colvin acting adjutant for him.

Mon. 29th

Terrible bad dust storm all day.

Capt. Fiennes brought in five prisoners from " Rosmead."

The Regiment played the 3rd Grenadiers at football for Lord Methuen's Cup, the Grenadiers winning by three goals to one.

Tues. 30th

The 16th Lancers, under Maj. Frewin, arrived. The

Cavalry Brigade played the Highland Brigade at hockey
and won by five goals to one.

The General inspected our lines.

Three Horse Artillery Batteries arrived, under Roch-fort.

A patrol, under Lieut. Lord F. Blackwood, chased a party of six Boers just before daylight out beyond No. 2 A Redoubt, but they got away through the bushes.

The 52nd and Cheshire Regiments arrived.

Lieut. Theobald, who was on patrol at " One Tree Hill," reported a party of 12 Boers advancing from the kopjes towards him. Two troops under Capt. Ellison went out to try and cut them off, but they had retired when he got out.

The officers played the men at hockey, the former winning.

The officers played the gunners at hockey and won by two goals to one. At 12 midnight we received orders to march at 5.30 a.m. to Fraser's Drift, the baggage to be ready at 3.30 a.m.

Paraded south of the river across the pontoon bridge with 62nd Battery, R. F. A., The Highland Brigade, Telegraph and Engineer sections, and two squadrons (" C " and " D ") 9th Lancers, the whole under Gen. Hector Macdonald. " D " Squadron covered the advance, and marched to Fraser's Drift. " D " and " C " Squadrons crossed the river and remained out till 12.30 p.m., when they were recalled, leaving one troop and a signalling party on Vaals Kop.

Marched at 6 a.m. for Koodoosberg, " C " Squadron

forming the advanced guard. A very rough march and terribly hot ; saw one or two small parties of Boers on the north side of the river. A party of 25 Boers were at the drift when the advanced troop, under Lieut. Lord F. Blackwood, arrived there and drove them back. At 10 a.m. the Regiment crossed the drift and advanced about two miles.

The Highland Brigade suffered intensely from the long march in the heat of the day, several dying of heat apoplexy and exhaustion, and the gunners had to send back wagons to bring the sick in. It was lucky we had no fighting to do, as the Highland Brigade were quite done up on reaching Koodoosberg.

Mon. 5th Patrols went out before daybreak, Lieut. Duckett proceeding with the signalling party to Koodoosberg Kop, which position commanded our camp at about 2,500 yards range. On arrival there he surprised a party of 17 Boers at the top, who luckily bolted at once and joined another party of 70 who were below. Our patrol opened fire, which was easily heard in camp, and Maj. Little ordered out " D " Squadron, and we found the Boers were occupying a low ridge on the east of the kopje about three miles north of the drift. We advanced gradually, dismounting and firing, and the remaining troops were ordered out in support, the infantry occupying the kopje. A patrol under Sergt. Smith, on the right of our advance, came under heavy fire at about 300 yards, and Pte. Crofts' horse was shot and they both rolled over ; however, Sergt. Smith got Crofts up behind him and they got safely away, the horse being subse-

quently retrieved by R. S. M. Grant and a party of four
men, who managed under fire to get up to the horse and
bring it in.

We returned to bivouac at 10 a.m.

About midday Lieut. Duckett's patrol was driven in
by an advance of Boers, and all troops were turned out,

KOODOOSBERG.

the Regiment galloping out to the same ground as we
were on during the morning. Our dismounted and
Maxim fire checked the Boers, and the infantry being in
position, we were ordered to try and draw the enemy on
by gradual retirements. The Boers advanced up the
northern side of Koodoosberg Kop, but would not be
drawn on by the east side and firing commenced on the
kopje, which the H. L. I. were holding. Pte. McNicoll,

of " C " Squadron, was shot through the head and instantly killed from the fire from the kopje. At dusk we returned and crossed the drift to bivouac.

A convoy came in with an escort of 11th Hussars and Life Guards, under Capt. Ferguson and Lieut. de Crespigny. Very bad dust storm all night.

Tues. 6th   Turned out at 4.30 a.m., Lieut. Carleton with one troop patrolling north, Lieut. Theobald's patrol going to Sands Drift, while the remainder of the Regiment dismounted and lined the track which ran north and south from Sands Drift, and afforded a good position.

Lieut. Carleton cleared the ridge of a few Boers who were holding it, but they were reinforced and the troop was obliged to fall back. Lieut. Theobald reported a large force advancing from the north of his position towards Maagersfontein, and several small parties of the enemy were seen moving round the north side of the river. " D " Squadron remained out all day.

Wed. 7th   Lieut. Sadleir-Jackson, with one troop and the machine gun, under Lieut. Allhusen, proceeded to Sands Drift at daybreak. Lieut. Skeffington Smyth, with one troop, went over Koodoosberg Drift to the north, and two patrols under N.C.O.'s went south-east and west respectively. Lieut. Skeffington Smyth came under fire from the kopje at 6 a.m., and Lieut. Sadleir-Jackson found a party of 70 Boers at Paynter's Drift. The enemy had meanwhile dragged a gun up on to Koodoosberg Kopje, and began shelling the camp. The Regiment galloped out to Paynter's Drift, and a section of guns in camp replied to the Boer gun, and another section proceeded towards Paynter's Drift and opened fire on Paynter's house, round which the Boers were concealed in the deep dongas close to the river. Four troops under Lieuts. Duckett, Sadleir-Jackson, Carle-

LIEUT. SADLEIR-JACKSON.

ton and Cavendish were dismounted and lined the ridge overlooking the drift. Lieut. Sadleir-Jackson, having worked down close to the river, was unable to get further. Lieut. Cavendish received a flesh wound in the side, and the following casualties occurred during the day.

Wounded : Pte. A. Frost, " D " Squadron.

Pte. J. Huxham, " D " Squadron.

Pte. T. Bayley, " D " Squadron.

Pte. T. Kelly, " D " Squadron.

The Cavalry Brigade, under Gen. Babington, consisting of 16th Lancers, 12th Lancers, Composite Regiment, one squadron 10th Hussars, one squadron Scots Greys, under Capt. Hawley, and two batteries R. H. A., arrived at 4 p.m. from Modder River on the north side of the river, and moved towards the east side of Koodoosberg Kopje.   The Composite Regiment endeavoured to charge, supported by gun fire, but got hung up in a wire fence and suffered some loss, seven men being wounded and several horses shot.   Maj. Little sent Capt. Willoughby off to inform Gen. Babington of the position and dispositions.

Maj. Briggs returned to duty as Brigade-Major, relieving Capt. Gordon.

Lieut. V. Brooke returned to Modder River from Douglas, having been away three weeks.

The " A " Squadron left Klokfontein to join the Regiment at Koodoosberg.

Thur. 8th   The Regiment left bivouac at 4.30 a.m., and went up towards Paynter's Drift, " A " Squadron covering the advance.   The Highland Brigade advanced along both banks of the river towards Paynter's Drift and over Koodoosberg Kopje, the Cavalry Brigade acting on the north bank east of the kopje.

The Regiment crossed Paynter's Drift unopposed,

followed by the H. L. I. and part of the Argyle and
Sutherland Highlanders in support. We received orders
to hold the drift and work round the west side of
the kopje, and communicate with Gen. Babington.
Paynter's house was completely wrecked by shell fire,
and the whole ground was strewn with shrapnel. Mr.
and Mrs. Paynter, both loyal Cornish people, had suffered
a terrible experience, which was increased by his being
a great invalid. All their furniture and things were
wrecked, but even in their distress they did all they
could for the troops, and produced bread and milk, which
one was most thankful to get. We remained holding
the drift until 4.30 p.m., Lieut. Brassey having taken
his troop round the kopje. A squadron of the 16th
Lancers relieved us at that time, and we returned to
Koodoosberg at 5.15 p.m., the " A " Squadron getting in
an hour later.

At 6.30 p.m. the whole of the Cavalry Brigade and force
retired from Koodoosberg, and reached Modder River at
midnight. One of the ambulances containing the
wounded upset into the Modder River when crossing the
pontoon bridge, which disaster proved fatal to several
of those who, after being badly hit, had undergone the
trials of the long and rough journey.

Lord Roberts and Staff having arrived at Modder
River on the evening of Wednesday, February 7th, we
expect a forward move at any moment.

The cavalry has now been formed into a Division,
composed of the following brigades, under Lieut.-Gen.
J. D. French.

*1900.
FEB.*

Fri. 9th

1st Brigade.—Colonel Porter.
 Carabineers.
 Scots Greys. " G " and " T " Batteries R.H.A.
 Inniskillings.
 14th Hussars.
 N. S. W. Lancers.

2nd Brigade.—Colonel Broadwood.
 Household Cavalry Composite Regiment.
 10th Hussars. " Q " and " U " Batteries R.H.A.
 12th Lancers.

3rd Brigade.—Colonel Gordon.
 9th Lancers.
 16th Lancers. " O " and " R " Batteries R.H.A.

M. I. Division—Two Brigades of four regiments each, under Colonels Hannay and Ridley.

Sat. 10th Lord Roberts inspected our Brigade, and afterwards addressed the commanding officers in the Division, saying that we were about to start on an expedition which we should remember all our lives. A British cavalry force of this size had never been employed before, and it rested with us to prove that we could maintain its traditions, and relieve Kimberley at all costs, as the town was in sore straits and suffering from severe shelling. He had wired to them to on no account surrender, and promised to relieve them within six days.

Capt. Willoughby had to go sick, and Lieut. Bell remains in hospital with enteric. All baggage was stored in the old mess hut we had built, and after the sick and debilitated horses had been weeded out, we were able to put 422 horses in the ranks.

Left camp at 1.50 a.m., the 9th and 16th Lancers, with " O " and " R " Batteries, R. H. A., forming the advanced guard to the Division. We reached Ramdam about 9.30 a.m. This is the commencement of a wide turning movement, with the relief of Kimberley as its object. An Infantry Division, under Gen. Tucker, is concentrating here with the object of holding the ground which the Cavalry Division makes good, and to bring on the convoy.

Lieut. Carleton went sick with sunstroke and fever and was ordered back to the lines.

This evening Lieut. Allhusen was lent to Gen. Tucker as a galloper, and Lieut. Abadie to Gen. French.

Turned out at 1.50 a.m. and after stumbling about in the dark joined the other brigades.

Our brigade had orders to act on the left and advance towards Waterval Drift, and there to make a feint at crossing the Riet River, the remainder of the Division moving in the direction of De Kiel's Drift.

At 6 a.m. our advance was checked by a party of Boers on our left front. These were shelled and cleared out of the kopjes, when we went on towards the river.

As the first shell was fired Lord Roberts appeared on the scene and was heartily cheered.

Lieut. Jackson with his troop worked his way down to the river and occupied a house close to Waterval Drift, with loss of only one man slightly wounded—Pte. J. Prescott (" D ").

The Boers brought up a gun which they cleverly concealed in the kopjes near the river. It commanded the open ground on which we were, and an artillery duel commenced.

At 10.30 we got news from Gen. French that he had gained De Kiel's Drift, and the Boers opposite us evidently got news at the same time, for they shortly afterwards retired.

About 3 p.m. we moved across De Kiel's Drift and went into bivouac. During the afternoon Gen. Tucker's Division began to arrive, a wonderful performance considering the heat and privation for want of water.

Tues. 13th   " C " and " D " Squadrons, with a section of guns, were sent to hold Waterval Drift and the kopjes the Boer gun occupied yesterday.

At 10 a.m. these squadrons got orders to rejoin the Division, which was starting for Randavel, a drift on the Modder River, about 25 miles off.

After joining the Division the Regiment covered the advance. There was slight opposition from the Jacobsdal ridge on the left and also from the right. On the latter our guns came into action, and a big veldt fire was started which burnt our field cable.

We then trotted on for some miles until the indication of the river was visible in the distance.

As clouds of dust were visible behind some low kopjes to our left front, Gen. Gordon moved our Brigade to the left to make them good, the remainder of the Division making for Klip Drift.

On reaching the kopjes we could see the laagers on

the river bank, and soon afterwards came under the enemy's fire. Our guns came into action and we saw the Boers streaming away. " C " and " D " Squadrons then galloped down to the river, the former crossing at the drift, and rushing and capturing Van der Merve's laager, which consisted of a lot of tents, stores, clothing, arms and ammunition. " D " Squadron, on their left, being unable to cross where they were, followed quickly behind " C " Squadron, both squadrons occupying the high ground behind the laager.

At the same time Broadwood's Brigade crossed Klip Drift and captured two laagers.

Fortunately there was any amount of forage, our horses having practically had nothing to eat all day, and no water for 24 hours. The Boers shelled us from a far ridge and kept up sniping till dark, when " D " Squadron went out on outposts together with a troop from " A."

By this day's work the passage of the Modder was in our hands, and the Maagersfontein Boers' direct line of retreat on Bloemfontein was cut off.

We were obliged to remain here until Gen. Kelly- Kenny's Division should come up, which they did at 10 p.m. with our supply wagons. We fortunately captured any amount of sheep, so the men had plenty of meat.

Soon after daylight a good number of Boers were seen galloping across our front, but dispersed on being shelled. A party of about 50, however, got into cover some 2,000 yards to our front, and annoyed us all day in spite of our shell fire.

About 8 a.m. they brought up a gun, and although

they got our range beautifully, there was not a single casualty ; then our guns knocked it out in three shots.

Later on a party of snipers crept up the river, and " D " Squadron, who had just been relieved off outposts, went out and drove them back. " C " Squadron night outposts.

Thur. 15th   Before leaving we heard that MacDonald had occupied Jacobsdal.

At 9.30 a.m. the Cavalry Division started for Kimberley, the 9th Lancers covering the advance, " C " Squadron in front, " D " on the right along the river, " A " on the left. We had proceeded about three or four miles when " C " Squadron was opposed by a heavy fire from a ridge of kopjes running north and south almost down to the river. At almost the same time a heavy shell fire was opened from the left and directed on our guns, which at once came into action. The " D " Squadron also came under heavy fire from the river.

As the Boer guns were doing such damage from their important ridge, Gen. French at once decided to clear it, and ordered Gordon's Brigade to make a dash for it.

" C " and " D " Squadrons quickly formed line to the left front, with two squadrons of the 16th Lancers on their left, charging direct for the ridge under a heavy cross fire for a good one and a half miles. Having successfully carried the ridge, we wheeled slightly to the left and took up a position on a line of kopjes further on. The Boers were now in full retreat towards Spytfontein, and those on the right in a north-easterly direction.

Gen. French, with the 10th Hussars and Composite Regiment, supported the charge. The remainder of Division coming on, we rejoined them, and made a short halt at Abon's Dam, where there was only a well. The General would not delay, and so pushed on, and we came

IN SIGHT OF KIMBERLEY.—CAPT. F. COLVIN AND
CAPT. G. ELLISON.

in sight of Kimberley, some nine or 10 miles off, about 2.30 p.m. The General here tried to communicate with Kimberley, after which we moved forward viâ Olifants-fontein, where we came under shell fire from a party of Boers who had abandoned their laager at Susannah and were retreating towards Boshof.

Pursuit was out of the question owing to the exhausted

5*

1900.
FEB.

state of the horses, so we marched in to Du Toit's Pan, where our Brigade bivouacked, Gen. French entering the town he had so brilliantly relieved.

The casualties were :—

Pte. G. Golding (" C "), died of wounds.
Pte. A. Bacon (" C "), wounded.
Pte. G. Dormer (" D "), wounded.
Horses—killed, 5 ; wounded, 15 ; died, 10.

Fri. 16th

Gen. French had orders to clear the Boers from their positions on the north and north-east.

Gordon's Brigade was ordered to make a wide easterly turning movement to endeavour to head off a body of Boers, who were trekking along the Leeufontein-Boshof road, and then to swing round the north side of Macfarlane's Farm, where we expected to get in touch with Porter's Brigade. He, however, was held up at Dronfield, and a force of Boers were holding Macfarlane's Farm, estimated at about 2,000 strong. After clearing the high ground east of Macfarlane's Farm, Boers could be seen trekking from that place. These we attempted to cut off, and at once came under heavy fire from the ridge covering the farm. The 9th Lancers then tried to work round on the north side of the farm towards the railway, while Capt. MacEwen's squadron of the 16th Lancers galloped straight for the ridge, but a wire fence at the top stopped them, and in the face of a heavy fire they were forced to retire.

In doing this the Boers opened a very heavy fire, at the beginning of which Capt. Gordon was wounded.

Maj. Little retired a short way, and then ordered Lord D. Compton with " A " Squadron to gallop straight at a party of some 40 Boers in front, supporting him with the other squadrons.

The Boers kept up their fire until the squadron was within 200 yards, and then mounted and galloped off, leaving five dismounted prisoners in our hands. The remainder of the Boers, although only some 60 yards ahead, were able to gallop away from our horses, which were absolutely reduced to a walk.

" A " Squadron crossed the railway line and went about half a mile further on, but seeing some Boers coming down from Macfarlane's Farm on his left rear, Compton collected his men, who were now reduced to 13 in number, and retired on the other squadrons, who had taken up a position in a stone quarry half a mile east of the railway.

It was in this advance that 2nd Lieut. Brassey lost his life. Lieut. Durand was badly hit during the earlier part of the advance.

Gen. Gordon retired us to Macfarlane's Farm, where an order came for us to go to Dronfield and support Porter's Brigade. On arrival there the men and horses were so completely exhausted from want of water and food, and the very long day in the saddle with continuous fighting, that Gen. French withdrew, leaving the local forces to watch the enemy. It was about 9 p.m. before Kimberley was reached.

The casualties :—

2nd Lieut. Brassey, missing (killed).
Capt. E. R. Gordon, wounded.
Lieut. H. M. Durand, wounded.
Sergt. J. Blatchley (" A "), wounded.
Pte. S. Mason (" C "), wounded.
Pte. C. Turnbull (" C "), wounded.
Pte. J. Jeffers (" A "), wounded.
Pte. J. Price (" A "), wounded.
Pte. J. Caister (" D "), wounded.
Corpl. J. Foord (" A "), wounded.
40 horses killed and died of exhaustion.

Sat. 17th   Maj. Little inspected the horses and found that we had
only 105 fit to go on out of the 422 we left Modder River
with.

Gen. French had started with Broadwood's Brigade
and the Carabineers for Koodoesrand Drift, so as to cut
off Cronje, who was making a bold dash for Bloemfontein,
pursued by Lord Kitchener. We received orders to
follow to-morrow morning.

Sun. 18th   After turning out at 4 a.m., we were delayed over
getting supplies, and finally got off at 6.30 a.m., Maj.
Follett, Capt. Ellison and Lieut. Skeffington Smyth being
left behind with 200 sick and exhausted horses. The
Brigade reached the kopjes overlooking the drift about
5 p.m., and found a party of about 200 Boers north of the
river, who evidently intended occupying the kopjes
which we had fortunately got to first. Our Maxim and
one gun were at once brought into action, which drove

them hastily back, part of them going eastwards along the north bank of the river.

The " A " Squadron were sent to reconnoitre the drift and went eastwards, but met with opposition from a long low ridge about a mile from the drift. Lieut. Sadleir-Jackson volunteered to ride down to the drift, which he reconnoitred by himself and found it unoccupied. However, it was within range of the Boers on the ridge. And as it was now dark, and the position being an unsuitable one for the night, owing to a considerable force of Boers being all round, we received orders to withdraw on Blinkwater Pan, where the rest of the brigade was. We blundered back in the pitch dark for some five miles and there bivouacked with the 16th Lancers.

It was then 9 p.m., and we had been 18 hours in the saddle and had covered quite 40 miles.

Got orders to rejoin Gen. Gordon at Blinkwater Pan, and to send a patrol again to Koodoesrand Drift, which Lieut. Sadleir-Jackson took. He surprised six Boers watering their horses at the drift, and shot two of them.

The Brigade moved south to Kameelfontein, where Generals French and Kelly-Kenny were holding Cronje, and joined the main body.

During the last two days the Boer laagers had been heavily shelled, and were now practically surrounded, the only danger being an attempt at relief from the south-east.

Gen. Gordon gave the " A " Squadron great credit for the way the drift had been reconnoitred on Sunday, February 18th, his words being : " I never saw anything better done ; it was executed like clockwork."

Gen. French decided to secure the two drifts—Koodoesrand and Makauw—to prevent any attempted relief
being successful, so our bivouac was moved to Koodoesrand and the 16th Lancers to Makauw's, whilst some of
Roberts' Horse held the kopjes on the south side of the
river.

Paraded at 4.30 a.m. on the south side of Koodoesrand
Drift, together with two squadrons Household Cavalry,
parts of Roberts' Horse and Kitchener's Horse, with
three batteries, for the purpose of clearing the hills and
farms south of the river round Kitchener's Hill, which
was also held by the enemy. Broadwood was ordered
to turn the position from the south and west, and join
hands with Gen. French.

" C " Squadron covered our advance to Bank's Drift
Farm, which they seized and came under fire from the
ridge commanding it. Our guns came into action and
shelled the kopjes on the west of the farm.

Gen. French quickly moved the Brigade eastwards,
leaving " C " Squadron (Capt. Lund) and the Maxim
(under Lieut. V. Brooke) at the farm. We got round
in rear of about 1,500 Boers. After doing so about
800 galloped out and started a hot fire on us within 900
yards, Capt. Campbell and Pte. Rowley both being
wounded. Our guns, which must have been partially
concealed by the long grass, promptly opened fire, and
together with our dismounted fire, proved too much for
them, and compelled them to make a hasty retreat.
Just at this time 40 Boers were coming up to a small
kopje on our left rear, and had it not been for the prompti-

tude with which it was seized by Lieut. Sadleir-Jackson 1900.
we should have suffered considerable damage.

Between 2,000 and 3,000 Boers were now in precipitate
flight, and streamed out in the direction of Makauw's
Drift, under heavy fire from Roberts' Horse and the party
at Bank's Drift Farm. Capt. Lund, who only had

BANK'S DRIFT FARM.

about 40 men there, dispatched nine men under Capt.
Fiennes and Lieut. Lord F. Blackwood to charge the
tail-end of the fleeing Boers, and every man had the
satisfaction of getting his lance " home."

We then joined hands with Broadwood and returned
to Koodoesrand Drift, " C " Squadron being left out,
holding Bank's Drift Farm.

1900.
FEB.

They had one casualty, Pte. Turner, shot through the head, and a curious thing happened in connection with this. When the squadron first arrived at the farm, Pte. Turner, who was searching the farmhouse, came across a coffin, and made the remark, " I wonder who this is

HEADQUARTERS 3RD CAVALRY BRIGADE, KOODOESRAND DRIFT ON
MODDER RIVER, PAARDEBERG.

for ? " Shortly afterwards he himself was placed in it for interment.

Our casualties were :—

Capt. D. G. Campbell, wounded.

Pte. L. Turner, " C " Squadron, killed.

Pte. A. Rowley, " A " Squadron, wounded.

Thur. 22nd   Capt. Campbell, with the rest of the wounded and sick, was sent into Jacobsdal. The " A " Squadron was

turned out at 1 p.m. by an alarm reporting that about 1900.
100 Boers had attacked the M. I. from the direction of
Blinkwater Farm, but seeing nothing of them they
returned to camp.

Eleven men and 20 horses rejoined, having come in
with Porter's Brigade. Lieut. Kincaid-Smith arrived
from England and told us that Capt. Bell and Lieut.
Gordon Stirling had gone home.

Heavy rain and thunderstorm.

The Queen's message and Gen. French's complimentary
remarks on the relief of Kimberley were published.

The following Divisional Order was published :—

1. The following extract from Field Army Orders, Jacobsdal,
dated 16th February, 1900, is published for information :—

The following telegram from Her Most Gracious Majesty the
Queen to Field-Marshal Lord Roberts, Commander-in-Chief, etc.,
has been received. "Pray express my satisfaction to General
French and those under him on his brilliant success ; trust sick
and wounded doing well, and that you and Lord Kitchener are
well. V.R.I."

2. In promulgating to the Cavalry Division Her Majesty's
gracious message, the Lieutenant-General desires to convey
to the commanding officers, officers, warrant officers, non-
commissioned officers and men, his warmest thanks for the
support and assistance he has received from them, and to express
his profoundest admiration for the skill and courage so abundantly
displayed by them at every critical phase of the operations and
for the cheerfulness with which they have endured much privation
and hardships.

To this alone he attributes the great success which must go far
to place the Cavalry and Royal Horse Artillery high in the
estimation of their Queen and Country.

EXTRACT FROM ARMY ORDERS, SOUTH AFRICA,
Dated Jacobsdal, Feb. 17th, 1900.

4. While the Field-Marshal Commanding-in-Chief is confident that all ranks of Her Majesty's Army in South Africa share the great satisfaction he feels regarding the success which has attended the efforts of the Horse Artillery, Cavalry and Mounted Infantry during the recent operations, he desires to record his opinion that their success would have been impossible without the material and moral assistance afforded to them by their comrades in the Field Artillery, Royal Engineers and Infantry, amidst great heat and under very trying circumstances. All ranks have pushed on in support of the Cavalry Division, and Lord Roberts feels sure that their Queen and Country as fully appreciate the value of the work they have performed as he does himself.

The results of the recent operations for the relief of Kimberley have demonstrated what can be achieved by a mobile and well-disciplined force, and whatever may be the difficulties or dangers to be faced before the present campaign is brought to a satisfactory conclusion, Lord Roberts trusts implicitly to the Army which it is his pride and privilege to command to overcome them.

Fri. 23rd   Capt. Lund sent in word to say his squadron had been under heavy fire at Bank's Drift Farm since 5 a.m., so a portion of Porter's Brigade was sent out to support them. The Boers, numbering some 400, were driven off, suffering considerable loss. Our Maxim gun did great work, and probably saved the squadron from annihilation. The bivouac was shifted to the south side of the river, and was completely washed out by the deluge of rain which fell all night. The spirits of the men were extraordinary under the excessive stress of the weather and privation.

Seventeen men and horses came in with a convoy. 1900.
Rain still continued, lasting all night, and we were FEB.
nearly drowned by the rain. Sat. 24th

Everything soaked with rain. Church parade for Sun. 25th
Cavalry Division at 6.30 a.m.

" C " Squadron came in from Bank's Drift.

9th Lancers strength.

" A " Squadron	..	60 men	56 horses
" D " Squadron	..	44 „	37 „
" C " Squadron	..	58 „	44 „
		162	137

Officers present : Maj. Little, Capts. Colvin, Lund,
Lord D. Compton, Stanley, Fiennes ; Lieuts. Kincaid-
Smith, Brooke, Theobald, Abadie, Blackwood, Caven-
dish, Duckett, Sadleir-Jackson ; Quar.-Mast. Laing ;
Capt. Forrest, R.A.M.C.

Just as we had turned in at 9.20 p.m. a fusillade was
opened by our infantry down by the river and went on
15 minutes. We turned out, and after waiting for half-
an-hour turned in again.

Stood to from dawn, with one battery R. H. A. and Mon. 26th
two companies M. I., under Maj. Little, to act as a flying
column if required. The Brigade got orders to turn out
and make a cordon from Kitchener's Hill to the river,
as it was thought Cronje would attempt to break out.
The 16th Lancers found this duty. Desultory firing
went on all night.

Majuba Day. Cronje surrendered unconditionally with Tues. 27th

1900.
FEB.

the whole of his force, some 4,000 strong. We turned out in the afternoon to hunt some Boers and got back to camp at 6 p.m.

Sixty-one men and 84 horses joined us to-day.

Wed. 28th

Fourteen men and 19 horses joined from Kimberley.

MARCH

Got news of the relief of Ladysmith.

Thur. 1st

Telegrams from H.M. the Queen, Prince of Wales, Duke of Connaught and Commander-in-Chief were published in orders, congratulating the troops on the successful operations round Paardeberg

EXTRACT FROM ARMY ORDERS, SOUTH AFRICA,
Dated Paardeberg, Feb. 27th, 1900.

4. TELEGRAM.—Lord Roberts has received the following telegram, dated February 27th, 1900, from the Rt. Hon. the Secretary of State for War :—

"Her Majesty's Government sincerely congratulate you and the forces under your command upon your great and opportune achievement."

In publishing it for general information the Field-Marshal Commanding-in-Chief desires to express to the troops under his command his high appreciation of their conduct during the recent operations. By the endurance they have shown through long and trying marches, and the gallantry they have displayed when engaged with the enemy, they have worthily upheld the traditions of Her Majesty's Army. Lord Roberts has every reason to rely on the spirit and resolution of British soldiers, and he confidently trusts to their devotion to their Queen and country to bring to a successful close the operations so auspiciously begun.

EXTRACT FROM ARMY ORDERS, SOUTH AFRICA,
Dated Paardeberg, Feb. 28th, 1900.

1. TELEGRAMS.—The Field-Marshal Commanding-in-Chief has great pleasure in publishing the following telegrams :—

"From Her Majesty The Queen, Windsor Castle,
"February 27th, 1900.

"Accept for yourself and all under your command my warmest congratulations on this splendid news."

"From Field-Marshal H.R.H. the Prince of Wales,
"London, February 27th, 1900.

"Sincerest congratulations."

"From Field-Marshal Viscount Wolseley,
"Commander-in-Chief.

"Well done.   I congratulate you and every soldier under your command with all my heart."

"From General H.R.H. The Duke of Connaught,
"Bagshot, February 27th, 1900.

"Our heartiest congratulations to you and your gallant troops."

The Regiment stood to from daybreak for flying column Fri. 2nd
if required.

Seven men and seven horses arrived from Kimberley.   Sat. 3rd

Porter's Brigade went out to the east and engaged the Boers near Leeuwkop, and located the Boer position at Poplar Grove.

Church parade 6.30 a.m.   Very dull morning, with Sun. 4th
showers of rain.

Thirty men and 32 horses arrived from Modder River. Terribly wet night, the whole place being completely

1900.   washed out and the shelters blown away like paper;
MARCH. things were floating about in all directions.   The men
kept up their spirits by singing " Home, Sweet Home."

Mon. 5th   Strength of the Regiment, 17 officers, 282 men, 266
horses.

Tues. 6th   Moved bivouac to Osfontein at 3 p.m., where the

BANK'S DRIFT FARM, SHOWING HOW THE LOOK-OUT MEN
WERE POSTED.

Cavalry Division, with two brigades of M. I. and seven
batteries R. H. A., concentrated to make a turning
movement on the left flank of the Boer position, and then
working round to the river so as to cut off their retreat
from Bloemfontein.

The 6th Division, under General Kelly-Kenny, was to
attack Table Mountain from Seven Sisters, while Gen.

Colville's Division moved along the north bank of the
river to attack the Boers on Leeuwkop.

Left Osfontein at 3.15 a.m. and followed the 2nd
Brigade (Broadwood's), which was leading the Division,
moving south-east by south.   About 6 a.m. we rounded
Seven Sisters kopjes and came under fire at long range,
but continued to work round behind the Boers.

The Boers were fully alive to the danger of holding on
to their position with their line of retreat thus threatened,
and at once began to retire.

The Division pushed on north towards Poplar Grove,
following up the retreating Boers.   At this time " C "
Squadron was ordered to make a flanking movement to
the left to try and drive off the Boers, who were holding
the ridge in front of the Cavalry Division.   Immediately
they saw this movement they concentrated a heavy fire
on the squadron, but were unable to check the advance,
and on reaching some stony ground about 450 yards
from the ridge, and almost in line with it, Capt. Lund
ordered the squadron to dismount, and try to drive them
off with carbine fire.   Just before we had actually dismounted, we saw what we imagined to be our own men
advancing towards us, but just as we were starting to
fire—and they were only about 200 yards or 150 yards
off—we discovered that they were Boers.   The order
was immediately given to mount, but both parties of
the enemy were able to give us a very hot time before
all the men got into the saddle.   The squadron then
retired.   There were about nine casualties, but only one
man killed.   Lieut. Duckett had his horse shot dead,

6

and was rescued in a most gallant manner by Corpl. Beadle.

The Boers retreated to a position extending from Schuin's Hoek to Stag's Kraal, out of which they were eventually driven about 5 p.m.

Horses and men were utterly exhausted.

Casualties :—

Killed : Lance-Corpl. J. Johns (" C ").
Died of wounds : Pte. H. Pyke (" A ").
Wounded : Sergt. F. Draper (" D ").
Pte. J. Reid (" A ").
Pte. A. Turner (" C ").
Pte. F. Clarke (" C ").
Sergt. G. Herrick (" C ").
Pte. J. Lavender (" C ").
Pte. G. Holben (" C ").
Pte. R. Morgan (" C ").
Pte. R. Thickpenny (" C ").
Pte. J. Ottley (" C ").
Pte. F. Ridewood (" C ").
Pte. A. Malthouse (" C ").
Pte. J. Elms (" A ").
21 horses killed, 11 wounded.

Lieut. Duckett's horse was killed and Lord F. Blackwood's severely wounded.

Kruger and Steyn were both reported to be present trying to urge the Boers to remain and fight.

The Regiment bivouacked at Poplar Grove.

The Regiment remained here all day. Porter's Brigade went some five miles up the river.

Lieut. Kincaid-Smith and the rest of the sick were sent in to Kimberley, while Major Follett, Capt. Ellison and Lieut. Skeffington Smyth, Vet.-Lieut. Tod, with 105 men and 106 horses, rejoined from Kimberley.

The Boers having taken up a position at Driefontein and Abraham's Kraal, an advance was made of the three Divisions, the left by Barberspan, the centre by Driefontein and Gen. Tucker on the right, with whom was the 3rd Cavalry Brigade, by Petrusburg. We started at 4.30 a.m., and reached the village about 10.30, bivouacking on the east side of it. On arrival a party of signallers was sent out to a high kopje to the east of the village, one of whom, Pte. J. Elms, was wounded.

We could hear the battle of Driefontein going on on our extreme left.

Left bivouac at 4.20 a.m., " C " Squadron in advance, " A " Squadron on flanks, and Capt. Fiennes with one troop in rear of the Division, and marched to Driekop, about 13 miles due east. On arrival the Regiment formed the outposts, and a Boer Field-Cornet, named Pretorius, with mauser and bandolier, was captured by Lieut. Duckett. This gentleman said he was only out buck-shooting !

Marched at 10 a.m. to Venter's Vallei. Had to leave 43 exhausted horses to come on with the infantry.

Did not reach camp till 8.30 p.m., where we rejoined the main army, and there heard the news of the Driefontein fight.

Marched at 4.45 a.m., " D " Squadron covering the
advance. Our direction was east to Leeuwberg, where
we halted, and " C " Squadron was sent south down the
railway, which they had to destroy.

They captured a German ambulance train, the engine
making good its escape under heavy fire from R.S.M.

LIEUT. SADLEIR-JACKSON'S TROOP, " D " SQUADRON.

Grant ! The remainder of the Regiment about 12 noon
were ordered to hold some kopjes overlooking Bloemfontein from the south. Just as we were getting there,
Capt. Brinton (2nd L. G.) galloped up and said the town
had surrendered.

Our men and the gunners cheered hard, and everyone
was delighted ; but what pleased us most of all was Lord
Roberts sending back word to say he wished the 9th

Lancers to form his escort on his entering the capital of the Orange Free State. Gen. Gordon had spoken to Lord Roberts in the morning and told him how pleased he was with the work of the Regiment, to which the Commander-in-Chief replied, " I know they have always been a splendid Regiment, and this is the third time they have been with me on active service."

Lieut. Jackson's troop led the way, then came Lord Roberts and Staff, Military Attachés and Bodyguard, then the rest of the Regiment, minus " C " Squadron, the R. H. A., 16th Lancers, etc.

The procession went up Monument Street, passing through the centre of the town, and received a great ovation from the Loyalists. Our brigade proceeded northwards out of the town to Rustfontein (about two miles) and there bivouacked.

Many Boers surrendered, and Steyn issued a proclamation to say that the Government was moved for the time being to Kroonstad !

" C " Squadron came in at 7.30 a.m., bringing in six Wed. 14th prisoners from Kaalspruit Farm, where they had spent the night.

Lieut. Jackson, who was on outpost duty, sent in 17 prisoners ; he also reported that about 3,000 Boers were holding the bridge over the Modder River to the north.

Lord Roberts issued the following address to the Thur. 15th troops :

" Cavalry Division Orders.

" Bloemfontein, 15th March, 1900.

" No. 1.. It affords F.M. the Commander-in-Chief the greatest pleasure in congratulating the Army in South Africa on the various events that have occurred during the past few weeks, and he would especially offer his sincere thanks to that portion of the Army which, under his immediate command, has taken part in the operations resulting yesterday in the capture of Bloemfontein. On the 12th of February this force crossed the boundary which divided the Orange Free State from British territory ; three days later Kimberley was relieved ; on the 15th day the bulk of the Boer army in this State, under one of their most trusted generals, was made prisoners. On the 17th day the news of the Relief of Ladysmith was received, and on the 13th of March, 29 days from the commencement of the operations, the capital of the Orange Free State was occupied.

" This is a record of which any army in the world may well be proud, a record which could not have been achieved except by earnest, well-disciplined men, determined to do their duty, and to surmount whatever difficulties or dangers might be encountered. Exposed to extreme heat by day, bivouacking under heavy rain, marching long distances (not unfrequently with reduced rations). The endurance, cheerfulness, and gallantry displayed by all ranks are beyond praise, and Lord Roberts feels sure that neither Her Majesty The Queen, nor the British nation, will be unmindful of the efforts made by this force to uphold the honour of their country.

" The Field Marshal desires specially to refer to the fortitude and heroic spirit with which the wounded have borne their sufferings. Owing to the great extent of country over which modern battles have to be fought, it is not always possible to afford immediate aid to those who are struck down. Many hours have indeed at times elapsed before some of the wounded could be attended, but not a word or murmur of complaint has been uttered, the anxiety of all when succour came was that their comrades should be cared for first.

" In assuring every officer and man how much he appreciates their efforts in the past, Lord Roberts is confident that in the future they will continue to show the same resolution of soldierly qualities and to lay down their lives, if need be (as so many brave men have already done), in order to ensure that the war in South Africa may be brought to a satisfactory conclusion."

Surrenders kept coming in all day. Fri. 16th
About 1,800 Boers are reported to have surrendered. Sat. 17th
Had a regimental " bon-fire " and " sing-song."
Church parade 9 a.m. Came on cold and wet. Sun. 18th
Everything soaked with rain. Mon. 19th
380 tins of tobacco sent by Miss Fiennes were distri- Fri. 23rd
buted amongst the Regiment. Heard that Maj. Little
had been gazetted to the command of the Regiment.

Got orders at 10.30 p.m. to march the following morning to Glen Siding, as the Boers were coming down

1900. on the farmers who had surrendered their arms, and
MARCH. Kruger had issued a Proclamation saying they would
be shot.

Sat. 24th   " D " Squadron marched at 5.30 a.m., the remainder
of the brigade followed at 9 a.m., and reached Glen
Siding at 3 p.m.   A very wet day and the ground terribly
heavy.   The Guards were encamped here on the south
side of the river, and had just lost one officer killed and
three officers and a scout wounded by five Zarps whom
they had chased.   We bivouacked on the left of the
Guards and fetched in some prisoners from a farm over
the drift.

Sun. 25th   " C " Squadron received orders to visit Brandfort,
about 22 miles to the north, accompanied by one
squadron of the 16th Lancers, under Capt. Sloane
Stanley, who moved on the west side of the railway.
Lieut. Duckett, with the advanced troop, got within
about 200 yards of the town, and could see the people
all coming out of church.   Almost directly afterwards
he came under heavy fire, and had to retire back on the
squadron.   The Boers were collecting in some force and
tried to get round the flanks, besides pressing them in rear.
Lieut. Lord F. Blackwood's patrol on the right flank was
also nearly cut off, and the squadron had to make a
running fight for ten miles.   At one time, the " C "
Squadron being somewhat pressed, Capt. Lund ordered
a troop to face about and charge.   This was well
carried out and checked the Boers considerably.
Sergt. Andrews and Corpl. Allin were both wounded
during the retirement.   Capt. Sloane Stanley was also

wounded in the head, and the 16th Lancers had several
casualties.

Sergt. Andrews, Corpl. Green, Sergt. Hart, Ptes.
Heanes and Shaw all brought men out of action, and
were reported for conspicuous gallantry. The squadron
returned to camp at 7 p.m., having had a very hard day.

Casualties :—

Wounded : Sergt. F. Andrews, " C " Squadron.

   Lance-Corpl. T. Allin, " C " Squadron.

   Pte. Brownrigg, " C " Squadron.

   Pte. J. Jones, " C " Squadron.

Missing : Pte. J. Dawson (wounded), " C " Squadron.

Prisoners of war : Pte. J. Warren, " C " Squadron ;

   F. Stevens, " C " Squadron.

Nine horses were killed and one missing.

The brigade crossed the drift and bivouacked at Klipfontein.

Col. Little and Lieut. Duckett went sick with fever
and dysentery.

Lieut. Sadleir-Jackson had to remain out with his Mon. 26th
troop on the river bank as sniping continued from the
farmhouse and bushes. Lieut. Cavendish went out on
patrol up the Springfontein road and had one man
wounded in the arm, Pte. G. Hill (" A ").   They
arrested some Boers at a farm and brought them in.

The ambulances brought in Ptes. Jones and Brownrigg.

The Zarps fired on our western patrol at Karree Tues. 27th
Siding.

1900.
MARCH.
Wed. 28th

Capt. Fiennes' patrol came under fire, and a patrol under Sergt. Johnson had one man captured.

"A" Squadron went out at 11 a.m. to strengthen the picket under Lieut. Lord F. Blackwood. The left patrol under Sergt. Andrews had a narrow escape of being cut off, and Corpl. Lapworth, whose horse fell with him, was taken prisoner, as also was Pte. Charlton, both of "C" Squadron.

Thur. 29th

Marched at 5 a.m. to concentrate with the Cavalry Division under Gen. French, in order to make a turning movement by the west and get round the kopjes overlooking Brandfort, while Gen. Tucker's Division attacked them from the south.

Proceeded about 12 miles and cleared the country to the north of Table Mountain. The Boers, numbering about 3,000, were holding the range of kopjes running east from Brandfort and had entrenched their position.

We received orders about 2 p.m. to return to the north side of the kopjes and co-operate with Gen. Tucker, whose shells were bursting over the Boer position. On our arrival we came under shell fire from the direction of Brandfort, and saw about 2,000 Boers on the kopjes and just below them. Our Maxim came into action at 2,000 yards range, and our guns came up and opened a hot fire, their shells bursting well amongst the Boers. The 1st Cavalry Brigade were on our left, and the Boers soon began streaming away along the ridge running towards Brandfort. The Regiment received orders to advance and charge, which we had started to do when Gen. French sent one of his gallopers to stop us. This

appeared reasonable, as the Boers were over a mile
away, had a line of kopjes behind them which they
held, and there were four wire fences between them
and us.

The Boers kept up a continuous shell fire, but no one
was hit.

Gen. Chermside on the east engaged the enemy till
dark. Le Gallais, M.I., and the 16th Lancers remained
out, but we were sent back to Klipfontein at 7 p.m.
very tired.

Maj. Follett commanded the Regiment as Col. Little
was still sick.

2nd Lieut. Vaughan Wynn joined the Regiment.

Paraded at 7 a.m., and marched back to Rustfontein, Fri. 30th
the Colonel and Lieut. Duckett going in by train. Capt.
Campbell and Lieuts. Brooke and Durand rejoined, and
Lieut. Allhusen returned from Gen. Tucker's staff.

An order came at 11 p.m. to turn out at once, as Sat. 31st
Broadwood's Brigade had got into difficulties at Sanna's
Post. We marched as far as Boesman's Kop, where we
joined the rest of the Cavalry Division.

Colville's Division had started to support Broadwood
at 3 a.m. APRIL.

Left Boesman's Kop at 9.15 a.m., and marched to Sun. 1st
Waterval, where Colville's and French's Divisions concentrated. Remained at the drift till 4 p.m., when the
whole Regiment was sent out on outposts for the night,
forming a ring round the Modder River opposite the
waterworks. Saw lots of Boers on the ridges and kopjes
in front, whose numbers we estimated at about 4,000.

1900.
APRIL.

They held all the positions that commanded the water-works.

Mon. 2nd The projected attack on the waterworks position fell through, principally owing to the weak state of the cavalry. Gen. French recommended that the Cavalry Division should return to Bloemfontein and refit. At 3 p.m. we received orders to go back to Boesman's Kop, which was reached at dusk.

Tues. 3rd Left Boesman's Kop 6.15 a.m., and marched back to our old quarters at Rustfontein. All the horses were very much done up.

Fri. 6th Seventy-two remounts arrived.

Sat. 7th Took over 96 Argentine remounts.

Col. Cameron (late Capt. 9th Lancers) came in with his Tasmanian contingent.

One squadron 17th Lancers also arrived.

Sun. 8th Church parade 9 a.m. Gen. French came round and inspected the horses.

Mon. 9th Strength : 367 men, 438 horses.

Tues. 10th The P.V.O. inspected the horses.

Wed. 11th Capt. Gordon with 12 men and eight horses arrived from Naauwpoort.

Sent away 38 remounts and 27 old horses to the depôt as unfit.

Distributed the gifts sent by Mrs. Henry Allhusen and Miss Colvin.

Took over an automatic Colt gun.

Thur. 12th Sergt. Connors, Sergt. Herrick and 13 men arrived.

Fri. 13th Gen. French saw some of our men and the 17th Lancers turned out in marching order. We are very much against the Argentine remounts they supplied us with.

Church parade 9 a.m.

Distributed gifts sent for the Regiment by Mrs. H. Allhusen, Lord W. Beresford and Lady Elliott.

Gen. French inspected the horses at 6.30 a.m.

Rained hard all day ; camp was in an awful state.

Distributed packages of socks sent by Lady Dorchester.

Grand concert at the Theatre in aid of " the Soldiers' Widows and Orphans," Lord Kitchener in the chair.

Messrs. Melton Prior and Woollen were very good in their " lightning sketches," which were sold by auction from the stage by Mr. Bennet Burleigh, and realized the following prices :—

Lord Roberts, by Melton Prior	..	75 guineas.
Kruger, by Woollen ..	..	33 ,,
Melton Prior, by Woollen	..	16 ,,
Woollen, by Melton Prior	..	10 ,,
Total ..	..	134 guineas.

Distributed more gifts sent by Mrs. H. Allhusen.

Capt. Willoughby rejoined from Cape Town. Gave out the gifts sent by Miss Little. Two chargers and seven troop horses were destroyed for glanders.

Paraded mounted for Gen. Gordon's inspection at 8 a.m., when he addressed the men who had been mentioned for gallantry in the field.

We were just parading for church at 8.30 a.m., when we received orders to turn out and march to Leeuwkop.

1900.   Left camp with 22 officers, 356 men, 327 horses ; two
APRIL.   officers, 74 men and 82 horses being left behind under
Capt. Ellison and Lieut. Lord F. Blackwood. 17th
Lancers covered the advance, followed by R. H. A., two
pom-poms, 9th and 16th Lancers. On nearing Leeuwkop we saw shells bursting to our left front, which were
probably Pole-Carew's gunners at work.

Bivouacked at 7 p.m.

Mon. 23rd   The 3rd Cavalry Brigade received orders to reconnoitre
Leeuwkop at daybreak, and report as soon as possible
if it was held. This was carried out, and the brigade
then marched on to Tweedieguluk.

Our objective was to march on Dewetsdorp, so as to
relieve the pressure on Wepener, which was being
besieged by the Boers.

Tues. 24th   Left Tweedieguluk at 6.30 a.m., "C" Squadron in
advance, with "D" Squadron on left flank, "A"
Squadron providing a patrol on the right. About 7.30
a.m. "C" Squadron came in touch, and was soon afterwards checked by a considerable number of Boers with
pom-poms. The left at the same time was being fired
on from the high kopjes on that flank. While this was
going on the main body was following the road which
here ran half right, and the head of it had got up to some
high kopjes, when "D" Squadron was ordered to make
good and hold a ridge that ran across the valley. Galloping to the left front the ridge was secured, and the
squadron started firing at the Boers who were seen
galloping away below. There was, however, a spur running away from the main ridge, and a troop coming up

under Capt. Stanley endeavoured to make this good, but unfortunately it had just been occupied, evidently by Boers coming up under cover from the left. The whole squadron was thus exposed and subjected to a very hot fire at only a few hundred yards' range.

Before very long there were a dozen or more casualties, including Capt. Stanley and his troop sergeant. Capt. Willoughby now gave the order for everyone to get back as best they could, ammunition having been exhausted, and sent for reinforcements. The " C " Squadron came up, as did also the 8th Hussars and 7th D. G. Extending on our right. The pom-poms were also brought up to very close range. It was not till about 10.30 a.m. that the whole ridge had been occupied and the Boers driven off.

Lieut. Brooke was wounded very soon after reaching the ridge, and it was especially bad luck for Capt. Stanley to be wounded, this being his first day under fire.

The " D " Squadron casualties were heavy.

Killed : Pte. W. MacDonald and Pte. H. Underwood.

Wounded : Capt. H. W. Stanley ; Sergt. J. Gratton, Corpl. A. Holmes ; Ptes. W. Lacey, G. Hemming, J. Scully, A. Kerr, G. Twyford, S. Taylor, J. Kerr, A. Hay, W. Webber, J. Elliott, J. McCrea, J. King.

Nearly all these were very severely wounded, also Lieut. V. R. Brooke, " C " Squadron.

The men behaved splendidly throughout the whole action.

Beyond this ridge was a large plain stretching away

1900.
APRIL.

to Grootfontein on the way to Thaba 'Nchu and Dewets-dorp.

After a halt the Division moved on to Grootfontein, where it bivouacked, throwing out very strong outposts.

Wed. 25th

" A " and " C " Squadrons were sent out on outposts last night, " D " being left in owing to its severe handling,

ON TREK, 9TH LANCERS EASING THEIR HORSES.

but between eight and nine o'clock it was also ordered out, and had to grope its way for a considerable distance, and cross two bad dongas before reaching its position. Three more of our men died of their wounds last night. The Division marched on about 5.30 a.m., and about 1 p.m. we saw a large force in the direction of Dewets-dorp. This turned out to be Rundle's Division going on to Wepener, the Boers having left Dewetsdorp 24 hours before.

Halted here for the night—Dewetsdorp.

Moved on at 6 a.m. towards Thaba 'Nchu, and halted for the night a few miles south of the mountains at Kopjes Kraal.

Moved on a few miles, leaving camp at 7 a.m., and then halted for a considerable time. In the afternoon our brigade and the 4th (Gen. Dickson) demonstrated towards the south-east end of the high mountain, where the Boers were found to be in force. Our guns had just started shelling them, when Gen. Dickson ordered a retirement of both brigades to last night's bivouac, leaving " D " Squadron out holding a ridge in front.

Our brigade was ordered to sweep round in an easterly direction and get at the Boers' left and rear if possible, while Dickson's went direct toward Thaba 'Nchu. The 16th Lancers were in front, and on coming in contact the " A " Squadron was pushed out to the right front. The Boers were in considerable numbers, and many were seen going back in a north-easterly direction, but the corner kopjes were well held with a pom-pom just round the flank. Going on we found the ground opening up to the north formed the neck known as " Springhaan Nek," at the south-east corner of the high Thaba 'Nchu mountain, and connecting it with the Ladybrand range of hills. On arrival here, a heavy fire was opened on us by pom-poms and rifles, but a couple of our guns coming up soon silenced them. Lieut. Theobald was then sent on with a patrol, supported by a squadron of 17th Lancers,

7

while the " A " Squadron got orders to rejoin.   The rest of the brigade with Gordon were away to the left under the hills.   Soon after this a heavy fire was opened and before long the squadron of the 17th retired.   Unfortunately Lieut. Theobald and part of his patrol were cut off.

Col. Little had to dismount a squadron to cover the retirement of the 17th, when the whole moved back over a rise, from which the Maxims and guns opened on the Boers, who pulled up and came no further.

Gordon, with the 16th, was busy on the left, the Boers having brought up a couple of guns.   Fighting was still going on, but it was getting late, and Gen. Gordon, finding the place we were in would be untenable as a bivouac, ordered a retirement of the whole brigade on our old bivouac.   It was a longish ride back in the dark with a nasty neck to get over, and camp was not reached till 9 p.m.   We had been in the saddle since 6 a.m., and then had to spend a miserable night—no food, or forage, or blankets, and cruelly cold.

The Regiment's casualties were :—

Wounded : R.S.M. W. Grant.
　　Pte. T. Crabtree (" A ").
Missing : 2nd Lieut. S. R. Theobald.
　　Lance-Corpl. C. Henty (" D ").
　　Pte. P. Swaffer (" D ").
　　Pte. H. Hinchcliffe (" D ").
　　Pte. W. Ferguson (" D ").
　　Pte. F. Norman (" C ").

Pte. T. Griffiths (" C ").

Pte. P. Keon (" A ").

Pte. C. Robinson (" D ").

Several of these men were stretcher-bearers helping the wounded, but the Boers detained them as prisoners.

Corpl. Henty was wounded and Pte. Norman died of his wounds, while Ptes. Ferguson and Robinson rejoined. Lieut. Theobald was reported by the Boers to have been killed.

Lieut. Allhusen went sick with fever.

Left bivouac at 7 a.m. to make our way to Thaba 'Nchu, but on getting to a gorge leading through the lower hills orders came for us to remain where we were, Gen. Gordon having selected a bivouac about 10.30 a.m., a squadron of 17th Lancers and the " A " Squadron being sent to hold some kopjes to the south-west of the high mountain.

Having just settled down and prepared for breakfast, a heavy rifle fire broke out from the direction of our outposts, upon which bivouac was struck at once, and the troops moved out to the support of the two squadrons. The 17th Lancers squadron retired from its position with loss of its Maxim gun, and then the " A " Squadron, under a heavy fire from each flank, was compelled to do so also, but came away slowly, and remained just out of range on the plain. While the fighting was going on, Maj. Lord D. Compton had sent two men back to the led horses for more ammunition, and these men returned up the kopje only to find the squadron gone. On hearing

7*

of this, Sergt. Mercer volunteered to go back and find them, and succeeded in bringing them safely down under a very heavy fire.

For this act Sergt. Mercer was recommended for the V.C.

The Boers were now seen working to the south to the kopjes held by the " D " Squadron on the night of Friday, April 27th. They had two guns with them.

While this was going on Gen. Gordon had received orders to fall back on Thaba 'Nchu, and detailed the Regiment to cover the retirement through the gorge. This was one of the prettiest pieces of work done so far. The " A " Squadron remained holding the ridge till all had retired, and then in turn retired past " C " and " D " Squadrons, which had taken up a position near the mouth of the gorge. Although the Boer guns had opened fire, the men were as steady as could be, and the retirement through the gorge was successfully accomplished, and fortunately with only one casualty—Pte. A. Clegg (" C "), wounded by a fragment of shell, and this in spite of the Boers getting the range of the gorge with a pom-pom before all had got through.

Mon. 30th   Everyone rather expected orders to return to Bloemfontein to complete refitting, but " C " Squadron was sent out to escort a convoy from Waterval, and at 1 p.m. the brigade got orders to move to Israel's Poort, where the Bloemfontein Road crosses the chain of hills which forms a semi-circle round Thaba 'Nchu from south-west to north-east, and here, some six miles from the town, got to bivouac at 5 p.m.

Early in the morning a Composite Regiment of one
squadron from each Regiment was sent to help Gen. Ian
Hamilton, who was forcing a neck to the north. The
" A " Squadron was the one sent from the Regiment.
About 9 a.m. a message came from Gen. Hamilton to say
that his left was being threatened. Gen. Gordon then
ordered Col. Little to take the other two squadrons and
a section of guns to the north-west, near Thaba mountain.
This was reached just in time to head off 300 or 400
Boers with two guns, who went off hastily in a north-
easterly direction, and just as we were starting off back,
a large column was seen in the distance coming from the
direction of Bloemfontein.

Crabtree, who was wounded on April 28th, died on the
30th. Heavy shelling all day to north-east. Got orders
to go in to Bloemfontein to-morrow.

A very complimentary message was received from Gen.
Hamilton thanking the cavalry for the assistance rendered to him.

Left bivouac at 5 a.m., and made a halt at the waterworks, where we heard that Capt. Stanley, Sergt. Grattan
and Pte. A. Kerr had died of their wounds while being
taken into Bloemfontein. Capt. Stanley was buried at
Bloemfontein by the Coldstream Guards.

Left Boesman's Kop at 6 a.m., and reached Rustfontein at 9 a.m.

This has been an expensive trip for us, the casualties
being 30, including one officer killed, one wounded, one
missing, and one sick with enteric.

One hundred and twenty-seven remounts arrived.

1900. Warm clothing and tobacco sent by friends at home
MAY.   were distributed.

Sun. 6th   Church parade 9 a.m.

Gifts from Lord W. Beresford and the Duchess of Marlborough were distributed amongst the men.

The General addressed the men after Church parade,

LIEUT. THEOBALD'S TROOP, "D" SQUADRON.

and told them how pleased Gen. French and he were
with their behaviour, especially mentioning the conduct
of "D" Squadron on April 24th, at Roodekop, where
they all behaved so gallantly.

Orders came for the brigade to march to-morrow and
pick up the army under Lord Roberts, which had begun
its general advance northwards.

Mon. 7th   Left camp at 7 a.m., with 21 officers, 384 men and 374

horses, and marched some 24 miles, halting at 5 p.m.
about four miles beyond Karree Siding.

Marched at 6.30 a.m., passing through Brandfort at
9 a.m., and reaching Wet River Station—28 miles—
about 5.15 p.m. Here heard that Lord Roberts was
only some seven miles on, and that the 3rd Cavalry
Brigade were to join him as Divisional troops.

Left camp at 7 a.m., and reached Welgelegen, where
Lord Roberts was already in camp, about 5 p.m., though
" D " Squadron as rear guard did not get in till after
dark. The march was about 20 miles, and much delay
was caused at the Wet River, owing to the drift being a
bad one and the bridge being badly broken up.

Marched at 6.30 a.m., " C " Squadron covering the
advance. The Sand River was crossed without opposition, but soon after doing this our advance was opposed,
as was also that of the M. I. on our left, and Ian Hamilton's force had hard fighting in crossing further to the
east. We were shelled from the kopjes to the north-east,
but after a short time the whole of the enemy's line began
to fall back, though they disputed the ground up to the
last, and kept their guns very active. The infantry
stopped at Riet Spruit, but the Cavalry Brigade pushed
on to Ventersburg Road, some 18 miles.

The railway line was badly torn up for many miles.

Lieut. Sadleir-Jackson was sent with a patrol to communicate with French, who was some 15 miles to the
west, and made out his journey successfully.

Skeffington Smyth got hold of a copy of the *Standard
and Diggers' News* at the station, which stated that

1900.
MAY.

Lieut. Theobald and 11 prisoners had passed through Kroonstad *en route* to Pretoria.   This was cheering news, after thinking he had been killed.   Capt. Gordon placed in charge of Maxim.

Fri. 11th

After a very cold night a start was made at 6 a.m., with the 16th Lancers in front.   They got in touch about 1 p.m. with the Boers, who had taken up a position on the Boschrand Spruit.

An artillery duel was kept up most of the afternoon, and we went into bivouac just as it was getting dark, the whole Regiment having to go out on outposts.

Sat. 12th

On moving out we found the Boers had evacuated yesterday's position, and a further reconnaissance proved that Kroonstad was also unheld.

Kroonstad.

Lord Roberts then came up and we marched on towards the town, crossing the Valsch River, where the chief watched the troops go by to their bivouacs, and then went on to the town with the Guards and Pole-Carew's Division.

Thus Steyn had deserted his second capital, and had now taken up his abode at Heilbron !

Sun. 13th

Church parade 9 a.m.

Everyone spent most of the day having a general clean up !

Mon. 14th

Horses inspected by veterinary officer.

Tues. 15th

Horses inspected by Gen. Gordon.

Thur. 17th

Gen. French inspected the brigade in the lines.   About 1.30 p.m. an order came for the brigade to turn out and go back to Ventersburg Road, as 500 Boers and three guns were reported to have gone back there.

On reaching Boschrand Siding we met some 800 M. I.
details, etc., which in all probability were the cause of
the report. Went into bivouac here.

Started back for Kroonstad at 8 a.m. and got in about
noon. Lord Roberts met the brigade as it crossed the
Valsch River and made some very complimentary
remarks about the Regiment.

H. Phelan, civil vet.-surg., arrived and was attached
to the Regiment.

The brigade marched at 6.15 a.m., going some 15
miles along the Heilbron road and then turned north
across country, bivouacking at Doornkop. Only small
parties of snipers met with, which were soon dispersed.

Capt. Ellison had to be left behind sick.

The Regiment marched out, 23 officers, 320 men and
308 horses strong.

Left bivouac at 7 a.m., and scoured a good deal of
country to north and east till midday, when we halted,
and later in the afternoon went into bivouac at Boschrand. Nine Boers came in and surrendered, and these
were sent in to Army head-quarters, under Lieut. Cavendish, Lieut. Duckett taking in three commandants, who
surrendered yesterday to Lord Roberts.

At 7.30 p.m. Lieut. Skeffington Smyth was sent back
to try and pick up the convoy that had left Kroonstad
by the Heilbron road.

The chief duty of the brigade in these parts was to
keep the country clear and the road open for this convoy.
Infantry marched up to Honingspruit Station.

Left bivouac at 6.15 a.m., marching north, the " A "

and " D " Squadrons covering the advance, and finally halted a few miles south-east of the railway bridge over the Rhenoster River, about 18 miles having been covered. Boers reported to have crossed the Vaal River. Heard that Mafeking had been relieved by a flying column under Col. Mahon.

VET.-SURGEON H. PHELAN, ATTACHED TO 9TH LANCERS.

Lieut. Durand was sent out with a patrol towards Vredefort to endeavour to communicate with Broadwood's Brigade.

Thur. 24th   Crossed the Rhenoster and marched on to Vredefort Road Station. Here a concentration of the main army and Ian Hamilton's force took place. Durand returned

from an unsuccessful search and Skeffington Smyth came
in with the convoy. The nights are getting very cold
now, and the horses are beginning to feel the effect of
it. All units paraded at 5 p.m. and gave three cheers
for Her Majesty.

The whole army moved on to Wolverhoek, which was
reached at 2 p.m. after an uneventful day.

Left bivouac at 6 a.m., and marched north across
Taaibosch Spruit, where a halt was made. About 3 p.m.
a convoy was reported to be some 12 miles off south-east,
and the brigade was sent out to try and cut it off. After
going some eight miles the " A " Squadron came under
fire from some small kopjes. As it was getting dark the
brigade withdrew and marched back to bivouac near
Viljoen's Drift Station, about four miles south of
Vereeniging, which is just across the Vaal. Sergt. Hart
was sent on with an American scout to try and save
the bridge, but one span was blown up before they got
there.

The brigade " stood to " at 6 a.m., but sent out patrols
eastwards, which were fired on about 9 o'clock, so we
went out in support. The Boers on being shelled soon
cleared out, and then some guns opened on us from
across the river, but could not reach us.

Remained on south side covering the army while it
crossed the Vaal, and then did so ourselves, going through
the filthy dirty station of Viljoen's about 4 p.m., and got
into bivouac just before dark with all the appearance
of " Christy Minstrels," owing to the coal dust.

This is a coal mining district.

1900.   The Boers were here in considerable numbers yesterday,
MAY.   but the crossing to-day was practically unopposed.

Mon. 28th   Marched at 6 a.m., " A " Squadron being in front and
" C " Squadron out on the right flank of the army. A
certain amount of sniping took place, especially from the
hills to the east which covered Heidelberg. Here Capt.
Fiennes, with a patrol, had an exciting gallop to save
themselves being cut off, and Lieut. Wynn in front
narrowly escaped being trapped. We bivouacked in the
evening to the east of Klip River Station after a very
long day. The Klip River runs down the centre of this
valley, which is several miles wide, and joins the Vaal
near Vereeniging.

There was a nasty line of trenches across the valley
near this station, but they were fortunately unoccupied.
Pte. J. Greig, " C " Squadron, was taken prisoner.

Tues. 29th   Did not leave bivouac until 9 a.m., and then the brigade
acted as a flank guard to the army. The M. I., under
Col. Henry, had been sent on first thing in the morning,
and came in contact with the enemy. The brigade then
got orders to support the M. I., but the fighting was over
when we arrived, and we were then sent to destroy the
main line and telegraph to Natal. After this had been
accomplished, we went on to Elandsfontein, and in to
bivouac at Rietfontein A mine, some eight miles east of
Johannesburg.

Lieut. Jackson was sent out with his troop to endeavour to bring in a train that had been cut off.

Wed. 30th   The " A " Squadron were on night outposts, and had
not been relieved, when about 8.30 a.m. there was a

sudden and determined rush made on them by a force
of Boers, who had evidently come from the direction of
Johannesburg under cover of a lot of dead ground there
was in these parts. The surroundings were imperfectly
known, as we did not reach bivouac until dark last night.
Gen. Gordon had started for Johannesburg as the brigade
was to go in to take part in a triumphal march through
the town.

Col. Little was thus left in command and had the
brigade out in a very short time after firing commenced.
A squadron of the 16th Lancers galloping up to the
outposts met with a very hot reception before they could
be dismounted, and had several casualties.

The Boers had three guns and a pom-pom with them,
and made it so hot for our gunners that one section was
unable to be worked.

However, the situation had been saved by Col. Little's
prompt action and the fine way in which the whole
brigade turned out, and in 30 to 45 minutes the Boers
were retreating. Had the attack been made a very
little later the camp would undoubtedly have been
rushed, for we should have been on our way to Johannesburg. The Regiment got out of this affair with only one
casualty—Pte. J. Nixon (" C " Squadron), wounded.

In the afternoon we got orders to work westwards to
co-operate with Gen. French.

Lieut. Jackson returned, having been unsuccessful
owing to the number of Boers about, but had the satisfaction of capturing a field-cornet.

The Regiment moved forward and occupied the

1900.
JUNE.

dynamite factory and its surroundings at Modderfontein without any opposition.

It was a treat to get hold of fresh bread and soda-water here.   We retired a short distance to bivouac.

BOER PRISONER CAPTURED DAY AFTER BATTLE OF
MODDER RIVER.

Fri. 1st   Left bivouac at 6.15 a.m., and halted near where we were yesterday—Mooifontein—the remainder of the brigade coming up to us.

At 6 p.m. got orders to turn out 100 mounted men to

act with a similar number from 16th Lancers and 20 from 17th Lancers.

Eventually 88 men and 98 horses paraded under Capt. the Hon. C. Willoughby, who had the following officers under him :

Capt. Campbell, Lieuts. Durand, Lord F. Blackwood, Pollok and Sadleir-Jackson.

The force that moved out last night was under the command of Maj. Hunter-Weston, R.E., of Gen. French's staff, and his orders were to endeavour to blow up the bridge at Bronkhorst Spruit by 2 p.m. to-morrow, as it was supposed that trains were in waiting to carry eastwards not only all the English prisoners but the President himself.

A start on their enormous undertaking was made about 8.30 p.m., and is here given in the words of Capt. Campbell who took part :

" We moved off, passing the dynamite factory, no one except Hunter-Weston knowing where we were going, or what we were going to do. After proceeding about a mile the column halted, and officers were called to the front, where Hunter-Weston and Burnham, the American scout, awaited them. Hunter-Weston then addressed the officers in somewhat the following terms. After telling them the object of the undertaking he said : ' It is about 65 miles to the bridge, and I propose we should lead our horses all night, and at daybreak we will seize the first farm we come to, and whilst the men and horses rest, Burnham and I will go on and scout. My plan is, *Mooifon-*
tein
Dynamite
Works.

if we meet a large force when anywhere near the bridge, Burnham and I will hide and we will try and blow up the bridge by stealth, whilst Willoughby tries to get the force safely back. If we come across any small force we must push through them and try to get to the bridge, and the bridge must then be rushed and blown up. After blowing up the bridge we must try and make the best of our way home!' Maj. Hunter-Weston then gave orders that if any men fell out they were to be instructed to make the best of their way to camp, and nothing was to be allowed to retard the march. The undertaking was of a somewhat stupendous character, as not only was the country full of Boers, but also the horses were in poor condition, and the journey of over 60 miles to the bridge was about as much as most of them would have been able to perform, and the return would still have to be done. In accordance with orders, we moved on in column of files, leading our horses. The squadron of 16th and 17th Lancers led the way, with Burnham continually working on in front. The night was cold and crisp, with a bright moon which greatly facilitated the march. All night long we led our horses with occasional halts, whilst Burnham made the ground good ahead. Several places were passed where it was anticipated Boer picquets would be found, but none were encountered, and day began to break without any signs of the enemy having been met with. It was now 6 o'clock and we all mounted. Scarcely had we done so when three heads appeared over a slight rise a few hundred yards to our right front. Immediately after-

wards three Boers galloped away, and almost simul- 1900.
taneously Burnham came in from the front and reported
three large laagers right ahead. ' I guess we shall have
a little scrapping,' he remarked—and we did ! At the
time the force was moving in line of squadron column,
the 9th on the left. We were 250 strong, 25 miles from
any support, and 1,000 Boers reported in our road.
There was nothing but to retire and seize a position in
rear. The 9th were ordered to occupy the left of the line
in retirement, and the 16th and 17th the right, both
retiring simultaneously by succession of troops. The
Boers began at once to press in front and to work round
both flanks, and it was only the rapid and orderly manner
in which the retirement was made, the cool and steady
behaviour of the men, and the excellent handling of the
troop leaders, that saved the force from being scattered
to the four winds, and having an enormous casualty list.
The Boers attacked in the most gallant manner, but were
always met by a steady fire, the last troop holding them
back till the last moment, and then retiring at a gallop to
the next position. The retirement was continued for about
10 miles, till we reached the first position it was possible
to hold, near a Kaffir kraal at Bapsfontein. This was
seized and all collected there. Burnham and Durand
(who had been wounded) galloped on to camp to have
reinforcements sent out ; these, however, were not
required, as the Boers, after reconnoitring the position,
retired, and after resting our horses Hunter-Weston gave
orders for a homeward move, and near camp we met the
force coming out to our assistance. On arrival about

8

1900.
JUNE.

11 a.m. Hunter-Weston addressed the men, and congratulated them on their fine behaviour, which alone had saved a disaster. Out of six officers with the 9th squadron Lieut. Pollok was mortally wounded, Lieuts. Durand and Sadleir-Jackson wounded, and Lieut. Lord F. Blackwood and Capt. Campbell had their horses killed. Lieuts. Durand and Jackson, after being wounded, continued to conduct the retirement of their troops, and Lieut. Pollok behaved most gallantly until overcome by weakness."

Lieut. Lord F. Blackwood was rescued by the gallantry of Ptes. Wright and Albert, " C " Squadron, both of whom had their names brought forward.

Casualties :—

Lieut. H. M. Durand, wounded right leg.
2nd Lieut. L. V. Sadleir-Jackson, wounded left leg.
2nd Lieut. J. F. Pollok, wounded body (died of wounds).
No. 3445 Sergt. J. Mercer (" A "), wounded.
No. 3979 Lance-Corpl. W. Joyce (" C "), wounded.
No. 3386 Pte. G. Lloyd (" C "), wounded.
No. 4082 Pte. J. Merriman (" C "), killed.
No. 3023 Pte. W. Leybourne (" C "), taken prisoner.
No. 3918 Pte. H. Letts (" D "), wounded.
16 horses killed, 6 wounded, 5 missing.

Sun. 3rd

The brigade moved on to Waterval, protecting the right flank of the army, which moved to Leeuwkop. As we were going into bivouac about 4 p.m., an order came from Lord Roberts for the three regiments of the brigade to push on and verify a report he had received that

Pretoria had been evacuated. Leaving the guns and the " A " Squadron, which had gone out on outposts, the remainder pushed on to Olifantsfontein, from which place the " D " Squadron was sent towards Vlakplaats, on the Six-mile Spruit, while " C " Squadron was to reconnoitre Irene Station, and in the event of its not being occupied, to push on towards Pretoria.

The remainder of the brigade moved on to Brakfontein, where they remained halted during the night. A patrol from " D " Squadron, under Lieut. Trower, ran up against a Boer picquet on the Spruit, and in the darkness could make no further way, and the " C " Squadron was likewise checked from further advance and fell back on the brigade.

The brigade moved on to within about four miles of Six-mile Spruit, where a halt was made to enable the guns and the squadrons that were out during the night to rejoin us, which they did soon after. It was here found that several men were missing from both squadrons. The rest of the army were beginning to appear on our left, but the Boers still maintained their outposts on the spruit, from which our patrols were fired on. The main army moved steadily on, driving all before them, and later on the brigade moved further eastwards towards Irene Station. Here there was a long line of hills strongly held and with long-range guns, which were dropping shells amongst us, while we could not touch them. The infantry worked steadily on and our heavy guns pounded the forts until darkness drew on. We bivouacked close to where we were.

1900.
JUNE.

Mon. 4th

8*

Advanced on Pretoria at 8 a.m., and on reaching the bridge over Six-mile Spruit heard cheers all along the line, which announced that the capital of the Transvaal had fallen. Moved on to near south-east fort, where the troops were halting preparatory to a triumphal entry.

One of the men here produced a lance flag, which he had carried specially for this occasion, so the Colonel promptly appointed him his orderly.

However, our ardour was very soon damped, for the brigade got orders to retrace its steps towards Irene and clear up the situation to the south-east of Pretoria, owing to a reported threatening by the Boers from that direction. After wandering about up and down the roughest of kopjes for the rest of the day, we eventually bivouacked on the south-east of the town.

It was found that most of the prisoners had not been taken away.

Several of our men who were missing from the night of June 4th turned up, and we found a grave at the bridge over the spruit, which was that of Pte. J. Briggs (" C ").

Wed. 6th   Lieut. Wynn on patrol reported the Boers in position near the distillery some eight or nine miles to the east.

Only some 800 men and 20 officers (prisoners) were got away from Pretoria.

In the afternoon loud cheers were heard coming from the Regiment, which turned out to be a welcome to Lieut. Theobald, who had got permission to leave the prison to come over and see us.

Though his experiences had scarcely been pleasant, there was a strong sense of humour about them, and a recapitulation may not be out of place. His story was somewhat as follows :

When he was out on patrol on April 28th, and found the Boers coming on in force, he galloped back, but his horse Carnac was beat and could hardly trot. A big Boer with a black beard galloped up to him, pointing his rifle at him and shouting, " Hands up ! " when he managed to pull out his revolver and emptied its contents into man and horse, killing both. His own horse was then killed, so he ran into a mealie field and hid while the Boers were looking for him. He lay there for fully three-quarters of an hour, and managed to bury his bandolier, sword and revolver, and took the lens out of his glasses. He then heard the Boers coming back, and they were almost giving up the search when one of them spotted him and he was taken prisoner.

He was taken straight back to the man he had shot, and thought they meant to have their revenge, when much to his relief they simply said, " You did rather well to shoot that man."

He was then taken before De Wet, to whom he reported that our stretcher-bearers had been made prisoners. Pte. Swaffer behaved very gallantly, and was taken prisoner owing to his stopping to pull a dead horse off Sergt.-Maj. Toones (17th Lancers), which had fallen on him and was suffocating him. Corpl. Henty, who was wounded, and Pte. Hinchcliffe were also taken prisoners.

He (Theobald) made an attempt to escape that night,

crawling out from under his wagon on "all fours," but unfortunately crawled into his guard, who asked him what he was doing and sent him back. He was subsequently taken on to Winburg and Kroonstad, and then by rail to Pretoria, where the officer prisoners lived in a tin house enclosed in a wire netting 12ft. high, with formidable wire entanglements outside, electric lamps about every 20 yards, and a strong Hollander guard.

On June 4th a commandant came into their house and told them that they must all get ready and leave at once with him.

Col. Hunt, after some consultation, went up to the commandant and said they were not going to move, and said, moreover, "You are our prisoner!" and they all surrounded him and took away his arms. Then another commandant came in and was promptly seized and disarmed, followed by an adjutant, who was treated in the same manner.

The Hollander guards said they would fetch up a Maxim, and went off to do so. Col. Hunt made terms with the commandant, who gave his parole that if he and the other two Boers were allowed to go, no harm should be done to the prisoners. This being done, the commandants were allowed to go, and soon afterwards the prisoners all got out and seized the Hollander guards, put them inside the caging and placed the officers' servants as a guard over them.

The Duke of Marlborough and Mr. Winston Churchill galloped into the town and up to the prison, and told them they were at last free.

3,500 prisoners were released, and a good many more from Waterval.

They were, however, not allowed to join their units until the official court of enquiry had been held.

A day of peace, except for outpost work.

Got the sad news that Lieut. Pollok had died of his wounds on June 3rd, at Boksberg, and that Capt. Ellison was very ill.

· The brigade received orders to join Broadwood's at Swavel's Poort, some eight or nine miles further east. Marched out at 1.15 p.m. and got into bivouac about 5 p.m.

Lord Roberts' congratulatory Army Order was published this evening.

"Army Order, Pretoria, 7th June, 1900.

" In congratulating the British Army in South Africa on the occupation of Johannesburg and Pretoria, the one being the principal town and the other the capital of the Transvaal, and also on the relief of Mafeking, after an heroic defence of over 200 days, the F.M. Commander-in-Chief desires to place on record his high appreciation of the gallantry and endurance displayed by the troops— both those who have taken part in the advance across the Vaal River and those who have been employed in the less arduous duty of protecting the lines of com-munication through the Orange River Colony.

" 2. After the force reached Bloemfontein on March 13th, it was necessary to halt there for a certain period. Through railway communication with Cape Colony had to be restored before supplies and necessaries of all kinds could be got up from the base. The rapid advance from Modder River and the want of forage *en route* had told hardly on the horses of the cavalry, artillery, M. I., and transport mules and oxen, and to replace these casualties a considerable number of animals had to be provided. Throughout the six weeks the army remained halted at Bloemfontein the enemy showed considerable activity, especially in the south-eastern portion of the Colony, but by the beginning of May everything was in readiness for a further advance into the enemy's country, and on the 2nd of that month active operations were again commenced.

" 3. On May 12th, Kroonstad, where Mr. Steyn had established a so-called Government of the Orange Free State, was entered ; on May 17th, Mafeking was relieved ; on May 31st Johannesburg was occupied ; and on June 5th the British Flag waved over Pretoria.

" During these 35 days the main body of the force marched 300 miles, including 15 days' halt, and engaged the enemy on six different occasions. The column under Lieut.-Gen. Hamilton marched 400 miles in 45 days, including 10 days' halt, and was engaged with the enemy 28 times. The flying column under Col. B. Mahon, which relieved Mafeking, marched at the rate of nearly 15 miles a day for 14 consecutive days, and successfully accomplished its object, despite the determined opposition offered by the enemy.

" The newly-raised battalion of C. I. V. marched 500 miles in 51 days, only once having two consecutive days' halt. It took part in 26 engagements with the enemy.

" 4. During the recent operations the sudden variations in the temperature between the warm sun in the day time and the bitter cold at night have been peculiarly trying to the troops, and owing to the necessity for rapid movements the soldiers have frequently had to bivouac after long and trying marches without firewood and on scanty rations.

" 5. The cheerful spirit with which difficulties have been overcome and hardships disregarded are deserving of the highest praise, and in thanking all ranks for their successful efforts to obtain the object in view, Lord Roberts is proud to think that the soldiers under his command have worthily upheld the traditions of Her Majesty's army in fighting, in marching, and in the admirable discipline which has been maintained throughout a period of no ordinary trial and difficulty."

Shifted our bivouac a short distance, and then sent back our sick horses to Pretoria.   Sat. 9th

The Regiment now being much reduced, it was formed into two squadrons under Capts. Willoughby and Lund.

Strength :—

		Men.	Horses.
" A " Squadron	..	87	55
" C " Squadron	..	85	47
" D " Squadron	..	90	57
		262*	159

* This included servants, men with convoy, etc., and 68 men without horses.

1900.
JUNE.

A section of our guns had also to be sent back, as well as men and horses from the other regiments. The brigade was now attached to Gen. Hamilton's Division.

Lord Roberts had ordered an armistice in order to confer with Louis Botha on the subject of surrender, but the latter would have none of it.

Maj. Follett had to go on the sick list.

Sun. 10th

Church parade 10 a.m.

Boers reported holding a strong position to the north-east.

Mon. 11th

Marched at 5.15 a.m., following Broadwood's Brigade towards Tiger's Poort. After the leading brigade got through, our advance (the 17th Lancers) came under heavy fire, losing two officers killed, and then two guns *Diamond Hill.* were opened on the main body from the kopjes to the south-east of the poort. These were, however, soon silenced by our gunners when we all got through the poort. Broadwood in the meantime had gone on and had got within striking distance of the left of the main position, but was here very heavily attacked and shelled, and the 12th Lancers and Household Regiment had to charge to save their gunners, Lord Airlie being killed here. Our brigade remained in support of Broadwood's, and carried on a certain amount of shelling to the flank during the afternoon.

Lord D. Compton was sent out at 4 a.m. with the dismounted men to hold the hills covering the defile we had to go through soon after leaving camp.

The convoys ordered in the afternoon to join their brigades, so this party went with them, and had a weary

time crossing several bad drifts, and on finishing one at
9 p.m. were told to take the wagons back to the other
side of it.

Broadwood's Brigade and ours remained out protecting
the left and left rear while the main attack was carried
out. As we were up fairly high amongst the kopjes, we
had a splendid view of Hamilton's part of the battle,
and watched the splendid work of the M. I. and infantry
with great keenness. They gained the crest about
5 p.m., piercing the main position, after which furious
fighting went on till long after dark, and the whole place
was blazing with grass fires.

Lord D. Compton's party had another bad day with
the convoys, and did not reach the 3rd Brigade till
11 p.m.

The whole Regiment was on outposts till 8.30 a.m.,
when we got orders to cover the front and right of Broadwood's Brigade, moving towards Bronkhurst Spruit.
Only a small party of Boers was encountered, but many
could be seen in the far distance, and a long-range gun
fired a few shells at the patrols from the line just beyond
Bronkhurst Spruit Station.

After a long round we swung to the left and bivouacked
at Elands River Station.

The whole force remained here for the day.
Started back at 12.30 p.m. for Pretoria with Ian
Hamilton's Division, passing over Donker's Hoek, and
so seeing what a tremendous position our troops had
successfully carried. Bivouacked just on the far-side,
near Christinen Hall.

1900.
JUNE.

Here we heard that De Wet had captured a train near Kopjes Station (Orange Free State), and burnt all our mails and warm clothing.

Sat. 16th   Waited till noon for orders, and at 1 p.m. marched on to Pretoria, not reaching bivouac till after dark.

Sun. 17th   Lord Charles Bentinck arrived, looking rather fine-drawn after his Mafeking experiences ; he is going on Col. Ridley's (M.I.) staff.

He also brought the sad news that we had lost yet another officer, Capt. Ellison having died at Kroonstad on June 7th.

Capt. Campbell took 84 men and saddles down to Kroonstad to get remounted.

Mon. 18th   Sent 31 horses and 19 men to the depôt, getting eight remounts in their place.

Gen. French inspected the Regiment in the lines, and again said nice things about it.

Tues. 19th   Together with the 2nd Brigade joined Ian Hamilton's force, and started for Heidelberg at 7 a.m., marching through the town and on to Olifantsfontein Station, where we bivouacked.

Maj. Follett left behind at Pretoria, sick.

Wed. 20th   Left bivouac at 6.30 and camped at Rietfontein, crossing *en route* the place where Hunter-Weston's party had their fight on June 2nd.

Lieut. Sadleir-Jackson rejoined from the Dynamite Factory Hospital, where he and Lieut. Durand had been left. The latter was not yet well, having narrowly escaped losing his leg from blood-poisoning.

Thur. 21st   Started at 6.30 a.m., but made quite a short march

and bivouacked at Springs. Rained in torrents the
whole afternoon and well into the night.

Marched at 6.30 a.m. towards Heidelberg, viâ the
Nigel gold mine. Here we came suddenly on a small
party of Boers, who were rather taken by surprise, but
were soon dispersed, while Lieuts. Jackson and Trower
caught some 16 Boers, amongst them being a field-cornet,
and got 36 rifles. We then saw a convoy some miles
off to our left front, evidently making for Heidelberg,
and were rather disappointed at not being allowed to
have a dash for it.

We were halted after going on a short distance, and
spent a frightfully cold afternoon in observation. Just
before dark our big guns shelled the Boers on the kopjes
which lay between us and the town.

Pte. Greig, who was taken prisoner on the 28th, was
found here. Lieut. Duckett appointed Prov. Marshal
to 3rd Cavalry Brigade.

Marched at 6.30 a.m., after a bitterly cold night, on
Heidelberg, which was itself evacuated. We were in
front on the left, with the 2nd Brigade in rear, while the
rest of the force made straight for the town. We found
the hills to the south-east occupied, and succeeded in
turning the Boers off, while the M. I., after going through
the town, went still further south and came into action
at rather close quarters, and had four casualties amongst
their officers, the Boers finally retreating towards Frankfort.

The Regiment went on outposts at 3 p.m., and remained
all night holding the hills to the south.

1900.   Gen. Hamilton unfortunately had a fall and broke his
JUNE.   collar-bone.

Sun. 24th   We did not come off outposts till 9 a.m., but were not
sorry to hear that we were to remain here.

Mon. 25th Sent a party of 49 men out to bring in a convoy. Gen.
Hunter arrived and took over command of the force.

Wed. 27th Left Heidelberg at 7.30 a.m., forming with the 2nd

CROSSING THE VAAL.

Brigade the eastern column, under Broadwood, while
Bruce Hamilton commanded the western. Crossed the
Zuikerboschrand River and bivouacked near Modder-
fontein and Malan's Kraal.

Thur. 28th The column moved on at 7.30 a.m., the Regiment
finding the advance guard. After a halt at Bierlaagte,
we bivouacked at Kalk Spruit.

Marched on to the Vaal River, and crossing it, once more entered the Orange River Colony, as the old Orange Free State is now called by Proclamation of Lord Roberts. Bivouacked at Villiersdorp, which is on the river.

It was a cruelly cold day, with biting wind.

Did not march until noon as the convoy had to be got across the river, and then only made some eight or nine miles towards Frankfort.

Marched in to Frankfort, some eight to ten miles, the Regiment covering the advance. The " A " Squadron on the left came in touch with a few Boers. On arrival the Wilge River was crossed at the bridge and camp formed on the south side.

Col. Little was sent out in command of a party of 100 16th Lancers, 200 M. I. and two guns, to look for Gen. Macdonald's force, which he met some 12 miles out. Another very cold day.

Capt. Campbell rejoined with 114 men and 140 horses from Kroonstad, and brought with them Lieut. Bell, who had returned from sick leave to England.

We also got our mail for May 11th.

De Wet had burnt those of April 27th and May 4th.

Officers with the Regiment :—

Col. Little.

Maj. Colvin.

Capts. Willoughby, Lund, Compton, Fiennes, Gordon and Campbell.

Lieuts. Bell, Skeffington Smyth, Blackwood, Cavendish, Duckett, Sadleir-Jackson, Wynn, Trower, Laing.

1900.   Capt. Forrest, R.A.M.C., and C.V.S. Phelan.

JULY.   N.C.O.'s and men, 291 ; horses, 313.

Wed. 4th   The whole force marched on to Marsala, the Regiment covering the advance.

Thur. 5th Did not march till 10 a.m., and bivouacked near Vlakfontein.

Fri. 6th   Marched into Reitz, where we found some 45 prisoners, chiefly sick and wounded Yeomanry and Derby Militia. The marches are short owing to our having infantry and a large ox convoy.

Sat. 7th   Marched to Viljoen's Hoek. The " A " Squadron being in front, Lieut. Cavendish's troop came on some 100 Boers, and managed to secure a few of them. Heard a good deal of firing towards Bethlehem, and saw a considerable number of Boers making off in the direction of Harrismith.

Sun. 8th   Left camp at 7 a.m., and went in to bivouac just outside Bethlehem at 11.30 near a beautiful stretch of water.

Gens. Paget and Clements had just got into the town after two days' fighting.

It has been very cold during the whole march from Pretoria.

Mon. 9th   Halted here, the rest of Gen. Hunter's force coming in.

Tues. 10th Got orders to march back to Heilbron to-morrow with 300 M. I., escorting a convoy and some 50 prisoners.

Wed. 11th Left bivouac at 8.30 a.m. and marched as far as Hartebeest Hoek.

Thur. 12th Left bivouac at 8 a.m. and marched to Reitz, the Regiment finding the rear guard.

Fri. 13th Orders arrived last night to say that the 3rd Cavalry

Brigade were to push on to Heilbron with as little delay
as possible, and there entrain.

Marched as far as Rustfontein.   •

Marched on as far as Varkfontein in the teeth of an
icy hurricane.

Marched on to Heilbron, getting there at 3 p.m. Here
Gen. Gordon found orders waiting for him. He was to
hand over the 3rd Brigade to Col. Little, who was made
a local brigadier, and proceed himself to Pretoria and
take over Gen. Porter's Brigade.

Our brigade was now to march to Winburg, viâ
Kroonstad.

Left Heilbron at 9.30 a.m., Maj. Colvin now commanding the Regiment, and marched as far as Vaalkrantz,
just beyond the Rhenoster River.

Left bivouac at 8.30 a.m., and on making a midday
halt about 12.30, found ourselves in the middle of a
large herd of blesbok. Needless to say, nearly every
officer went after them, not to mention a good many
irresponsible men, and soon there was a great battle
raging, often more dangerous to the brigade than the
buck ! Although a certain number were bagged, it is
to be feared that many more got away wounded, owing
to hardened bullets being used.

Marched on to Paardekraal, where we bivouacked,
and received orders to change our course and make for
Lindley, as De Wet, with some 2,000 men, had broken
away from the cordon being formed round Prinsloo, near
Bethlehem, and was travelling westwards, pursued by
Broadwood's Brigade.

1900.   We got a welcome supply of tobacco by this mail,
JULY.   most of the men having been out of it for weeks.

Wed. 18th   Had to send in 51 men and 23 horses to Kroonstad,
and Lieut. Sadleir-Jackson sick.

A weary march of 20 miles to Doornkop, the Regiment
doing rear-guard.

THE POM-POM—CAPT. POWELL, R.H A.

Thur. 19th   Marched at 8 a.m. towards Lindley, the Regiment
being in advance, with " C " on the left and " D " on the
right. About noon the " C " Squadron advance came
under fire from their left front, and a patrol narrowly
escaped being completely ambushed. They, however,
escaped with the exception of Pte. Albert ; and then two
guns were turned on to them, so Maj. Colvin was sent
up in support with the " A " Squadron and the pom-pom,

under Capt. Powell, R.H.A. The pom-pom getting the range of these guns soon silenced them. Our guns had just come up ready for action when the Boers split up, part going round each flank, being well shelled in doing so. The regimental Maxim and the M. I. had come up on the right flank and were tackling those coming that way, when suddenly firing started on the left rear. It seems that the party who went by our left did so in dead ground, and managed to make good a ridge, from which they were making it hot for the transport. However, Lieut. Wynn collected our dismounted men and Capt. Vawdry, A.S.C., all other hands, and endeavoured to hold up the attack. Col. Little, seeing what was taking place, at once sent the " C " Squadron and pom-pom to reinforce this point and recalled the M. I. from the right flank. These latter came in for rather a warm time, but eventually the ridge was carried, though the Boer guns were still playing on it.

As the Boers on the right were still hanging about a gun was sent for, which soon dispersed them.

After this they retired in driblets towards the Rhenoster, and so ended a very successful afternoon, though had we only been a couple of miles further on, it might easily have been otherwise, and to make matters worse a convoy from Kroonstad was only one march from us and under a very weak escort.

All the country in this district is very trappy. As it was dark soon after firing ceased, the force was collected and went into bivouac.

This farm was called Paarde Plaats.

We could hear Broadwood's guns, but failed to get into touch with him.

Two officers were wounded and several men, while many had narrow escapes, Corpl. Neeld having his pipe taken out of his mouth, and Vet. Surg. Phelan's horse was so badly wounded that he had to destroy him.

The Regiment had the following casualties :—

Wounded : Ptes. J. Scully (" C ") and P. Martin (" C ").

Missing : Ptes. S. Albert (" C ") and H. Sullivan (" D ").

Fri. 20th　The brigade got orders to reconnoitre the country thoroughly, and then about midday started for Doorn Kloof, in order to render assistance to the convoy and also to fill up our supply wagons. We made Doorn Kloof about 4 p.m., the convoy arriving safely shortly afterwards.

The " A " and " D " Squadrons both went out on outposts.

Sat. 21st　The 17th Lancers and the pom-pom started at 6 a.m., in order to try and get in touch with De Wet's force, which they did some four miles out, but the pom-pom soon scattered them. The brigade marched at 10 a.m. and got to Welgelegen about 4 p.m., from which place the Boers could be seen trekking away north. The convoy being some way back, we were forced to bivouac here. Steyn was reported to be with De Wet.

Sun. 22nd　The Regiment went out with the pom-pom at 6 a.m. to reconnoitre towards the Rhenoster. The " A " Squadron was on the right and " D " on left. The patrols from the former came in contact with a few Boers near the spruit, but no numbers were met with, and afterwards turning west, we rejoined the brigade—which had marched at 1 p.m.—at Kaffir's Kraal.

Got orders from Lord Roberts to go to Rhenoster.

After a very wet night we marched on towards Roode- val, and when within four or five miles of it got into communication with Broadwood, who told us to come in to Rhenoster camp, and follow him next day, as he was now going on after De Wet, who had crossed the line on Saturday night, destroying it near Honings Spruit and capturing a train of medical stores, etc., with some 50 infantry details.

We did not reach camp till 5.30 p.m., Capt. Willoughby having again to go sick, and owing to our reduction in numbers, the " D " Squadron was once more broken up. We were very badly off for horses, and the men's clothes were in a terrible state.

Left camp at 8.30 a.m. to join Broadwood, which we did about noon, and found him engaged with the Boers at Wittekopjes, near Vredefort. He sent word to us to support him on the left, but we had little to do, only our guns firing occasionally at long range.

Broadwood's right, however, was heavily engaged all the afternoon.

We went into bivouac at Paardekraal, and here Jackson rejoined us from Kroonstad with a welcome addition of 53 newly-equipped men and 62 horses.

Remained here all day, and very cold it was, with five hours' pelting rain in the evening.

1900.
JULY.
Thur. 26th
Fri. 27th

Both brigades remained in camp all day.

The M. I. were left to hold the place we were at, while our brigade moved south at 9 a.m., and crossed a spruit at Wonderheivel, halting shortly afterwards, when we got into action, the Boers shelling us from Wittkopjes. The bursting of their shells was bad, but one of their guns was so well concealed that it was never silenced throughout the afternoon.

The 2nd Brigade remained near here, while we went on some two miles and then bivouacked. De Wet's laager was reported to be at Rhebokfontein.

Sat. 28th

Remained here all day.

Gen. Little took Lieut. Sadleir-Jackson on to his staff as A.D.C.

Sun. 29th

Remained here.

Had to send in 22 men with 29 horses and 8 sick men to Kroonstad.

The Regiment now reduced to 205 men and 177 horses.

Mon. 30th

Heard last night that Prinsloo and 5,000 Boers had surrendered near Bethlehem.

In the afternoon the brigade moved further south to Kopje Aileen across the Rhenoster Spruit, while the 5th Fusiliers and two cow guns joined Broadwood. Hart's Brigade is waiting to come out, and Brabant's Colonial Force is coming up from Kroonstad.

Tues. 31st

The " A " Squadron, under Lord D. Compton, accompanied by the pom-pom and Maxim, went out at 6 a.m. on a reconnaissance south-west, first crossing the Honing Spruit at Klip Drift and then going on towards the Rhenoster.

The Maxim and a small escort were left at the drift to cover their retirement in case of necessity. Having gone some three miles the Boers appeared along a rise running across their front and left, and opened a considerable fire. The pom-pom was splendidly handled and enabled the squadron to get back to the drift with only one casualty—Pte. J. Lanham, evidently captured, as he was one of the advanced points. Having crossed the spruit, the party met the rest of the Regiment coming out to their support. Compton then sent Lieut. Wynn with a small patrol to the Roodeval Drift, up stream to the east, and they later on found themselves nearly surrounded by a party that had evidently worked along some dead ground round their left. They had to gallop through the Boers, and here S.Q.M.-Sergt. Ankers behaved in a very plucky manner, for seeing Pte. Daniels' horse shot, he slipped off his own, which was already wounded, and covered Daniels until he got back to him, when they both managed to get safely back on foot.

AUGUST.
Wed. 1st

Got orders in the middle of the night to march at 5.30 a.m. to Shepstone, as De Wet was supposed to have crossed the Vaal at Parys. Having gone some distance, we were told to return, the report being untrue. On the way back we met Hart's Brigade going out to Kopje Aileen, as some M. I. had been attacked by a party of Boers, but by the time we got there they had disappeared.

Thur. 2nd

Furnished the outposts and saw Gen. Knox's Brigade at Rhenoster Kop, and the Boers going north.

Fri. 3rd

Sent 22 men and 18 horses back to Kroonstad.

Sat. 4th

Gen. Knox advanced towards Rhebokfontein and

1900.
AUGUST.
shelled the kopjes across the Rhenoster. Our brigade turned out to support him, the 16th Lancers in front making good a portion of the kopjes. Remained out till 3.30 p.m., when the brigade was withdrawn.

Lord Kitchener arrived and took over command of the operations against De Wet on the south side of the river, while Lord Methuen was at Potchefstroom.

Sun. 5th
Left bivouac at 7.30 a.m., and marched to Paarde-kraal, close to where Col. Ridley's M. I. were, while Broadwood's Brigade made a demonstration westwards and Knox closed on Winkel's Drift. The cordon round De Wet should now be pretty complete.

Mon. 6th
"A" Squadron "stood to," but was not used. The Boers could be seen in occupation of the kopjes in front of us.

Got 20 more men and 18 horses out from Kroonstad.

Tues. 7th
Had to send back six men and nine horses.

16th Lancers went out to reconnoitre the kopjes towards Reitzberg, and came under fire. A Welsh Fusilier, captured when De Wet crossed the line, managed to escape, and got to our outposts at 3.30 a.m., when he reported the Boers crossing the Vaal at Schoeman's Drift and going eastwards. Heard heavy shelling all day in Methuen's direction and in the afternoon saw some 300 or 400 Boers trekking away, evidently De Wet's rear-guard.

Wed. 8th
Left bivouac at 11 a.m., the "C" Squadron covering the advance; marched through Vredefort and joining Broadwood's Brigade went on to Parys.

Thur. 9th
Left bivouac at 6 a.m., and marched through Verseilles

and Modderfontein, nasty mountainous country, crossed
the Kromellboorg Spruit, and shortly afterwards Broadwood's guns opened on the Boers across the river. On
going on towards Lindeque, saw the Boers going away
north-east for all they were worth, and their wagons away
in the far distance.

The Regiment now got orders to cross the Vaal, and
hold the kopjes on the far side for the night. We must
have seen nearly half De Wet's force. It was not till
6.30 p.m. that we got the outposts out.

Rejoined the brigade on its crossing the river, and Fri 10th
marched across the Houtboschberg towards Doornkloof.
De Wet had left the Losberg, travelling north all night.
This was a trying day for the transport, as the pull
across the range of hills was very long and steep in parts.
It did not reach bivouac till 9 p.m.

Marched at 6.30 a.m. and crossed the Gatrand range Sat. 11th
of hills, then turned west and did not get into bivouac
at Welverviend until 6.30 p.m., after one of the worst
marches we have ever done—about 25 miles, in the teeth
of a biting cold wind and blinding dust the whole time.
The unfortunate transport did not get in till 9.30 p.m.,
more dead than alive.

De Wet had crossed the line between Frederickstad
and Blaauwbank.

De Wet is now going north, closely pursued by Sun. 12th
Methuen. The 2nd Brigade and ourselves are following
them up as quickly as possible. Left bivouac at 9 a.m.,
and shortly afterwards heard Methuen's guns. He ran
into a party of Boers with three guns, capturing one and

1900.
AUGUSTan ammunition wagon and setting free most of the prisoners, amongst whom was Pte. Albert, who had been taken prisoner on July 19th, and who had had anything but a pleasant time, also Pte. Lanham. We went on till after dark, bivouacking at Schoolplaats.

Mon. 13th The unfortunate transport wagons did not get in until 6 a.m., and after filling up we moved on, marching the whole day and bivouacking at Groenfontein about 6 p.m.

Tues. 14th Marched at 2 a.m., reaching Lord Methuen's camp at Rietfontein at 4 a.m.

Had only gone three miles further on when the advance was checked by the Boer picquets. It being still quite dark, a halt was made. Soon after starting again the advanced squadrons of 2nd Brigade, with De Lisle's M. I. on their left, went forward and cleared the bushy ridge. The Megaliesberg range lay ahead of us, with nasty wooded country in between, and it was thought we again had De Wet, but soon learned to our disgust that Ian Hamilton, who had been holding the passes, had withdrawn. Thus De Wet was enabled to get over the passes scot-free.

We were bothered a lot all morning by isolated snipers amongst the bushes. In the afternoon we went into bivouac, as further pursuit was useless.

Wed. 15th Left Vlakhoek with the 2nd Brigade at 6 a.m. to the relief of Col. Hore, who, with some 300 Australian troops, was besieged at Brakfontein on the Elands River by Delarey.

Marched to Tweefontein, some 25 miles, not getting into bivouac till after dark.

Marched at 6 a.m., and reached Brakfontein about 10 a.m. A certain amount of sniping was going on to the north, so " C " Squadron was sent out to drive the Boers off.

This unfortunate garrison had been escorting a huge convoy, and had just time to take up a position before being surrounded. They had a terrible experience during the first day, until they had dug themselves into trenches. In order to secure the water supply Capt. Butters, with 81 men and a Maxim, were posted across the stream.

Delarey had some 2,000 men and seven guns, and commanded the place from all sides, shelling it unmercifully, no less than 1,500 shells being fired the first day. However, the plucky garrison held on for 11 days, having 65 casualties.

The whole of their horses were killed and nearly all their oxen, the stench from the dead animals being awful.

It was one of the finest performances of the whole war.

The Regiment " stood to " all day, the " A " Squadron being sent some 10 miles up the Elands River on reconnaissance.

The brigade remained here to await Lord Methuen, who arrived in the evening. The remainder went back with Lord Kitchener to Pretoria.

Started at 5.45 a.m., in company with Methuen's force, for Mafeking, viâ Zeerust.

Marched as far as Rondavel's Kraal, where we bivouacked.

1900.
AUGUST.
Mon. 20th

Remained here all day, and indulged in a game of "rounders" against the gunners.

Tues. 21st

Left Rondavel's Kraal at 5.15 a.m., and after a very trying march of some 17 miles over a very rocky, hilly and bushy country, bivouacked at Wilgeboom Spruit.

Wed 22nd

Left bivouac at 5.30 a.m. and marched to Zeerust, getting there about noon.

The whole of this country is scrubby and hilly, with numerous nasty gorges and defiles.

Captured a laager and a lot of oxen that were hidden amongst the bushes.

Lieut. Jackson hauled down a Transvaal flag which was flying in the town, although Gen. Carrington had only left a short time before.

Thur. 23rd

The Regiment was sent out on reconnaissance towards Jacobsdal, and some four miles out took up a line of outposts.

Small parties were met and sniping went on all day.

They kept worrying our picquets by continually sending in women, evidently to act as scouts.

Sat. 25th

Had to send in 70 men, 23 horses and 43 saddles with Methuen's force to Mafeking, and started towards Pretoria with only 16 officers, 153 men and 109 horses. The Colonial force under Col. Dalgety was not much better off, nor were the other regiments of the brigade. A start was not made till 2 p.m., and after going some four miles, the 17th Lancers, who were in front, encountered parties of snipers in the thick bush just beyond Botha's Farm.

On the Regiment coming up, both squadrons and

some of the Colonials were dismounted to clear the bushes and the pom-pom opened on the left. Gen. Little here got a very nasty flesh wound high up in the thigh, and the command of the force fell on Col. Dalgety.

After clearing the bushy country it was too late to go further, and so we turned into bivouac to the east of the farm.

Started at 7.30 a.m., the Colonials being in front. Sun. 26th We off-saddled at Jacobsdal for a short time, and then went on to Doornhoek, where the advance ran into some 200 Boers, who were chiefly holding a kopje across a spruit in front. The guns and pom-pom were sent up, and after about two hours' fighting the Boers suddenly made a dash and were off in every direction.

It was a very nasty piece of country, and we were practically emerging from a defile. Bivouacked a little further on at Doornhoek.

Left bivouac at 5.30 a.m. and marched till 9.30 a.m., Mon. 27th when we off-saddled and went on again at 1 p.m. to Grootfontein.

Marched at 6 a.m., the Regiment doing rear-guard. Tues. 28th The road ran through an extremely nasty defile to and from the lead mines, where we crossed the Great Marico Spruit, and the rear-guard was much delayed here owing to the empty supply wagons waiting to fill up with oat hay. No one was sorry to leave this beastly place behind, especially as all sorts of reports were current as regards the Boer strength and intentions.

1900.   We bivouacked at 2 p.m. at a Kaffir location and mis-
AUGUST.   sionary station at Mabalstad.

Wed. 29th   An early start at 6 a.m., after a very wet night, the
Regiment being in front.   Marched as far as Doorn-
poort, when we encountered a terrific thunderstorm,
being at the time among enormous iron-stone rocks, and
got drenched to the skin.   Halted here till 1 p.m., and
then went on to Kleinfontein, where we bivouacked.

Thur. 30th   Another tremendous storm during the night.   Left
bivouac, and after a short but wet march, bivouacked
at Vlakfontein.

One squadron of 16th Lancers and two guns were
sent out in afternoon to drive off some Boers, who were
annoying the outposts.

Fri. 31st   Started at 5.30 a.m., and shortly afterwards ran into
a thick mist.   The 17th Lancers were in front, and Lieut.
Skeffington Smyth had one of our troops on the left
flank.   The advance was just clearing the mist when its
left became involved, the Boers having taken up a position near Quaggafontein.   Maj. Colvin sent the " A "
Squadron under Lord D. Compton, with the Maxim
under Capt. Gordon, on to support the left advance,
while the " C " Squadron was on the right.   Part of the
" A " Squadron and Maxim were able to make good the
grassy slope and were enabled to check the Boer fire to a
certain extent, while the rest went on with the pom-pom.
The Maxim was here being fired at a range of only about
600 yards, but the party had managed to find a fold in
the ground, and owing to the long grass were fairly well
screened.   The Kaffrarian Rifles had in the meantime

come up to where Skeffington Smyth was, and were
hotly opposed in a rather exposed position, and suffered
considerable loss.   Col. Dalgety then ordered the Border
Horse to rush the hill from the roadside, but their C.O.,
Maj. Robertson, was wounded and they could advance
no further.

Our guns were now blazing away at pretty close
quarters, but little impression could be made on the
Boers.

Col. Dalgety, seeing that a withdrawal could not be
effected without serious loss, ordered those involved to
hang on till dusk and then withdraw.   Under this cover
he moved the convoy on some four miles to Zandfontein,
where we eventually bivouacked.   Lieut. Skeffington
Smyth was reported as having behaved in a most gallant
manner, binding up the wounded and carrying water to
them, and it was not till late in the afternoon that he
was badly wounded himself, being hit in several places,
in spite of the risks he ran.   At dusk all withdrew under
a heavy fire, fortunately with little more loss added to
what had already taken place.   The casualties were
pretty severe considering our numbers, being over 50,
and many of them bad cases.

The doctors went back with the ambulances, but were
detained by the Boers, who were under Lemmer.

The Regiment had the following casualties :—

Wounded :   Lieut. G. Skeffington Smyth.
             Sergt. T. Atkins (" D ").
             Lance-Corpl. H. Cook (" A ").

1900.
SEPT.
Sat. 1st

Moved on towards Cyferfontein at 5.30 a.m., and on reaching Buffelsfontein the advance—the C. M. R.—ran into the Boers holding the far edge of the plateau. They soon dismounted, and, supported by the " A " Squadron

SERGT.-MAJOR PRAEGER.

on their right, worked their way across the open, where only a few anthills served as cover. Our guns then got to work, and afterwards the whole of the dismounted men rushed the far edge, when the Boers cleared out, a few going round by the right, whilst the majority gal-

loped away north under heavy fire from the 16th Lancers
and some of the guns. We afterwards learned that
Delarey had been here with reinforcements for the Boers.

The column then pushed on to Vlakfontein. The
Transvaal has to-day been proclaimed British territory
by Lord Roberts.

Marched into Krugersdorp, some 20 to 22 miles, and Sun. 2nd
so finished what has been anything but a pleasant march.
Had Delarey had more go in him, we ought to have been
smashed to pieces, as we were very weak. Our orders
were now to go on to Johannesburg and there leave all
crippled horses and entrain for Kroonstad, there to
re-equip.

Capt. Gordon and Quar.-Mast. Laing proceeded at
once by rail to make the necessary preparations.

Capt. Porter, R.A.M.C., arrived with all the wounded.
The strength of the Regiment is :— Mon. 3rd
15 officers, 150 men, and 93 horses, only 35 of which
are fit for work.

Left Krugersdorp at 6 a.m., and marched to Johannesburg, going through the town and bivouacking between
it and Rietfontein.

Remained here all day. Tues 4th
Col. Porter took over the brigade, which left bivouac Wed 5th
at 9 a.m. for Germiston, the Colonials cheering us out of
camp.

Lieut. Trower left at Johannesburg sick. Thur. 6th
Entrained for Kroonstad at 10.20 a.m. and were loaded Fri. 7th
up, wagons and all, by 12 noon, the men having worked
splendidly.

1900.
SEPT.

The train left at 1.30 p.m., reaching Viljoen's Drift at 4.40 p.m., where a halt had to be made for the night, as trains had been stopped running at night.

Sat. 8th

Left Viljoen's Drift at 6.30 a.m., and arrived at Kroonstad at 4.30 p.m., getting into bivouac at 6 p.m.

2nd Lieuts. The Earl of Leitrim and Chadwick joined the Regiment.

Lieut. Sadleir-Jackson rejoined from Mafeking, whither the Colonel had been taken. The latter's servant (Pte. Wilson) was killed during a thunderstorm while there.

Sun. 9th

Sent 53 horses to the sick depôt, which leaves the Regiment with 36 !

Got 185 horses (including 15 chargers) from the Remount Department.

Mon. 10th

Lieuts. Sadleir-Jackson and Wynn, with 50 men, were sent up the line to join Gen. Knox at Paardekraal, while the brigade " stood to " at 4 a.m.

Capt. Fiennes arrived with 48 men.

Tues. 11th

Moved camp to west of railway close to the Scotch Hospital.

Sat. 15th

Gen. W. Knox inspected the brigade. The Regiment turned out 101 mounted, and 141 horses led (remounts).

Jackson's party returned in the afternoon.

Boxing match in the evening, between Sergt. Morley, I.Y., and Pte. Keir, 9th Lancers, the latter, however, being knocked out in three rounds.

Sun. 16th

A squadron from each regiment and four guns went out under Maj. Bannatine-Allason, R.H.A., to join Gen. C. Knox to the eastward. Capt. Lund commanded our squadron.

Gen. W. Knox ordered us to shift camp again !

Maj. Allason's party returned, having had a fight on September 18th, when the 16th Lancer squadron, which was in front, had several casualties. Nothing of importance occurred in camp since September 17th, but since the brigade arrived from Johannesburg, it has had no easy time. What with training almost raw remounts, chiefly Hungarians, re-clothing, and equipping generally and fitting saddles, besides outposts and patrols, everyone has been pretty busy, and the continual changing of camps has been rather annoying.

Great polo match held !

Yeomanry beat Garrison.

1st team, 17th Lancers beat 9th Lancers.

2nd team, 17th Lancers beat Yeomanry.

1st team, 17th Lancers beat 2nd team, 17th Lancers.

Regiment represented by Fiennes, Blackwood, Cavendish and Duckett.

The Regiment is fairly strong once more, and is again made into three squadrons in the field.

" A " Squadron, Capt. Lord D. Compton.

" C " Squadron, Capt. F. Lund.

" D " Squadron, Capt. E. R. Gordon.

Strength : 15 officers, 301 men, 287 horses.

Sergt. Casebow takes charge of the Maxim.

The brigade marched at 6 a.m., moving on till 11 a.m., when we off-saddled at Hautkop, where Gen. Knox was. Went on again at 1 p.m., getting to Welgelegen just before dusk. Our object is to head the Boers from the south and south-west, while Hunter and Macdonald come up from the east and south-east, and De Lisle and Dalgety from the north and north-west.

Started at 6 a.m., but only made a short march as far as Vaalbank. Vechtkop reported held by the Boers.

Left bivouac at 5.30 a.m., the " A " Squadron covering the advance. On reaching Vechtkop, which was just over the Rhenoster, the Boers opened fire on us. The " A " Squadron at once dismounted and commenced operations, while " C " was sent to the left front and " D " and the Maxim to the right front to work round that flank. As soon as the guns came up and opened fire, the Boers began to quit, and our line advanced, " D " Squadron being now sent away to the extreme right to support a squadron of the 17th Lancers.

The Maxim, under Sergt. Casebow, here did very good work.

Sniping continued on the extreme right until Rietfontein was reached about 1 p.m. The " A " Squadron then went out on outposts, and when everyone was getting comfortably settled down sniping was heard to the north where Lieut. Wynn was in charge of the outposts, and then a shell came hurtling over the camp, followed by a second, which went plump into the middle of the gunners.

The shells were only received by roars of laughter from the whole brigade, who, nevertheless, saddled up and turned out wonderfully quickly.

The Regiment was first off to reinforce the outposts, and reached Wynn none too soon, for he was getting very hard pressed.

Some six or seven shells were fired into the camp at a range which must have been between 7,000 and 8,000 yards, but fortunately only wounded two men, though the 16th Lancers' horses had rather a bad time.

" D " Squadron went to the immediate support of Wynn's party, while " C " went away to the ridge running north from Spitzkop to where the Boer gun was.

After our guns got into action, and we were seen on the move, the Boer gun disappeared and the burghers fell back rapidly everywhere. We all remained out till nearly dark, when we returned and changed bivouac.

Gen. Porter was very pleased at the smart way in which the men turned out, and also with Lieut. Wynn and his party for holding on so well.

Marched towards Heilbron at 5 a.m., the 16th Lancers in front. After going some distance the advance came under fire from some kraals, when the guns were ordered up and galloped into action splendidly. The Boers retired, and " D " Squadron were then sent out to the right.

The General now moved west to Heilbron, taking most of the brigade, but leaving Maj. Colvin with two squadrons and two guns, with orders to withdraw gradually.

" C " Squadron and the pom-pom were sent to support a squadron of the 16th Lancers, which was turning the Boers off a hill to the north, and all this time a certain amount of sniping was going on on the right, while the main body and wagons could be seen trekking away to the east.   Gen. Porter shelled a lot of Boers out of the vicinity of Heilbron.

After reaching Heilbron we off-saddled till 11 a.m., and were none too pleased to hear that we had to go on

OFFICERS, " A " SQUADRON, 9TH LANCERS.
CAPT. LORD D. COMPTON, LIEUT. H. CAVENDISH, CAPT. D. CAMPBELL,
2ND LIEUT. A. TROWER.

another 14 miles or so to Groenvlei on the Vredefort road.

Bivouac was reached at 4 p.m.

Thur. 27th   Remained here all day, and got a pleasant surprise in the evening by Lieut. Gordon Stirling returning from England.

Remained here all day waiting for the supply wagons to come out.

Left bivouac at 6.30 a.m., and marched to Uitkyk.

Moved about five miles to Doorndraai and there bivouacked. " D " Squadron was from here sent in to Rhenoster as escort to the convoy.

List of officers now with the Regiment :—

Maj. Colvin.

Capts. Lund, Lord D. Compton, Fiennes, Gordon and Campbell.

Lieuts. Bell, Stirling, Lord F. Blackwood, Duckett, Jackson, Wynn, Earl of Leitrim and Chadwick.

Quar.-Mast. Laing.

Capt. Forrest, R.A.M.C., and Vet.-Surg. Phelan.

" A " Squadron was sent out some 15 miles south to Kaffir Kraal, collecting cattle and searching farms. No end of stock brought in.

" D " Squadron and the convoy returned from Rhenoster.

Marched at 6 a.m., viâ Vaal Krans, to Cyferkuil, and made a terribly long journey of it owing to the zig-zag way we moved.

Remained at Cyferkuil.

Marched at 6 a.m. to Rhenoster, which was not reached till 6 p.m., after a march of some 30 miles.

Remained at Rhenoster.

A troop under Lieut. Sadleir-Jackson sent out to reconnoitre towards Kopje Aileen.

Had to send 14 sick horses down to Kroonstad. Got

1900.
SEPT.
Fri. 28th
Sat. 29th
Sun. 30th

OCTOBER.
Mon. 1st

Tues. 2nd

Wed. 3rd

Thur. 4th

5th & 6th

Sun. 7th

1900.
OCTOBER.

Mon. 8th

Tues. 9th

Wed. 10th

Fri. 12th

Sat. 13th

Sun. 14th

orders for the brigade to start at 2.30 p.m. for Rooikop, which was reached at 6.30 p.m.

The 16th Lancers and pom-pom were sent out at 6.30 a.m. to seize Kopje Aileen, while the rest of the brigade followed at 8.30 a.m.

Had been in bivouac only a short time when a report came in to say that there were 500 Boers along the spruit at the foot of the hills near Rhebokfontein.

The brigade was turned out and forming line, 9th Lancers on the right, 17th Lancers and guns in centre, and 16th Lancers on left, galloped down towards the spruit, but only a few Boers were seen.

Jackson returned this afternoon.

Twenty-six men and 59 horses joined from Kroonstad.

Remained at Kopje Aileen, the 17th Lancers reconnoitring Rhenoster Kop.

" C " Squadron reconnoitred towards Rhenoster Kop, only a few Boers being seen, whom Blackwood's patrol dispersed.

Got orders at 10 a.m. to march to Kroonstad and by 11 a.m. were on the road.   Made a halt of three-quarters of an hour at Honing Spruit, and did not get into camp till 7.30 p.m., it being pitch dark.

Sixty-one horses and 33 men joined from cavalry depôt, and we had to send 28 horses sick.

Strength of Regiment now : 16 officers, 337 men, 316 horses.

Marched at 8.30 a.m. for Boschrand.

De Wet, with 500 men and four guns, reported to have

occupied Rhenoster Kop after we marched from Kopje
Aileen.

The General received his orders concerning the farm burning and clearing, and communicated the details to all officers.

The 17th Lancers went out reconnoitring and devas-
tating, while we amused ourselves in camp by taking the gunners on at hockey.

" A " Squadron was sent on to reconnoitre Cyphergat
Kopje near Geluk. They came in contact with the Boers, but drove them back, the Maxim gun doing good work. Lord D. Compton reported the place to be held by about 300 Boers, but after rejoining the brigade, which had marched at 7.30 a.m. for Graspan, some native scouts came in and said that Cyphergat Kopje was evacuated. The " A " Squadron was sent back to verify this, and, as was only to be expected, their advance guard came under a pretty heavy fire, but fortunately withdrew with only one casualty—Pte. G. Williams, wounded. Several horses were, however, shot.

The brigade bivouacked at Rietgat.

Marched at 6 a.m. towards Otto's Spruit. The left
had become engaged, when Rimington, who was away in front of Hunter's force, sent back an urgent message to say he required strong reinforcements. Unfortunately the messenger came on us first, so Maj. Colvin went off with the " C " and " D " Squadrons, and after trotting some five miles, saw about 20 Boers away in the distance !

Many of the Boers seen to-day were dressed in khaki, and some carried lances.

1900.
OCTOBER.
After destroying a good many farms we bivouacked at Nel's Farm.

Thur. 18th
The brigade was out all day farm burning.

Fri. 19th
Left Nel's Farm at 8 a.m., and marched to Tweefontein Drift on the Valsch and some six miles short of Bothaville.

"D" Squadron advance guard. Only a few Boers were encountered by the advanced troop under Jackson.

Sat. 20th
Marched into Bothaville, Hunter's force coming in in the afternoon.

The 16th Lancers and pom-pom went on in advance, and were only slightly opposed by some 60 Boers.

The orders were that the whole town was to be razed to the ground.

Sun. 21st
Left Bothaville at 4.45 a.m. with orders to effect a junction with Gen. Settle's force at Commando Drift, some 30 miles off on the Vaal River.

Halted at 9 a.m., for a couple of hours, and then went on, but saw nothing until nearing the drift, when the advanced guard had a little opposition, and afterwards nearly tried conclusions with some of Settle's people, who had crossed at a drift lower.

Eight hundred Boers under De Wet had intended opposing Settle here, but retired in direction of Wolmaranstad.

Mon. 22nd
Left bivouac at 8 a.m., and marched as far as Welgelegen, where the General decided to bivouac. Water supply bad and horses very much done up. It is a tiring march, as water is scarce everywhere, and the soil is sandy, while the whole country is undulating.

Boers were hanging about everywhere, and fired on our rear-guard as it left the drift.

Left Welgelegen at 5 a.m., and marched into Botha-ville, which we found in flames.

After watering and feeding we went on to Visser's Kuil.

Marched at 6 a.m. to Nordebeeste Kraal, crossing a large bend of the river, which area had to be devastated. A squadron of the 17th marched up either side of the river as far as Tweefontein Drift, with the third one moving along the banks, in order to try and capture 40 Boers reported to be in the bed of the stream.

The brigade left bivouac at 5.30 a.m. for Bester's Kraal, " A " Squadron in front, " C " on right flank, and " D " on left flank. After burning a considerable number of farms, the kraal was being approached when the " A " Squadron came under fire. As the " A " Squadron was making good the ridge, " D " Squadron received orders to work to the left and endeavour to cut off some 30 or 40 Boers who had broken that way. They had a running scrimmage with these for several miles, and finding it useless, pulled up, and sweeping round burnt some farms.

The men worked very well indeed, and Maj. Colvin received a note from the General to say that he was very pleased at the work of the two squadrons.

On returning to the kraal the " D " Squadron found that the brigade had turned right-handed, and were going to bivouac at Doorn Spruit, some eight or 10 miles further.

1900.
OCTOBER.
Fri. 26th

Left Doorn Spruit at 6 a.m., " C " Squadron being told off to do right-flank guard to Bruce Hamilton's convoy. Kroonstad was reached about 10 a.m. Maj. Follett rejoined and took over command of the Regiment.

We are very short of horses, having 96 sick and exhausted, and wanting 136 to complete.

Sat. 27th

Only marched out as far as Boschrand.

Sun 28th

Marched at 5.30 for Geneva Siding, " D " Squadron in advance. Scarcely a couple of miles had been covered, when loud reports were heard ahead, so the advance was hurried on to Geneva, where it could gather little information. Gen. Porter came up here and ordered the advance guard to trot right on to Holfontein, and on arrival it was found that the tail of the Boers was being shelled by the armoured train, which had arrived from Ventersberg Road just after the garrison of volunteers had surrendered. The " C " Squadron pushed on to the left front, but were eventually withdrawn.

Mon. 29th

Marched at 6 a.m. to Ventersberg Road Station. Gen. Hunter came down in the afternoon and decided to march that night and make an attack on Ventersberg at dawn.

Our brigade with some M. I. were to make a long round by the north side, and then swing south, while Bruce Hamilton's Brigade was to march straight there.

Tues. 30th

A start was made at 8 p.m. last night, and nothing happened until we were within a few miles of the town, when the head of the column lost touch with the party of guides in front. We were halted for some time, and then the officer who was with the guides turned up, they

having run into 200 Boers at a farm we ought to have
passed. They were all caught except himself. Soon
after dawn heavy rifle fire opened on the north-west
side. We trotted on down a valley and then swung
right-handed on to the ridges between the town and the
high hills, and there got slightly engaged. Boers were
now seen to be going away north-east, so " A " Squadron
was sent over to what was our right to hold the ridge,
while the " D " Squadron and Maxim were sent still
further to the right. The " A " and " C " Squadrons
then went further on to a high ridge to the north. A
considerable number of Boers were coming across the
" D " Squadron front, and another party looked sus-
piciously like trying to get at their rear. The former
were held off by the Maxim, while the flank troop sent
the others to the right about.

The Boers evidently did not intend waiting, for the
fighting was of short duration, and then the convoy, etc.,
was seen some miles off trekking north-east. We went
into bivouac near Ventersberg at 10 a.m. One unfortunate man of " D " Squadron (Pte. S. Chapple) lost his
life through going to sleep when we halted during the
night, and not coming on when roused. He ran into
the retreating Boers, who wounded him severely, but
he managed to get within a few hundred yards of our
line. He died during the afternoon.

The brigade was sent out farm burning in a south-
easterly direction, and during most of the time sniping
went on in all directions. Returned to bivouac 1 p.m.
Halted near Ventersberg.

1900.
Nov.
Fri. 2nd

Orders to march at 7 a.m., but it commenced raining at 6 o'clock last night and continued steadily throughout the day. Lieut. Theobald once more rejoined. He had had bad luck, for after being liberated at Pretoria he was sent with a composite squadron eastwards with Gen. French's force and there contracted enteric.

Sat. 3rd

Marched at 7 a.m. for Virginia Siding. It rained most of the time. Found the Zand River in flood, and could not get the wagons across.

Sun. 4th

Made a start at 9.30 a.m., but did not leave the far side of the river till 11 a.m., as the transport found great difficulty in crossing the drift, while the troops had to lead in single file across the deviation bridge. Bivouacked at Welgelegen Siding.

Mon. 5th

Marched to Winburg—24 miles—to assist in protecting the railway while undergoing repairs. The left advance came into touch with some 200 Boers, but they were soon dispersed.

Tues. 6th

Remained here all day.

Wed. 7th

Received orders for the brigade to march back to Smaldeel and there refit, but at 1 p.m. this was changed to march at once to Bloemfontein. Started at 2 p.m., and went on till after dark, when we bivouacked at Welcom, a rather nasty place to have to dump down in after dark without having seen it by daylight.

Thur. 8th

Marched on as far as Nooitgedacht, where we bivouacked. We passed some kopjes where three guns are supposed to have been buried, but it would have taken a long time to find them.

Fri 9th

A long march to the Modder east of Springfield.

Marched in to Bloemfontein, after being kept waiting outside for a considerable time, and then had to go right through the town to the west end.

Got orders for the Regiment to go out to Kruger's Drift on observation duty, accompanied by a section of guns. This is the break up of the 3rd Cavalry Brigade. The order was, however, cancelled in the evening.

Some 62 or 63 officers of the brigade dined at the Club this evening on the break up of the brigade, the guest of the evening being our brigadier—Gen. Porter.

General Hunter received orders from Lord Roberts that the 3rd Cavalry Brigade was to be split up, and the troops available in the part of the country divided into three columns.

The " A " and " D " Squadrons were posted to Col. Barker's column, which consisted of : Lovat's Scouts, two companies Dublin I.Y., two guns, one pom-pom, two companies infantry (Seaforth Highlanders), while the " C " Squadron went to Col. Herbert with the 17th Lancers, etc.

Col. Barker's column was to work westwards from Springfontein, while Col. Herbert's was to move eastwards from Edenburg.

" 9th and 17th Lancers to draw rifles at once and be prepared to move by rail this afternoon. All lances and carbines to be returned to store ! "

Received orders at 10 a.m. to pack up and march down to the station as soon as possible. The " D " Squadron started at 11.30 a.m., followed shortly by the " A," but it was not till 1.30 p.m. that entraining could be com-

1900.
Nov.

menced. After being muddled about a good deal the train with the " D " Squadron was started off at 5 p.m. The " A " Squadron, though loaded up, did not start.

Thur. 15th   The first trains only ran on till dark last night, starting at daybreak again, but were once more pulled up at

ARRIVAL OF THE ENGLISH MAIL.—SORTING LETTERS.
[Reproduced by permission of *The King* and *Navy and Army Illustrated*.]

Bethanie at 7.30 a.m., owing to the line being destroyed. Moved on at 2 p.m., finally reaching Edenburg about 4 p.m.

The " A " Squadron started at 4 a.m. and reached Edenburg about 4 p.m.

Fri. 16th   Our orders were now to escort a large convoy to Jagersfontein, so that the original idea did not last long.

Sat. 17th   Marched at 5.30 a.m. for Jagersfontein and reached

Taaiboschfontein, on the Kromellboorg Spruit, about
4.30 p.m.   Lieut. Chadwick left behind sick.

Left bivouac at 5 a.m. and marched into the town
about 10 a.m., bivouacking in the market square.

Started back again at 5.30 a.m. with a considerable
number of prisoners, undesirables and Kaffir families
from the mine.   Made a midday halt at Proces Spruit,
and reached Kalverfontein in the afternoon, where we
bivouacked.

Left bivouac at 5 a.m., and after a false alarm about
Boers got into Edenburg at 10 a.m.   Found Herbert's
column still here, and news that De Wet was working
south with a considerable following.

Both columns sent out patrols owing to a rumour that
the place was to be attacked to-day.   The line was blown
up last night and a letter to Fourrie to this effect found
at the place, but it was evidently only a blind.

Got orders at 11.30 a.m. to be ready to march at 1 p.m.,
in conjunction with Herbert's column to Dewetsdorp,
which place was reported to be surrounded by 1,200
men and four guns under De Wet and Fourrie.   Reddersburg, where we bivouacked, was reached about 6.30 p.m.

Started at 5 a.m., and at about 8.30 a.m. the " A "
Squadron, who were in advance, had a slight brush with
some Boers.   A halt was now made till 1 p.m. to let the
ox-convoy up, after which a further advance was made
to Oorlogs, where we bivouacked about 6 p.m.

Marched at 5 a.m., the 17th Lancers being in front,
and after travelling a few miles came up to the position
which lies to the south of the town.   The main position

runs roughly south-east and west, but a branch runs south from this for some distance. Herbert's column managed to make good the end of this, and later on Barker's column started a demonstration on the west. The " D " Squadron was sent towards a prominent kopje on the position, supported by the " A " Squadron and pom-pom. A further advance was made by Lieut. Theobald with Lieut. Jackson on his outer flank. The pom-pom and Maxim were hard at it, making very good shooting against a Boer gun that was near the kopje. After a while this gun was shifted to behind a kraal wall.

Both Theobald's and Jackson's troops, the Maxim now being with the latter, were creeping forward, but were much bothered by well-hidden snipers. It was now getting late and at 6.15 p.m. orders to withdraw were received, and bivouac not reached till about 8 p.m. Some Kaffirs reported that the garrison had surrendered last night.

Failed to get into communication with Thaba 'Nchu or anyone.

Sun. 25th　　" Stood to " at 4.30 a.m. The Boers had if anything strengthened the position where Herbert's column was, and about 9 a.m. most of the Regiment and pom-pom were sent out to reconnoitre to the north.

The patrols worked a good way ahead, after which a withdrawal was ordered.

Herbert's column had some stiff work in the morning. Heavy storm in the afternoon.

Mon. 26th　　" Stood to " at 4.30 a.m.

The place was reconnoitred in the morning and found

evacuated, so everyone moved forward at 2 p.m., only
to find the *débris* of the four days' pounding. Meanwhile Pilcher's column had been seen coming up behind
us. De Wet, Haasbrook and several others, with some
2,500 men and one gun, had attacked the place, and
finally captured the garrison, about 400 strong, with two
guns.

The Boers were reported to have bivouacked only some
nine miles off, so Gen. Knox ordered the two columns
to march at 7 a.m., while Pilcher, with whom he was,
cut in.

Got in touch with Pilcher, and also the Boers, near
Aasvogel Kop. After a little skirmishing the march
was continued, and all three columns went into bivouac
at Helvetia.

Gen. Knox, with the other two columns, went on by
the main road to Smithfield, while our column was sent
more to the south-east by a track that passed Leeuwkop,
Kaffir's Kopje and Franz Kraal, where we got into communication with Smithfield.

Here we went into bivouac about noon, but sent out a
patrol under Lieut. Wynn eastwards towards Spitzkop.

Started at 5 a.m. by a very rough country road to
Waterval, Pilcher's column going on to near Carmel.

Did not leave camp till 9 a.m., but Herbert's column
went on at 5 a.m. Halted to water and feed at 11.45
a.m., and then moved on to Rietpoort, where we were
once more checked, owing to an escaped Basuto prisoner
telling Pilcher that the Boers were not very far off.

This is a terribly mountainous country.

Left Rietpoort at 4 a.m. for Bethulie, which was reached about noon.

Sat. 1st
Herbert's force left at Slik Spruit, so as to watch De Wet, who was reported to be at Klein Bloemfontein.

Sun. 2nd
Our column left Bethulie at 6.45 a.m. for Slik Spruit, while Pilcher's started out on the Springfontein road. Herbert's column had gone back to Carmel. Arrived at the spruit soon after 11 a.m., and had just off-saddled, when we heard Herbert's guns in the distance, and shortly afterwards a message came in to say that Herbert was being heavily attacked on front, left, and rear. We saddled up and moved out towards Badfontein, the " D " Squadron being in front with Lieut. Theobald's troop in advance. They being opposed by Boers to the left front, our guns came up and cleared the way for them. A good many Boers were now seen to the front and right front. Lieut. Jackson's troop was sent to the right front, so as to give Theobald's troop time to work round by swinging right-handed. The opposition was now pretty general, and as the Boers saw us coming on rapidly, they opened a gun on us. However, the ridges overlooking the farm and the valley under the Boer position were gained, which caused the Boers to retire from Herbert's left and rear. The " A " Squadron had come up in support, while the Yeomanry were sent to hold the kopje from which the Boers originally opened on Theobald.

While this had been going on Lieut. Theobald had been working round, but had got stranded by wire not many hundreds of yards from the position. Here he was shot through the thigh, as were also two more men.

Capt. Forrest made endeavours to get to him, but was unsuccessful, owing to the heavy firing. Later on, however, Ptes. Leutchford ("D") and Vincent ("D") made another plucky attempt to get Theobald into a safe place, but although they managed to get to him, could do no more, as any attempt was met with a heavy fire. They all had to lie there for several hours until late in the afternoon, when an ambulance was allowed to go out. Both these men's names were forwarded to the General. Firing kept up all the afternoon along the whole line, and later on the "D" Squadron were sent up the donga to Middelfontein Farm, which lay close under the kopjes, but no good could be effected.

We got no food or blankets till 11 p.m., as we all bivouacked on the ground we held, and the carts had been ordered to remain behind until 8.30 p.m.

The Regiment's casualties were :—

Lieut. S. R. Theobald.

Lance-Corpl. J. McCrea ("D") and Pte. G. Pickford ("D").

"Stood to" at 4.30 a.m. while the transport was brought across the spruit and packed just behind us. We were ordered to move on, but Maj. Follett asked to be allowed to reconnoitre the position first, as we were sure it was still held. The "A" Squadron sent Sergt. Mercer out with a patrol, which was very soon knocked about. Firing then became general. Gen. Knox had

turned up with some M. I. and Strathcona's Horse. The
Seaforths (two companies) and the " A " Squadron were
now sent up the donga to endeavour to get up the kopjes
near the farm, and then the Strathconas dashed up, and
got well hotted as they bunched up at an impossible
place for entering the donga. However, they did get
into it ! The Boers had now brought a gun up on their
right, and started shelling the convoy. Fortunately
Capt. Montgomery with the pom-pom made most excellent shooting, and made the gun shift its position
before it had done much harm. The wagons were soon
turned about and did not take long to disappear, though
not without several more effective shrapnel in their
midst.

Firing all along the line was kept up most of the day,
and in the afternoon the howitzers, which had come up
with Knox, plied the ridge and beyond with lyddite.

Soon after this, about 5 p.m., our people crested the
ridge and within a very short time not a Boer was left.

They had all trekked off towards Boesman's Kop.

Casualties :—

Ptes. H. Frisby (" A ") and A. Sear (" A ").

" C " Squadron with Col. Herbert's column.

Lieut. J. G. Stirling.

Lance-Sergt. A. Creighton and Pte. T. Heights.

Tues 4th   After a wet night all the columns started off this
morning towards Boesman's Kop.

We started at 5 a.m. and travelled in rain over a
terrible road, which knocked our transport about
terribly. Off-saddled here, but got orders to go on at

11.45 a.m. towards Haasfontein to join Gen. Knox and
Williams' column.

The rain now came down in sheets, so much so that we
had to halt and turn our horses round, as they would not

LIEUT. GORDON STIRLING.

face it. While thus halted Knox sent us word to say
that De Wet had now gone across us, making in a south-
easterly direction for the Caledon River. Our course
was altered viâ Klipfontein and Grydam to Carmel,
where we off-saddled, but did not expect to remain.

1900.
Dec.

There were fortunately several large barns at Wessel's Farm, into which the men crowded and endeavoured to get dry by lighting huge fires. The transport crawled in anyhow, completely done up, while the Seaforths and Strathconas never saw theirs, so we had to fix them all up as best we could.

Wed. 5th

Marched at 3.30 a.m. to Karree Poort Drift. Williams' column was on ahead of us, and on arrival at the drift we found them just getting the last of their things over. They had surprised a small party of Boers at the drift, and had made them drop a 9-pr. Krupp gun, with 25 rounds of ammunition, besides seven rifles and 25,000 rounds small-arm ammunition, taken at Dewetsdorp, I suppose.

The Caledon was rising fast, so we were sent across at once, and had just got the last of the guns over when, about 5 o'clock, it became evident that it was dangerous to try any more. The far bank was so steep, and of course slippery, that double teams had to be used for everything, so our transport remained on the far bank.

Thur. 6th

All idea of getting anything over was now at an end, as another bad storm during the night had further increased the river, so the transport was ordered to march round by Smithfield.

About 5 a.m. we marched on to Odendal's Drift, passing no end of De Wet's dead and dying ponies. It was the first time we had ever seen anything like this. Here we found Williams' column, and got news that the Dewetsdorp prisoners, except the officers, had been

liberated yesterday. After an hour's halt, everyone
moved on and eventually bivouacked at Kromdraai.

De Wet had been reported as going to Aliwal North, but was now making for Rouxville.

We had fared rather badly as regards food for the horses, they only having 2lbs. of oats apiece, but we managed to supplement this a little with some barley, wheat, flour and a little bran.

Marched at 4.30 a.m. for Rouxville, Strathcona's Fri. 7th
doing the advance. Reached the town about 12.30 a.m., the advance guard having seen a few Boers going away.

Rouxville and Commissie Bridge were both held by some of the H. L. I., and although De Wet tried to drive out the little garrison of 45 at the bridge, they laughed at him. He had camped last night six miles north of the town, but made for Bastard's Drift as soon as he heard we were approaching.

Managed to get a little forage from the garrison.

Did not leave here till 5.30 p.m., and arrived at Com- Sat. 8th
missie Bridge at 10.45 p.m., fortunately with the aid of the moon. Crossed the bridge and were delighted to find all the transport waiting for us.

We had received orders to march at 8 a.m., but an Sun. 9th
after order said we should not do so before noon. Patrols had been sent out, as reliable information about the Boers was not to hand. Strathcona's Horse located them eventually north-east of Smithfield, but we remained here all day.

Gen. Knox's idea now seemed to be to corner the Boers in the angle made by the Thaba 'Nchu–Ladybrand

range of hills and the western border of Basutoland
Pilcher and Herbert were to come up from Aliwal North,
White going to Helvetia, while we and Williams were
south and other columns would come in from the west.

Mon. 10th   Started at 5.15 a.m., and got to Smithfield about
9 a.m. Halted here till 10.30 a.m., and went on as far
as Groningen, where we found White's convoy parked.
Halted for an hour to water and feed, and then moved
on to Weltevreden, where we bivouacked. Our guide
—Bethune—here brought in information that Steyn and
De Wet with 800 men, two guns, and six wagons, had
left Helvetia at noon to-day, going north along the main
road.

Lieut. Sadleir-Jackson was left behind at Smithfield
with 30 men to bring on some ammunition wagons.

Tues. 11th   Marched at 3 45 a.m., Williams' column being a short
distance ahead of us. It ran into the Boer picquets
about one and a half miles short of Helvetia and was
held back. We were halted, and not for some time were
we sent away to Williams' left, where after a long, heavy,
uphill pull, we saw the whole of De Wet's force going
away west, and only a few miles off. We were now
opposed along the open plateau, but had we only been
sent there sooner, could have hammered away unmolested
at the retirement, for the Boers were taken completely
by surprise and only had the one picquet out.

After clearing the left of the plateau and getting to
the far edge of it, we remained inactive for a considerable time, and could see their wagons through a gap in
the hills at Ninavelspost. After a time orders came for

Strathcona's Horse and the 9th Lancers to get down off the plateau, and a nice game it was. Having done this, we made good a large kopje to the south near Uitzicht. In the meantime the Boers had moved on to Alsemfontein, to which place Col. Steele, commanding Strathcona's, now led us. We soon found ourselves almost on top of the laager, but were far too weak to make any attempt on it, and had to sit there patiently (?) waiting for the others to come up. About 4 p.m. De Wet trekked off towards Reddersburg with the whole of his force, except some 300 or 400 men, who marched off south in a very orderly manner.

There being no signs of our people coming, we retraced our steps, and after going back several miles, met them about 6 p.m., and were none too pleased to find that we were to move on to Alsemfontein, where the Boers had been outspanned, and it was dark before we got there.

We had been dying to have a smack at the Boers, but of course did not know the General's plans, which certainly now looked as if he were nursing the Boers quietly up to an undoubted trap.

Jackson's party had a stiff time, for they did not leave Smithfield till 6 p.m. last night, travelled all night, and got on to the field soon after the fighting began, not getting to bivouac till 7 p.m., 25 hours straight off the reel.

Started at 3.45 a.m., the Regiment covering the Wed. 12th advance ; crossed the Hex River and went on towards Reddersberg, following the Boers' tracks. Some miles short of the town they had turned right-handed, and

gone north again. Col. Parson's camp could now be
seen at the town, and we saw his Yeomanry returning
from the direction the Boers had taken. The advance
troop got within a few miles of the Boer rear-guard, but
as it was now 11 a.m., and we had had no halt, orders
were given to off-saddle. This we did till 1.30 p.m.,
when we went on, crossing Mosar's Hoek, and from here
saw the Boer trek some eight miles off, moving close to
the Bulsberg and going in an easterly direction. It was
getting late, so we were ordered to move across to the
Bulsberg, some five or six miles to our right, and there
bivouacked under the hills about 7 p.m. It was a long,
trying day, and some 33 to 35 miles must have been
covered.

Thur. 13th   Patrols having gone out first thing in the morning to
make sure of the way the Boers had gone, we started at
5.30 a.m., Williams' column being in front. The main
body seemed to be working towards Ladybrand. About
11 a.m. we made a halt, and then went on northwards
between Dewetsdorp and Wepener, and finally bivouacked just before dark at Daspoort. The Boer outposts could be distinctly seen a few miles further on.

Fri. 14th   Left bivouac at 5 a.m., and went on together as far as
Saaifontein. After a bit of a delay, owing to not knowing exactly which way the Boers had gone, we started
towards Thaba 'Nchu, the three columns working in
line, Williams to the right, White to the left, and Barker's
with Gen. Knox in the centre. About 10 a.m. the hopes
of all were raised by a helio message from Thaba 'Nchu
Hill, saying De Wet had tried to force his way through

Springhaun Nek to the south-east, but had failed.   Away
went everyone in the best of spirits, all hardships forgotten, for it really seemed as if Gen. C. Knox was to
be at last rewarded for his perseverance and patience
during the last three weeks, with country and weather
against him.

De Wet was now in a very precarious situation, and
it should have been a net difficult to get out of

Our spirits were soon, however, to receive a damper,
for at 11 p.m. another message came to say that De Wet
and 2,000 Boers were galloping over the nek for all they
were worth.

The disappointment was intense, and it was indeed
hard luck on the General as well as the troops under him.

Everyone had worked hard, had had long marches
over bad ground and in torrents of rain, and were now
at the last moment robbed of a well-merited reward.

On arrival we found the place weakly held by an
infantry post and Thorneycroft's M. I.

Of course the early morning affair was simply a reconnaissance on De Wet's part, and finding the place not
strongly held he determined to try and rush it.

A certain amount of damage was done, as Thorneycroft's M. I. captured 30 prisoners, nearly all the wagons
and ambulances, 60,000 rounds small-arm ammunition,
one gun of the 68th Battery and a pom-pom.   Six Boers
were killed, and a lot of saddles covered with blood were
brought in.   We bivouacked here at 4 p.m.

Haasbrook's commando would not face the nek, but
turned westwards, and in so doing ran into White's

1900.   column, the 16th Lancers and the Welsh Yeomanry
DEC.   getting well into them, and here was felt the want of
lance and sword.   They accounted for eight killed, and
captured between 20 and 30 prisoners.   Col. Thorneycroft went out this morning and followed up the Boers,
whom he located near Lokoala.   We had to wait for
supplies, but unfortunately got no fresh horses.

Sun. 16th   Marched a little before 6 a.m. to Maseru (not the
capital of Basutoland), getting there about 10 a.m.
Here we found Thorneycroft's M. I., who were in
observation of the Boers, the latter having taken up a
long and strong position on the line Lokoala-Vlakplaats-
Vaalkop.

Col. White went to Alexandra, Col. Pilcher to Rietfontein, while Col. Williams and the General were at
Brakfontein.

Mon. 17th   White's column and ourselves marched at 8 a.m. for
Lokoala, which was reached about 12.30 p.m.   Here we
halted till 2 p.m., and then moved east to Zamenkomst
Drift, and got into bivouac about 4 p.m.

The Boer laager was reported to be at Annandale,
some 12 or 14 miles north.

After a wet night " stood to " at 4.30 a.m., and eventually remained here all day.

Tues. 18th   De Wet with 1,500 men reported at Thaba Mountain,
and Mequatling's Nek reported held.

Wed. 19th   Rained hard all last night, and all to-day.

Information having been received that Hertzog and a
large following had got into the Colony, the following
columns were withdrawn : Parson's, Williams', Thorney-

croft's, and Byng's. The remainder got orders to stay
in these parts and endeavour to keep any more from
getting south.

The Regiment was sent off at 4.30 a.m. to reconnoitre
Mequatling's Nek, the " D " Squadron being in front.
Capt. Montgomery and his pom-pom accompanied us.
Lieut. Jackson's troop surprised a party of eight Boers
at a Jew's store a few miles short of the Pass, but they
all managed to get away

Some 40 with pack animals were then seen amongst
the lower hills. This is one of the nastiest places we
have come across during the whole war, a lot of low
kopjes and small plateaux, with a semi-circle of high
hills behind, over which the pass leads, and of course
the inevitable dongas and spruits. Every ridge being
covered with boulders makes it impossible to see whether
the place is held or not until fired on.

After a certain amount of firing, we halted for a time
as there was nothing to be gained by going on. The
pom-pom came forward later on, when Corpl. H. T.
Elliot made some beautiful single shots at separate Boers.

Later on in the afternoon Maj. Follett decided on
pushing on further, so Jackson's troop went on to the
right front and was accompanied by the commanding
officer. It was necessary to send a troop to the left front
to cover the other. This one was under Sergt. Draper,
and came in for a pretty hot time getting to its position
and back. The whole place was now held, and the Boers
were making things pretty warm for us when Maj.
Follett decided to withdraw.

Curiously enough not a man was touched. We now went back a few miles and bivouacked just as it was getting dark, Col. Barker bringing the rest of the column up to within four or five miles of us.

Fri. 21st

The " A " Squadron went off at 4.30 a.m., accompanied by the pom-pom.

The Earl of Leitrim was leading the advance troop, and had anything but a pleasant time, never knowing when he might come under heavy fire ; fortunately only a very few Boers remained, and the pom-pom soon dispersed these.

The rest of the Regiment followed at 7.30 a.m.

About 9 a.m., Compton was told to move on, and by 10 a.m. his scouts had reached the nek without further opposition.

We waited on top of the Pass until the convoy and the rest of the column got up, and from here saw what turned out to be Pilcher's column a short way on, they having come round by the left.

A forward move was made at 2.30 p.m., and we reached the Mission Station at Evening Star about 6 p.m. Here we went into bivouac.

Sat. 22nd

" Stood to " at 4.30 a.m. and marched at 7 a.m., going into bivouac at Clocolan to wait for our convoy.

Clocolan consisted of a large store which was practically empty !

Sun. 23rd

Again " stood to " at 4.30 a.m.

Pilcher's column went out north, while Strathcona's Horse reconnoitred in a north-easterly direction, we following at 9 a.m. Passed a very pretty and well-kept

property with nice house, owned by a Mr. Newbury, and
then turned north for a time, eventually returning to
bivouac at 3.45 p.m.

To our astonishment Lieut. Stirling once more turned
up, having joined a squadron of the 16th Lancers who
were escorting a convoy.

FARM CLEARING BY "A" SQUADRON.

"Stood to" at 4.30 a.m. "D" Squadron was Mon. 24th
ordered to go out towards Peka Drift, as Hogg, our
intelligence officer, had gone in that direction to collect
and bring in some Basuto ponies. The squadron went
by way of Newbury's House, and a few miles beyond
came in contact with some 70 or 80 Boers. It being
unnecessary to go any farther, as far as Hogg's safety

was concerned, attention was simply paid to those Boers in front, chiefly by the pom-pom. Others could be seen on the further hills and to the left, and it was known that their main body was at Ficksburg, so that there was every chance of being cut off had the squadron gone on. It remained out till 5.15 p.m., and got back to camp about 7.30 p.m.

Tues. 25th   "Stood to" at 4.30 a.m.

Lord Leitrim took a patrol out beyond and to the left of Newbury's and destroyed a mill.

We tried to imagine it Xmas day.

Phelan and Bell had their mile match over again, the latter winning, and then the men had a five-shilling sweepstake on commandeered ponies. This was won by Pte. Callaghan; Pollard, second; and Devine, third. Won by a short head; good third. Distance, four furlongs.

Numerous "sing-songs" took place in the evening.

Wed 26th   Left bivouac at 5.30 a.m. The two squadrons and pom-pom, with the companies of the Seaforths, under Capt. Bradford, went on to Dreiyer's Verdreit, which was reached about 11 a.m., while Barker with Strathcona's Horse, the guns and Irish Yeomen went to Somerset, preparatory to crossing into Basutoland by Peka Drift and thus getting at Ficksburg in the morning.

Pilcher's column came up in the evening, while Gen. Boyes and White were further north. On reaching bivouac, Compton's squadron, which was in front, went on, and ran up against some 100 Boers, with whom they had some rather good fun, especially with the pom-pom.

Got orders from Col. Barker to march at noon, and rejoin him at Ficksburg, which we did by 4 p.m., having to go through a very bad defile, in the middle of which lay the Victoria Flour Mills, a very large business.

Our columns met at Ficksburg early this morning, only to find that the Boers had divined our intention, and had left the place at 11 p.m. last night for the hills and caves beyond, taking with them their families and any quantity of flour and mealies, not to mention an enormous amount of ammunition that had been buried here, local native labour being foolishly used for the purpose.

Started at 4.30 a.m. with orders to secure Commando Nek. This was done, with only slight opposition, by the " A " Squadron, which was in front. The column halted near Dwars Kloof till 10 a.m., when the Regiment was sent up the Fouriesburg road to reconnoitre as far as Bamboes Hoek. A few Boers were encountered, but retired. Remained in occupation of Generals Hoek the rest of the day, and awaited orders, which did not reach us till 6.30 p.m. We then saddled up and made a short cut across the mountains, which few of us will forget. There were two very bad dongas to negotiate, one taking our carts, only nine small ones, and the pom-pom three-quarters of an hour to cross. Then came the climb by a track (!), much of it smooth rock and a descent of the same class.

It was 10 p.m. before we reached camp at Long Thom's Farm, the carts with Leitrim's troops and Bell and Forrest just managing to get off the hills before the

12*

1900.
Dec.

moon gave out. They had, however, to settle down where they were, as it was impossible for them to find the camp.

Sat. 29th   " Stood to " at 4.30 a.m., but did not march till 9 a.m., when we crossed a drift and then had a nasty pull over a mountainous country in a westerly direction till noon, when we halted for one and a half hours, and then went on in a northerly direction, bivouacking at Rovi Krantz about 4 p.m.

Sun. 30th   A very bad thunderstorm last night. The rain-water swept through the bivouac like a river.

Started at 4.30 a.m., " D " Squadron in advance. After covering several miles we got into a valley with a very boggy stream, and here the transport experienced very considerable difficulties, and a bridge had to be extemporised. While this was going on the advanced squadron had moved forward to make good the high ground beyond, and here a certain amount of opposition was shown, but ceased as soon as a supporting squadron was seen coming up. Then came some very bad uphill pulls until Palmietfontein was reached about 5.30 p.m.

Mon. 31st   Marched at 5 a.m., Strathcona's covering the advance. We had only gone a short distance, and had turned right-handed over the Zand river, when considerable firing began. Strathcona's moved forward, working beautifully, and threw out parties to right and left, managing to secure a ridge. We came close up to support and to get cover, for the bullets were beginning to fall pretty thickly. After a time the guns were brought up and a party with a pom-pom was sent to the left. The Boers now began to give way and we were able to get across a nasty donga and on to the ridges beyond, from which the passage of the transport could be covered. Getting clear of the worst part of the kopjes the road swung round to the left, and a mile or two on the advance once more came under heavy fire from the left front, but this was soon stopped by the guns, and then the Regiment and guns were sent on to the right front, when we saw some 400 Boers with a good many led ponies streaming down the valley. The guns were turned on to them, but at their maximum range. The " A " Squadron then went on, supported by the rest, but found it was only a waste of horseflesh, and were soon afterwards ordered to rejoin. At 2 p.m. we moved on from Barnfontein, and bivouacked at Bankfontein, said by our guides to be five miles short of Lindley !

The rear-guard was much harassed throughout the day.

1901.

MARCHED at 5 a.m. towards Lindley and made a halt near Palmietfontein, when the " A " Squadron, which was doing rear-guard, sent in word to say that they were engaged and that some 70 or 80 Boers were evidently trying to get on our right flank. Along this flank and close to the road ran a long, low ridge. About the same time a message came in from the Yeomanry in front to say that a convoy was passing us to the north and only about four miles off.

To save time, Col. Barker turned everyone about, parked the convoy, and sent " D " Squadron forward to cover the new advance, supported by the " A " Squadron. Scarcely had the left made good the ridge when sniping broke out, some Boers having got close up. They wounded one of our men, Pte. H. Wilkinson (" D "), and shot Lieut. Jackson's pony, he having gone on with his troop. The Yeomanry came up on a ridge on hearing the firing, and evidently mistook the squadron for the Boers, and started a pretty hot enfilading fire. As the double report of their rifles was most distinct, the conclusion was come to that they must be Boers, so the Maxim was brought up and turned on to them. After

the mistake had been discovered, an advance was again
made, one prisoner being captured. After going some
miles along a high plateau, the Boers could be seen going
away across the plain below. Lieut. Wynn was then
sent on to a farm, under cover of our guns, but too much
time had been wasted, and further pursuit being useless,
all were recalled and Lindley reached as it was getting
dark, a distance of some 17 miles, instead of five as our
guides had said !

Remained here all day in company with White's and
Pilcher's columns. There are a great many Boers
around this district.

White's column went on towards Reitz at 4.30 a.m.,
followed by ours at six. After going a few miles our left
and left rear were attacked. Wynn was detached from
" A " Squadron to the left, while Jackson took his troop,
covered by the Maxim, to the left rear, as " D " were
doing rear-guard. A considerable amount of sniping
went on, after which a move forward was made, the
Boers hanging on our flank the whole time. Shortly
afterwards a halt was made, and the " A " Squadron
was sent away to the right with orders to go to Piet De
Wet's Farm, and escort him and his family back into
Lindley. The farm was being held by some of the body-
guard, but these were driven off by the Boers.

Col. Barker moved the whole column towards the
farm, sending on Strathcona's Horse, who recaptured
De Wet's wagons, and at 2.30 p.m., after Lord D. Compton had rejoined, moved on and went into bivouac near
Schietmakaar, White's column being in front.

1901.
JANUARY.
Fri. 4th

Marched at 4.15 a.m. and reached White's camp about 6 a.m., in time to stop a second attack on part of his outposts.

We remained here till midday, while White was burying those of the body-guard who had been killed yesterday, the corps having walked into a trap and suffered heavily. Moved on at 1 p.m., the " D " Squadron covering the advance. Sniping all round during the whole march, especially against the advance squadron. Towards evening, just before returning off march outposts, Boers could be seen scattered about in every direction.

Bivouacked at Riet Vallei, three miles from Eland's Kop. At 9.30 p.m. the camp was disturbed by heavy firing, apparently from White's outposts.

Sat. 5th

The firing last night was evidently caused by parties of Boers meeting each other in the dark, as none of the outposts had fired a shot.

Marched at 4.30 a.m., the Irish Yeomen in front. Did some 15 or 16 miles, being sniped at from every direction. After making a halt, a message arrived from Gen. Knox ordering us to return to him at Eland's Kop. The march back was begun at 3.45 p.m. and it was 8 o'clock before we reached bivouac, the rear-guard having had a bad time of it the whole way.

Sun. 6th

Left bivouac at 5.30 a.m., moving towards Reitz, and then went to Rietpan, after making a midday halt at Longwerwacht. The Regiment had to send a squadron out on each flank, covering the march of our convoy as well as White's. Sniping was going on everywhere, the

Boers being split up all over the country, evidently trying
to get away all the cattle.

We eventually bivouacked near Schietmakaar, after a long and annoying day with the transport.

Marched at 5.30 towards Kroonstad, and made a   midday halt at Lindley from 11 a.m. to 2 p.m. Having started off again, White's column found that they could get their transport no further that day, so we all went into bivouac just beyond the town.   •

Marched at 5.30 a.m., White's column leading.

On reaching the Eland's Spruit, where it runs into the Valsch river, a midday halt was made, and the semicircle of hills beyond held.   The Boers were on the kopjes beyond, and began firing as soon as they noticed the forward move begin, but our guns and pom-poms held them back.

The transport had a difficult job getting across the spruit, and then had to cross the Valsch by the bridge.

As soon as this was accomplished, and the troops began to withdraw from the kopjes, the Boers came down on Strathcona's Horse, who were doing rear-guard and gave them a merry time. Bivouacked a few miles on at Waterval. Pte. White (" A ") had a narrow escape, being hit on his bandolier, which was fortunately a double one. Several cartridges were smashed up, and as the bullet hit him just over the heart, he was completely " knocked out of time."

Left bivouac at 5 a.m., " A " Squadron in advance,   and after a halt some five or six miles short of Kroonstad,

1901.
JANUARY.

got into bivouac on south side of Bloem Spruit about 4 p.m.

Here we heard that Lord F. Blackwood, with the " C " Squadron, had been severely wounded on Xmas Eve near Burghersdorp.

Thur. 10th   Remained here all day.

Lieut. Gordon Stirling left us to join Capt. Lund's squadron at Hanover Road, Cape Colony.

Fri. 11th   Strathcona's Horse left us, preparatory to being sent home.

Sun. 13th   Moved over to Col. White's column, to which we have now been transferred, Col. Barker proceeding to Winburg to take command there.

R.S.M. Grant has been offered a Quarter-Master's commission in the Remount Department in Natal.

Mon. 14th   Left camp at 9 a.m., but were terribly delayed, owing to the time the transport took to get through the town. Our objective was Lindley, with orders to bring back the small garrison and accumulated stores. " D " Squadron was in front and came into touch on the left just before reaching the spruit at Doornkop, where a wood overlooked the drift. The advance now worked to the left, while " A " Squadron took the right of the wood. A certain amount of sniping went on on the left all the afternoon, and the squadron did not get into bivouac till 9 p.m.

The whole of this country is very trappy and is infested by the Heilbron Commando, who are rather desperadoes.

Tues. 15th   After a wet night a start was made at 5.30 a.m., and almost before the advance guard (Yeomen) had got out,

sniping began and continued the whole way to Doornkloof, where we made a midday halt.

The " A " Squadron on the left flank and the rear-
guard were annoyed to a very considerable extent by
these snipers, and continued to be so until bivouac was
reached, some five or six miles short of Lindley.

Remained here all day, as the original orders were
altered. The " A " Squadron escorted Col. White into
Lindley.

Started back on the return journey at 6 a.m., going by
Groenfontein. " D " Squadron was in rear. A midday
halt was made after crossing the Eland's Spruit, and on
resuming the march sniping began, when the Yeomen
and a pom-pom were sent out to the right, and after
stirring up the Boers, returned to the column at a fair
pace, thus leaving the rear-guard to bear the brunt of
their deeds. The column had been going on all this
time, and seeing their way pretty clear, the Boers came
at the rear-guard in a most determined manner. The
whole fell back quietly, Lieut. Jackson's troop on the
right-rear coming in for a pretty hot time, as also did
Sergt. Draper's. Although the Maxim gun was with the
squadron, it was impossible to set it up until camp was
nearly reached. The Boers pressed on, evidently thinking the column had crossed the spruit, but were soon
dispersed, when the Maxim was able to work and a
pom-pom and the other squadron turned out from
bivouac at Doornkop.

The mounted troops crossed Quagga Spruit at 6 a.m.,
when the Yeomen were left holding Doornkop and the

near ridges, the remainder going roughly south to clear farms. A few Boers were encountered and driven across the spruit, and after clearing out some farms, the whole swung round in a northerly direction, but did not go far enough, the direction being again changed towards the east. Here the advanced guard ran into a lot of Boers "lying up" in the spruit, and got rather a warm reception, as also did the pom-pom, but fortunately only horses were damaged. All this resulted in another move northwards, the "A" Squadron being first sent across the spruit.

A very considerable number of Boers were encoun-tered and then their convoy was seen going away in the distance from behind the kopjes we had turned short of.

Farm clearing now continued while the guns and pom-pom kept the Boers moving slowly back, but as soon as we turned to go back to camp about 4.30 p.m., down they came and followed us for some three or four miles until the pom-pom made it too uncomfortable for them. Encountered a heavy hailstorm before getting back about 7 p.m.

Sat. 19th
The mounted portion of the column once more moved out at 7 a.m. to clear farms in a north-easterly direction. On returning the Regiment was told off to look after the wagons, the "A" Squadron doing rear-guard. They were much bothered by snipers all the way back.

Sun. 20th
Despatches arrived in the middle of the night, with orders for us to see them safely through to the C.O. at Lindley. The place was to be evacuated, and we were to return to the line, as De Wet was reported to be once more in

the Witkopjes district.   Marched to within six miles
of Lindley, when the 16th Lancers took on the despatches.

Officers present with the two squadrons now :—

Majors Follett and Colvin.

Capt. Lord D. Compton, " A " Squadron.

Capt. E. R. Gordon, " D " Squadron.

Capt. D. G. M. Campbell.

Lieuts. Sadleir-Jackson, Wynn, Earl of Leitrim.

Quar.-Mast. Laing.

Capt. Forrest, R.A.M.C., and Vet.-Surg. Phelan.

Left bivouac and marched back as far as Doornkop,
only a little sniping having taken place.

The Regiment was left at Doornkop to assist the Lindley garrison under Munro to cross the drift, the rest of
the column going on to America Siding.

We started for that place about 10.30 a.m., and after
a peaceful march got in about 4 p.m.

During the morning everyone received a great shock
on the arrival of a telegram to say that our much
revered Queen was dying, and a little later another to say
that the end had come yesterday.   It was most unex-
pected, as no one had even heard of her being ill.

Paraded at 2.45 p.m., and then got orders to join Col.
C. Maxwell's column and proceed with it to Witkopjes.
Honing Spruit was made good just as it was getting
dark.

Left Honing Spruit at 2 a.m., and reached Kop Aileen
at daybreak, then trotted right on to the Rhenoster.
From here Rimington's Guides (in front), the Regiment
and two pom-poms went on to Witkopjes, but only saw

1901.
JANUARY.
a few Boers and learnt that De Wet had gone south on January 18th. Returned to bivouac at Wanderheuvel at 11 a.m.

Fri. 25th
Marched at 5 a.m., halted at Honing Spruit, and reached America Siding about 1.30 p.m.

Sat. 26th
Marched at 2 a.m. and reached Kroonstad about 7 a.m. Here we had to entrain for Ventersburg Road Station, which was reached about 10 a.m., and found a large force assembling under Gen. Bruce Hamilton.

Sun. 27th
All the columns started off early, Maxwell's column covering the advance, and halted just beyond Ventersburg, after an uneventful march. Going on again, Maxwell's column got orders to return, and at 4.45 p.m. were told to be ready to start as soon and as light as possible. We were away by 6 p.m., making for Junction Drift on Zand river, which was reached about 11 p.m. after a nasty march in pitch-darkness.

Mon. 28th
On halting last night a terrible thunderstorm came on and it poured with rain incessantly. It was no use trying to bivouac, so everyone remained where he was, soaked to the skin and shivering with cold.

After getting through this ghastly night, a forward move was made at 5 a.m., the Zand river crossed and a halt made at Bloemplaats. During the afternoon we got orders to march at 6 p.m. for Smaldeel and entrain.

Tues. 29th
We reached Paardekuil about midnight, where a halt was made till 4 a.m. and another for breakfast a few miles out of Smaldeel. After all this hustling we did not entrain until late in the afternoon, and it was 9 p.m. before the last train got away.

The " A " Squadron and C. M. R.'s marched out from
Bloemfontein for Thaba 'Nchu about midday, the " D "
Squadron not getting to Bloemfontein till 1 p.m.   After
numerous orders and counter-orders, the squadron, guns
and Rimington's Guides made a start at 7.30 p.m.

After a march of 22 miles the waterworks were reached
at daybreak.

The " A " Squadron had gone further on at 3.30 a.m.,
and had seen the whole of De Wet's force, about 3,000
Boers, some miles off, trekking south at a great pace.

They rejoined with the C. M. R. in the afternoon, just
as the rest of the column were starting back for Bloemfontein at 5.30 p.m., and after a rest followed on at
7.30 p.m.

We reached Springfield soon after 10 o'clock last night,
" A " Squadron getting in after midnight, and all started
again for Bloemfontein at 5 a.m., arriving at 7 a.m.

Once more the order was to entrain, this time for
Bethulie. After a considerable amount of delay, the
" D " Squadron started at 1.30 p.m., accompanied by
Gen. Bruce Hamilton and staff. After a tedious and
trying journey for men and horses, Springfontein was
reached at 10 p.m.   " A " Squadron followed at 4 p.m.

This train did not go on from Springfontein until 2
a.m., and got to Bethulie at 6 a.m.   The " A " Squadron
arrived at 3 p.m., were detrained south of the river and
marched back into bivouac at 6.30 p.m.

All Bruce Hamilton's columns are assembling here, and
much rearrangement of transport is necessary, owing to
the train with White's wagons being captured and burnt.

1901.
FEB.

The squadrons increased to about 80 for field work, thanks to being able to collect stray men. Maj. Colvin left us here to join Col. Crewe's column as staff officer.

Mon. 4th

Gen. Bruce Hamilton's three columns (Maxwell's, White's and Munro's) marched out for Slik Spruit, and arrived there about 10 a.m., when we all went into bivouac.

Tues. 5th

The force remained here all day.

Lieuts. Tooth and Trower, who had been sent out with 50 men from Bloemfontein to augment the Thaba 'Nchu garrison, rejoined to-day, and we were not sorry to find they had brought our mails, which had been accumulating for six weeks.

Wed. 6th

Remained in camp, but White's column went out on reconnaissance.

7th & 8th

Remained here.

Sat. 9th

Maxwell's column went out to reconnoitre towards Tafelberg, and soon after getting there received a message to say that our transport was following, and that White had moved to Vaal Kop, Munro to south of us.

Sun. 10th

During the night orders arrived for the column to move on to Prior Siding. It was a long march of some 30 miles, but was accomplished before dark. Munro's and Crewe's columns were also here. Heard that De Wet had safely crossed into Cape Colony by the Zand Drift, his rear-guard having gone over this morning.

Mon. 11th

Munro's and Maxwell's columns started at 4.30 a.m. on a march which was through defiles nearly the whole way, and over much bad ground. A halt was made about 8 a.m. to water, the march being resumed at 9.30

and Phillipolis reached at 2.30 p.m. Here a halt was
made for an hour, and bivouac at Kaliesfontein, some
eight miles from the drift, was reached just as it was
getting dark.

It was a very hot, dusty march and must have been
nearly 40 miles in length.

We were delayed in starting, having to get rations and
forage from Pilcher's supply wagons, ours not having
turned up.

The approach to the drift for the last three miles was
so bad that leading by files had to be resorted to. The
river was in semi-flood and several of Pilcher's carts
were upside-down in mid-stream. The troops were got
safely over, and then everyone had to set to to get the
transport over and up the far bank, which was very
steep indeed and heavy with deep sand. Everything
had to be double-teamed with ropes manned as well.

As soon as the Regiment got its light carts over, it
was ordered to go on with two guns some five miles to
Holfaar Farm and take up a position there, so as to cover
the crossing of all the transport. We got there about
5.30 p.m. and heard heavy gun and rifle fire further on.
Some 300 Boers were knocking about, but did not dis-
turb us.

Remained holding this position all day, and soon after
noon Pilcher's and Munro's columns began to go by.
Outposts came pretty heavy on the two squadrons, we
being the only part of the column over the river.

The firing yesterday was Gen. Plumer attacking De
Wet.

1901.
FEB.
Thur. 14th

Baggage and troops kept passing all through the early morning, and then we got orders to march at 8.15 a.m. Went on to Venter's Valley, which was reached about 11.30 a.m., and were prepared to resume the march at 2 p.m. ; but Gen. Bruce Hamilton had to halt his columns here until the transport could get up, as there was no corn for the horses and practically no grazing, though we were getting away from the awful kopje country near the river.

A horribly wet afternoon and evening.

Fri. 15th

Did not start till 7.30 a.m., having had to wait for the forage and feed the horses. Marched on till 11.30 a.m., making a halt till 2.30 p.m., and reached Phillipstown about 5.30 p.m., but owing to muddling of the transport did not get into bivouac till dark.

Sat. 16th

Started at 5 a.m., and went on till 10.30 a.m. over very heavy sandy soil, made worse by the heavy rain. Went on again at 12.30 p.m. still over very trying ground, and now began to see the effects of the hard work and practical starvation on the horses, the country being strewn with dead ones, chiefly from Knox's columns. We expected to bivouac some seven or eight miles north of De Aar, and were preparing to do so when a message came in from Lord Kitchener to say we were to come on to De Aar, so a long tiring day was not brought to a close until 7.45 p.m. The unfortunate baggage crawled in at all hours.

Sun. 17th

Remained here all day.

Mon 18th

Last night was one not to be easily forgotten, for late in the evening the rain came down in a perfect deluge,

and swamped the whole place. We had to turn out at
5 a.m., with everything sodden, upside-down, and filthy
from mud.

Marching on until a tributary of the Brak river was
crossed, we halted, and then went on at noon to Spreeuw-
fontein, which was reached about 2 p.m. At 8 p.m.
orders came for us to go on at 9 o'clock, and unfortunately the Regiment was to form the rear-guard, an
ox convoy coming with us as far as Britstown.

The rear-guard did not get off till 10.30 p.m., and had
scarcely gone four miles when another terrible storm came
on. The road was, of course, in an awful state, and halts
were continuous, and then came a longer one than usual.
We sat in our saddles or dismounted, drenched to the
skin and shivering with cold, sleepiness being absolutely
unbearable, from 1 a.m. till 6 a.m. Time went on and
on, and daylight broke only to find that all the other
troops had gone on, the convoy for some unaccountable
reason having remained.

It took some time to rout out all the Kaffir drivers, Tues. 19th
etc., and was 6.30 a.m. before we were once more on the
move. The going was cruel, and although only some
seven or eight miles had to be covered to Britstown, the
rear squadron did not get in till 10.15 a.m. Rest was
not to be ours, for, leaving the convoy, the column moved
on again at 2 p.m., with Prieska as its ultimate destination. Lovemore was reached about 5 p.m., and having
watered and rubbed down the horses orders came for us
to go on at 6.15 p.m. Dog-tired and sleepy to a degree,
we dragged along in a northerly direction until Houwater Wed. 20th

13*

1901.
FEB.

was reached about 1 a.m. Nothing was up but the troops, so having picketted the horses as best we could in the dark, everyone lay down where he was.

The column went on again at noon, and bivouacked at Mochas Dam at 5.30 p.m. Here we got news of Hertzog's Commando in front. The whole of this country is too cruel for words. Where not a bog, it is covered with ironstone rocks and scanty " Karroo " heather, or is a series of small stony hillocks.

Thur. 21st

We started this morning at 6.30 a.m. and halted at 8.15 a.m. to water everything, then went on till 1.30 p.m., when we outspanned. Soon afterwards we went back a short distance to Beer Vlei, and moved into bivouac later on in the afternoon.

Fri. 22nd

After several delays, a start was made at 9.15 a.m., and Groot Vrach Kuil was reached at 2.30 p.m. Here we went into bivouac to wait for our supplies.

Sat. 23rd

Marched at 3.30 a.m., and reached Karree Kloof at 10.15 a.m. Here we remained till 4 p.m., and finally got into Jantjesfontein about 7.30 p.m.

Sun. 24th

Started at 5 a.m., and reached Strydenburg about 8.15 a.m. Just after reaching the town a small party of Rimington's Guides, under Capt. Harvey, made a very plucky attack on a party of Boers, which they handled severely, but it cost them dear, as Harvey was mortally wounded and another shot.

Were very much afraid that an ox convoy sent to us had gone astray, but it fortunately turned up just after dark.

Mon. 25th

The column started at 6.30 a.m. for Potfontein Station,

and did not reach Blikdam till nearly 2 p.m., owing to the column in front moving so slowly. Went on again at 4.30 p.m. for about eight miles, going into bivouac at Quagga Pan.

Started at 5.30 a.m. and reached Potfontein about 9.30 a.m.

Although this last trek has been a very hard one indeed, both for man and horse, and to many seems to have been of no use, chiefly on account of having to work in the dark as regards the scheme, it is very evident that Bruce Hamilton's force being sent in the way it went effectually prevented De Wet working south, and compelled him to turn back eastwards in his tracks, as there was every prospect of his being cornered in the angle of the river between Douglas and Prieska. It was naturally disappointing to the column not to fall in with the Boers, though the other columns did great execution.

Got orders at 3 p.m. to march at 3.30 p.m., but the horses were out grazing and the supply train had only just arrived. However, we were off by 4.30 p.m., and first marching east, turned south, making Bosberg at 8.30 p.m. Heavy thunderstorm.

Left bivouac at 8 a.m. and made Leeuwberg at 10 a.m. Here we settled down, but had an uncomfortable afternoon owing to the heavy rain.

Started at 5.30 a.m., and marched steadily on for some 14 or 15 miles, until Philipstown was reached about 10.30 a.m. Halted here till 3 p.m., going on to Winkel Hoek and arriving at 8.30 p.m.

Left bivouac at 6.30 a.m., and reached the Sea Cow

river near Onvervacht about 11.30 a.m. A halt was made till 4.30 p.m., when we went on to Nachtegaalsfontein, and there bivouacked in sight of the famous Cole Kop.

De Wet with some 400 men had crossed into the Orange River Colony, west of Colesberg bridge, but had to swim the river.

Sun. 3rd   Orders had arrived for us to go to Colesberg and once more entrain. Starting at 6 a.m. we got into camp at 9 a.m. Maxwell and staff, with pom-pom and 25 men of "D" Squadron, went off by train, but there was such a congestion that no more of the Regiment got away to-day.

Mon. 4th   Got orders to go down to the Junction at 7 a.m., but the " A " Squadron did not begin entraining till 1.30 p.m., and did not get away till 6.30 p.m. The " D " Squadron were ready entrained by 10 p.m., but the train was not allowed to go on in the dark.

Thur. 7th   Aliwal North was reached after as bad a railway journey as could possibly be wished for.

Fri. 8th   Most of to-day was taken up examining and casting horses, and got a very poor class of country-bred as remounts. We cast 56 out of 100 of them !

Sat. 9th   Had a very wet night last night, and spent most of the day refitting men and horses. We were fortunately augmented by a party, who arrived under the Hon. A. Macdonald.

Sun. 10th   Bruce Hamilton's three columns started out at 8 a.m., moving north, and commenced the systematic clearing of the country of all inhabitants and stock, as Lord

Kitchener had threatened. After going a few miles a
nasty donga had to be negotiated, and here the " A "
Squadron left advance met with slight opposition, the
first for a very long time, from some kopjes, but soon

CAPT. E. GORDON, " D " SQUADRON.

cleared them. We marched on till about 2 p.m., when
we went into bivouac at Driefontein.

Started at 5.30 a.m., and moved on to Vlakplaats, Mon. 11th
where a halt was made from 8 a.m. to 12 noon. Then
moved on to Dauncey's Nek, where the column bivouacked. Two troops of the " D " Squadron were sent

1901.
MARCH.

from Vlakplaats to Karreepoort, viâ Kaffir Kop, along the Orange river to verify a report that 100 Boers were at the former place.   They returned about 7 p.m., having neither seen nor heard anything of the Boers.

Tues. 12th   Started at 5.30 a.m. for Hetcamp under Vecht Kop, near Zastron, and reached the place about noon, after a soaking wet march.

Wed. 13th   Did not move out till 2 p.m., and then only went as far as Trafalgar, south of Leeuw Kop, getting in at 5.30 p.m.

Thur. 14th   The C. M. R. were doing the clearing, and as we only had a short march, a start was not made till 11 a.m., Bushman's Kop being reached at 2.45 p.m.

Fri. 15th   Left camp at 5.30 a.m., and halted at 10 a.m. till 12.30 p.m., when we went on to Wepener by the eastern road, the fighting part of the column getting there at 2.30 p.m., as a message from Bruce Hamilton's staff officer led Col. Maxwell to understand that Boers were ahead of us, and so we trotted on.

Sat. 16th   Stayed at Wepener all day.

Sun. 17th   Moved over the Caledon, some five miles on, in the morning, and started destroying the contents of two mills, but at noon got orders to make a start at 1.30 p.m. Marched as far Gelegenfontein on the Ladybrand road, and there bivouacked.

Mon. 18th   Started at 8 a.m., and marched on to another Gelegenfontein, near Gras Vlei, which was reached at 11.30 a.m.

Tues. 19th   Started at 7.30 a.m. for Twyfelfontein. The " A " Squadron cleared farms, while 50 men of " D " Squadron and pom-pom escorted Maxwell to the Don-Don Flour Mills to have them destroyed or disabled.

Remained here all day and received orders that the columns were to turn about and work back again.

Started once more at 7 a.m., and cleared farms as far as our old camp near Gras Vlei. A very hard day's work, there being an enormous quantity of grain to destroy.

Camp remained in same place, but most of the troops went out farm-clearing, and had a long day.

All moved on at 7.30 a.m., and camped just to the west of Leeuw Kop at Constantia.

Orders had been received that camp would not be moved, so both squadrons were sent out clearing. In the afternoon, however, a forward move was made to Bokpoort. Pouring rain in evening, everyone wet through, particularly the refugees in open wagons.

Hearing that some Boers were again on the Jammersberg, near Wepener, Col. Maxwell took nearly all the fighting portion of the column with him. On nearing the river a few shots were fired, and again on our galloping down to some kopjes close to the bridge. However, the few Boers that were there soon cleared out, and the force returned, but left the C. M. R. and guns there for the night.

Everything moved on towards the river, and after a halt there bivouac was formed at Nottingham on the Dewetsdorp road.

Moved on at noon as far as Daspoort, where we bivouacked.

Started at 6.30 a.m., and reached Dewetsdorp about 10 a.m. Went into bivouac at " Gun Hill " at western end of position, and found that Munro and White had gone on after some 200 Boers, who were here when they arrived yesterday.

Our column was none too pleased last night when an order was received for it to take over the gatherings of all three columns and escort " the menagerie " into Edenburg.

A start was made at 6.45 a.m. and Kelly's Farm reached by the head of the column about 10 a.m., though it was 5 p.m. before the rear-guard got in.

The following details of " the menagerie " speak for themselves, and will give some idea of what this work is like, particularly for the rear-guard.

33,000 sheep and some 1,000 head of cattle, and a certain number of ponies.

1,100 white and 900 odd black refugees.

Boers still lurk about the place, the rear-guard being attacked by about 50 on coming off " Gun Hill."

Started at 6.30 a.m., the intention being to reach Reddesberg, but the travelling was so slow that a halt had to be made at Rosendal. " A " Squadron was rear-guard and " D " on both flanks. It was 9.15 a.m. before the rear-guard was able to move off, and by 1 p.m. had only covered some four miles, and did not get in till 5 p.m. The unfortunate sheep are absolutely cooked from want of water.

The chief portion of the column was to go to Edenburg, while " the menagerie " made for Bethanie. A halt was made just beyond Reddesburg from 10 a.m. to 2 p.m., and Maxwell decided to take the whole force on to Bethanie.

By 2 p.m. things seemed hopeless, so Col. Maxwell detailed part of the " D " Squadron to wait and bring on the guns when they arrived. These did not turn up till 4 p.m., and the last sheep not till 5 p.m. It was impossible to get them further, so Col. Lukin decided to stay where he was with everything. At 7 p.m., however, a message was received to say we were all to come in, simply leaving 30 unfortunate C. M. R.'s to struggle in with the sheep as best they could. We jogged along at a fair pace and reached Bethanie at 9.30 p.m.

Started at 10 a.m., after catching some horses for remounts, down the line to Edenburg, having a very wet march.

Found Lieuts. Durand, Cavendish and Theobald waiting for us.

Went on at 8 a.m., and reached Jagersfontein Road about 5.30 p.m., having made a midday halt at Kruger's Siding.

Started at 7 a.m., and got to Springfontein about 4 p.m., having made a halt at Kuilfontein. " C " Squadron was here waiting for us, and Sergt.-Maj. Wardell also rejoined, he being now appointed regimental sergeant-major.

After exchanging a few horses, a start was made at 11 a.m., and Providence, down the line, reached about 4.15 p.m.

Made a short march to Spitz Kop, while farm-clearing

1901.
APRIL.

went on. Capt. Campbell, with a patrol of 30 men and one from the C. M. R., went out in the afternoon to try and get intelligence of Kruitzinger.

Sat. 6th

"D" Squadron out farm clearing. Fell in with Capt. Campbell's patrol, which had remained out all night, but only saw a Boer patrol. Heard to-day that Maj. Colvin had been given the command of a small column under Gen. Plumer.

Sun. 7th

Received orders to move north and join Gen. Hamilton at Winkel Hoek.

Started at 6.45 a.m., and at 9 a.m. "D" Squadron was sent on ahead to join the General. Having decided to go on to Cyferfontein, we started at 1.30 p.m., being followed by the rest of the column at 3 p.m.

Mon. 8th

Started at 7 a.m., making a midday halt at De Bad about 11.15 a.m. Went on again at 1.30 p.m., reached Snyman's Post at 4 p.m., and pushed on to Nooitgedacht, getting there about 5.15 p.m. Very conflicting information about Kruitzinger.

Tues. 9th

Left camp at 6.30 a.m., Bruce Hamilton, ox convoy and other columns to Dewetsdorp, our column moving on to Uitzicht, which was reached about 11 a.m., and a halt made till 1.30 p.m. Camp was formed between Helvetia and Roodepoort about 5.15 p.m. Swamped out once more soon after getting into bivouac.

Wed. 10th

We left camp at 1.30 p.m. with orders to go to Nottingham. After going some five or six miles "A" Squadron in front came in touch with some Boers and pushed on, supported by the "D" Squadron. Soon afterwards saw Munro's column a few miles ahead, they

having just finished a fight, in which they successfully
captured 91 prisoners and some wagons.

Bivouacked at Ruitefontein 6 p.m.

" A " Squadron and C. M. R. farm clearing, while the
rest only went on as far as Riet Spruit. The " D "
Squadron was, however, sent out to the right flank on
what turned out to be a false report, and there spent
the rest of the day farm clearing.

The three squadrons started out farm clearing in
different directions at 7.30 a.m., and collected late in the
afternoon at Jackalsfontein. The C. M. R. were away
to the west.

Continued farm clearing and bivouacked at Vaalbank.

Having filled our wagons, we started for Helvetia at
8 a.m., the stock having gone on early. Got in at 11 a.m.
Rejoined the C. M. R. here

Went on to Koetzee's Post, farm clearing *en route*,
and encountering a little sniping.

Started this morning at 7 a.m. for Vertkraal, which
lies in the centre of a large plain with a horse-shoe-shaped
line of kopjes round the borders. The C. M. R. with
pom-pom were away to the right, under Maxwell, while
Maj. Follett had the remainder and convoy.

After crossing the kopjes, we could hear pom-poming
going on on the right, and then saw about 100 Boers
streaking across the plain, apparently making for some
bushy kopjes, so Maj. Follett sent the advanced squadron
(" D ") on at a gallop to get there first. This was done,
and soon afterwards the Boers came into view, but did
not mean stopping except to water. Sending for the

1901.   guns, we unfortunately restrained ourselves from firing,
APRIL.   and the former for some reason not starting soon enough,
a golden opportunity was lost, and they got away with
only a sound frightening.

The C. M. R. burnt their camp and then we went into
bivouac about 4 p.m., having got drenched through
owing to a storm suddenly coming up.

Wed. 17th   The C. M. R.'s had received orders to return to the
Colony, and started for Edenburg this morning, Col.
Maxwell having a dismounted parade to bid them farewell. At 8 a.m. the rest of us moved off, two troops
" D " Squadron being sent to the right and two of " C "
to the left to clear farms. Unfortunately one of the
latter, under Macdonald, got into difficulties running
into a party of Boers, who had laid a trap for them by
hiding on a kopje and sending one or two of their number
to canter past the kopje in the open. Macdonald
charged them, only to find his mistake too late, but
gallantly refused to surrender, and when Lieut. Stirling
arrived with the other troop, he found the Boers galloping
away, Lieut. Macdonald and three men killed, Sergt.
Hart dying, and seven more, including the Rimington
Guide (interpreter), severely wounded. All were brought
into camp at Vaalkop (Boutjesfontein Farm), where two
more died of their wounds during the night. Col.
Forbes, with the Welsh Yeomanry, joined us here.

Casualties :—

Killed : 2nd Lieut. Hon. A. Macdonald ; Sergt. W.
Hart ; Lance-Corpl. R. Heanes ; Ptes. A. Banks. E.
Lavers.

Wounded : Ptes. P. Moody, J. Cook, P. Bothing, A. Prior, G. Elliott, W. Philp.

All belonged to " C " Squadron. Capt. Campbell appointed S.O. to Col. Maxwell, vice Collyer, C.M.R.

The day commenced with the funeral of the poor fellows killed yesterday, and then the refugee convoy, stock, and the wounded in charge of Capt. Forrest were sent into Edenburg, while the rest went on to Foster's Kop, keeping a southerly course in order to support a party of Rimington's Guides. After a halt here, Kruger's Siding was reached about 2 p.m.

Capt. Fiennes, who had escorted the convoy into Edenburg, returned this afternoon and brought the welcome addition of Lieut. Kincaid-Smith and 139 N.C.O.'s and men.

The column marched at 1 p.m. as far as Poortje, getting there about 4.45 p.m. A section of guns of 39th F. B. have joined us in addition to the Yeomanry.

Moved on to near Ospoort at 9.30 a.m. and got into bivouac at 2 p.m., having come in for a little sniping.

A move was not made till midday, owing to clearing work to be done at the camp.

The " A " Squadron was sent out to reconnoitre to the left front, when Lieut. Wynn found a party of Boers at their old camp on the Hex river. He had to clear out, but the Boers were checked on finding they were running into the rest of the troop in position. Got to bivouac at Ninavel about 4 p.m.

As the Boers had been located at Hex river, and

White's column was coming out from the west, Col. Maxwell decided on going that way and endeavouring to catch the burghers. Leaving the I. Y. in charge of the column, the remainder went on towards the drift on the Hex river. When nearing it, " D " Squadron, who were in front, were told to make good the drift. This was done by Lieut. Jackson with a little opposition, and when the support came up, the 16th Lancers were seen coming round the kopjes. They, thinking us the Boers, promptly opened fire, and very nearly destroyed our staff with their Hotchkiss gun. Our gallant young gunner promptly let them have five shells before firing could be stopped. Fortunately no damage was done, except a few horses wounded, but the Boers had managed to slip away.

Wed. 24th   Started at 8 a.m., and went as far as Helvetia, where we had to take in supplies, and remained here all day. Received orders to once more cross the Caledon river and clear that part of the country thoroughly. Small parties of Boers still hanging about.

Thur. 25th   Marched at 7 a.m. for Bastard's Drift, halted at Vaalbank, and then went on to within a couple of miles of the drift, when we bivouacked at Kalkoen Kranz about 5 p.m. Again, small parties of Boers encountered.

Fri. 26th   The ox part of the convoy with the " A " Squadron started at 8 a.m. for the drift. On getting there they were opposed, so we all saddled up and went on. The country beyond was a very nasty piece of hilly country, backed by a high mountain. The " A " Squadron was having very difficult work reconnoitring it, and having

a running fight all the time. The drift was now tried,
but the colonel thought it too sandy for the heavy wagons,
so we went back to our old bivouac.

White turned up and crossed before dark and
Williams also came in.

The ox convoy started off at 6 a.m., followed later by
the rest. Everything was safely over by 9 a.m., and we
then marched on to Sweetwater, and afterwards to Bushman's Kop, and arrived just before dark.

All three columns are now temporarily under Williams.

" C " and " D " Squadrons farm clearing along the
Basuto border. The marches of the main body of the
columns are now much shorter, which gives the clearing
parties time to do their work thoroughly, instead of
rushing through it as we had to do before.

Remained here all day, while Lieut. Jackson was sent
out with his troop to reconnoitre the vicinity of Leeuwkop and Grysberg. He was accompanied by Lieut.
Wynn. He was unable to ascertain anything. Several
unarmed Boers were taken at the farms to-day, their
arms evidently being hidden.

" A " and " C " Squadrons out farm clearing, while
the column moved on to Houtconstant.

Moved on to Delft. A new system has been inaugu-
rated, the squadron not out farm clearing is called the
" emergency squadron," and together with the pom-pom
is always in readiness to got out at any time.

Marched on to Hooglanden.

Went on to Eland's Kloof, which was reached about
2 p.m. The " emergency troops " were called away to

14

1901.
MAY.

co-operate with White's column against some Boers near Zastron.

At 4 p.m. had to move everything over to where White's camp was at Draaifontein.   Did not get in till dark.

One or two Boers were captured during the day.

Sat. 4th

Col. Maxwell sent the transport under escort of "D" Squadron back to Eland's Kloof, and took the rest of the column to assist Col. White.   After getting about six miles beyond Zastron, the 16th Lancers, who were in front, came under heavy fire from a ridge, which was, however, soon cleared by our guns and pom-pom.

Lord Leitrim was sent to another ridge, where he found some 200 Boers galloping away.   Unfortunately they were at extreme gun range by the time the rest got up.   The 9th Lancers with guns and pom-pom and I. Y. then advanced rapidly to a third ridge, but only to find the Boers still going hard towards Elandsberg. Further pursuit was useless, so the whole force was withdrawn and camp reached at 5.30 p.m.

Little damage was done to either side, beyond some horses, and only two prisoners were taken, although a large number of sheep and cattle were secured.

This party were evidently driving the stock north, and managed to get through between White's and Williams' columns, the latter having been recalled to Springfontein,

Sun. 5th

The column marched on at 11 a.m. for Zandfontein, which was reached at 2 p.m., and all stock, etc., handed over to empty convoy returning to Aliwal.

Mon. 6th

Moved to Vlakplaats.

Tues. 7th

Started at 7 a.m. for Aliwal, it being an awfully cold

morning. Halted at the drift some eight miles from the
town, and went on again at 12.30 p.m., getting to bivouac
at 3.45.

Remained here during the last two days, and got the Thur. 9th

REGIMENTAL SERGT.-MAJOR WARDELL.

list of the clasps that are to be issued with the medal.
The majority of the Regiment get six or seven.

Started off on another trek at 9 a.m., and got to Roux- Fri. 10th
ville at 4.30 p.m.

Remained here all day, very cold and windy. Sat. 11th

As it was thought that Scheepers was going to try and Sun. 12th
get back to the Orange River Colony through the native

14*

1901.
MAY.
territory of Herschel, our columns got an order to watch the river.

The Regiment and pom-pom were sent out towards Damers Hek to cover the river from there (Karreepoort) to Aliwal North. Marched at 2 p.m. and got to Rietfontein at 5 p.m. The rest of the column stayed at Rouxville.

Mon. 13th
Two officers and 24 men had to be sent to Kaffir Kop to entrench themselves and watch the river. In the afternoon camp was moved some four miles nearer Damers Hek. A gale of wind and very cold. " D " Squadron found the above party.

Tues. 14th
This morning all the Herschel hills covered with snow. " A " Squadron went on in relief of river party.

Wed. 15th
" C " Squadron on observation.

Thur. 16th
" D " Squadron on observation. At 12.30 p.m. orders came for Regiment to rejoin at Rouxville. Started at 1.45 p.m., and got in at 5 p.m.

The G.O.C. (Gen. Bruce Hamilton) published following order :—

" The Major-General commanding much regrets that he has to record the death of 2nd Lieut. the Hon. A. R. A. Macdonald and four men of the 9th Lancers, who were killed in action at Werfkraal on April 17th. 2nd Lieut. Macdonald with his troop, consisting of 12 men only, galloped to a kopje held by the Boers, who were hidden behind sangars. They were outnumbered by the enemy, but refused to surrender and held their ground until without exception every man was hit.

" The whole party behaved in a most gallant manner,

and the Major-General commanding deeply deplores
their severe loss."

Started at 10 a.m., and marched direct to Sterkfontein, getting there about 3 p.m.

The I. Y. and " C " Squadron and pom-pom, under
Col. Forbes, started at 8 a.m. in a northerly direction,
and then had to work east through the Elandsberg
mountains. The remainder of the column started at
10 a.m. for Elandsberg Farm, but while the troops were
crossing the donga that runs up to this place, Col. Maxwell met with a severe accident. He had been knocked
up with the severe cold lately experienced, and while
sitting mounted and watching the donga being crossed
evidently fainted, for his pony came over backwards,
and he was found quite unconscious. He could not be
moved, so we halted between Olievenrand and Harvey's
Hoek. Col. Forbes' party did not return till after dark
—6.30 p.m.

Orders came for us to return south, having to be on
the road half way between Rouxville and Commissie
Bridge by noon to-morrow.   Moved back as far as Sterkfontein in the afternoon.

Started at 8 a.m., and went as far as Leeuw Spruit,
whence the ambulance with Col. Maxwell went on to
Rouxville and the column to Vishgat, which was reached
at noon. It was with the deepest regret that we heard
of the death of our gallant column leader in the evening.
Though in extremely delicate health he never flinched
from the hardest task.

Remained here all day awaiting orders.

1901.
MAY.
Wed. 22nd
Started at 7.30 a.m. and marched on to within a couple of miles of Smithfield, where we made a midday halt, resuming the march at 2.30 p.m., and making Klipplaatfontein about 4 p.m.

Thur. 23rd
Moved out at 8 a.m. and marched to Weltevreden, where we bivouacked alongside of Col. Du Moulin's column.

Fri. 24th
Farm clearing began once more. We moved out in a westerly direction and had a certain amount of sniping. Two of our black scouts were killed first thing in the morning, and later in the day we had to shell the Boers out of Leeuwkop. Du Moulin's on our left was also engaged.

Sat. 25th
The column started at 9 a.m., the farm clearers having already gone out. After reaching Ventersfontein, where the bivouac was to be, Maj. Follett took the "D" Squadron and pom-pom on towards Bushman's Kop, and here came across a few snipers. All this time Du Moulin's was heard shelling away to our left front. After getting through the gorge in the hills the other two squadrons came up, and from our elevated position the Boers could be seen trekking away north, but out of range, with the exception of some 50 going along the foot of the hills ; these the pom-pom was only just able to reach. Camp was reached soon after 4 p.m.

Sun. 26th
Moved on to Twyfelfontein, having to get the transport through the gorge in the hills, which was bad going. The sheep were an awful nuisance. The Yeomen found seven women, 10 boys and 24 girls living in hiding up in the hills.

"A" and "D" Squadrons were farm clearing, and as "A" would eventually have to get over the neck in the hills overlooking Ospoort, the emergency squadron ("C") was sent to support them. While the clearing was going on Lieut. Stirling was sent with his troop to occupy the neck, covered by the pom-pom. The three advanced points were allowed to go right through the neck and the remainder of the troop to get right underneath the kopjes, some having already dismounted, when there was a shout of "Hands up!" followed by heavy firing, as Stirling shouted, "Files about!" The men all took what little cover they could find, while reinforcements were sent up on both flanks. The pom-pom getting to work effectually cleared the kopjes, and Lieut. Kincaid-Smith, who had been sent up to the right, saw some 200 Boers going away north, besides a certain number leaving the different parts of the kopjes.

Lieut. Stirling very pluckily returned under heavy fire to help Sergt. Sharples get under cover, his horse having been shot.

The casualties among this troop were pretty heavy, and all belonged to "C" Squadron :

Killed : Pte. R. Winn.

Wounded and died of wounds : Ptes. J. Ridge, C. Baker, C. Ward, T. Allen.

Wounded : Pte. J. Powers, Shoeing Smith A. Hersey, Lance-Corpl. W. Murrant.

We camped at De Put, a few miles further on, and just before reaching this place the Yeomen, who were in front, came on another lot of Boers, who had evidently

1901.
MAY.

gone away in the opposite direction to the others and were rounding up stock, all of which was captured, except the ponies.

Tues. 28th Started at 8.30 a.m., and as there was a nasty range of kopjes for some miles along our right, with a gorge at the end through which we were bound to go, the column was kept together and the stock closed up. It had been increasing horribly, and we now had from 25,000 to 30,000 sheep and nearly 1,000 cattle, besides families.

Palmietfontein was eventually reached without mishap.

Wed. 29th " D " Squadron (emergency) and pom-pom accompanied the " A " Squadron while farm clearing. Found some saddled ponies, but could not find their owners, though we got the stock they had been collecting, namely, some 1,000 sheep, 30 donkeys and 100 head of cattle. On reaching Zwaartlaagte, where we bivouacked, orders were received from the General for us to go to Edenburg instead of Kruger's Siding, and for the Regiment to entrain for the south. Two troops of the " D " Squadron took the ambulances straight on to Kruger's Siding.

Thur. 30th The I. Y. started off at 7.30 a.m. with all the stock and refugees for Kruger's Siding, while the rest left for Edenburg at 9 a.m., getting in at 12.30 p.m. " C " Squadron entrained at 2.30 p.m., and the rest began at 5 p.m. We only went as far as Kruger's Siding, as the trains are once more not running after dark.

Tried to get the General to let our old friend Capt. Montgomery and his pom-pom come with us, but were refused.

Capt. Campbell goes as staff officer to Col. Du Moulins and Lord D. Compton is still out with Yeomanry, he having been given command of them on return from short leave, as the column was still on the veldt.

The trains went on again at 7 a.m., and reached Fri. 31st Burghersdorp, after many delays, late in the evening. The four trains were here converted into three, and, thanks to the railway authorities, a whole train of horses sent on with only one troop in attendance.

The " C " Squadron got down to Queenstown, but the Sat. 1st remainder were stopped at Bowker's Park, our destination having been changed to Dordrecht.

After a most unpleasant journey Dordrecht was made Sun. 2nd good this evening, the first train getting there at 4 p.m., and " C " Squadron not till 8 p.m.

Moved over to the camp, and there found that we were Mon. 3rd to be part of Col. Scobell's (Scots Greys) column, and that our companions were the C. M. R. once more.

Kruitzinger and Fouchee, with some 700 Boers, are causing much annoyance in these parts, and have been fighting at Jamestown.

News came in that Jamestown had surrendered, Tues. 4th and with the garrison an enormous amount of ammunition.

The column started at 7 a.m., the " C " Squadron being detached to go straight towards Jamestown, while the remainder went north. On the way out we picked up the detached post of C. M. R.'s at Labuscogne's Nek and 30 miles. halted at 1 p.m. near Toom Nek. A fresh start was made at 2.30 p.m., and the rest of the way made by a

1901.
JUNE.

bad road running through a horrible piece of country full of defiles and traps. It was quite dark before we settled into bivouac at Laf Krans, having done some 30 miles. The Boers under Kruitzinger, Fouchee, Lotter, and Greyburg were here at 5 p.m. last night.

Wed. 5th

The column moved off at 6 a.m., " D " Squadron in advance. The road ran close to the Holle Spruit, with high hills on each side. This continued till Flaauw Kraal was reached. As it was not certain which way the Boers had gone, Scobell sent the " D " Squadron on towards Roode Nek, following with most of the others.

12 miles.

It was discovered that Fouchee had passed through here yesterday evening, but with only a portion of his men, so Lieut. Theobald was sent on with a patrol, but could not find out anything definite. We got in about 11.15 a.m., but owing to the stiff collar-work, the transport did not arrive till 4 p.m., Lund's squadron turning up soon afterwards.

Thur. 6th

In consequence of information received, Scobell decided to make a night march, and we accordingly started at 9 p.m. as soon as the moon rose. After a long, steep, downward journey to Waschbank a bad spruit had to be negotiated, and soon afterwards the column halted. Scobell now told squadron leaders his plans, which were that he intended to cross the Kraai river at Abbots Ann, about a mile further on, as he was led to understand that the Boers were at Myburg's Farm. As the descent to the drift was a very bad one, the transport was to come on as best it could. After about an hour's halt the column moved on, crossed the river and bore

away to the left front, when the road reached the
semi-circular hills which ran out from Abbots Ann.
The C. M. R. were in front, and climbed up the very bad
and steep ascent on to the hills, which formed a plateau
on top and were followed by the Regiment, " D "
Squadron in front.   The latter were just on the top when
a shot rang out from in front, and it turned out that the
C. M. R. had run into a picquet.   Maj. Follett sent the
" D " Squadron to hold different points while the rest
were coming up, and then " C " Squadron came up on
left of part of " D " Squadron, " A " Squadron being on
left of plateau.   Scobell now ordered the C. M. R.'s to
rush the farm (Wildefontein) which was in the hollow
beyond, while he himself took what he could find of
" D " Squadron and slid down the steep side, horses and
all, while the " A " Squadron felt its way round the
kopjes on the left.

Firing was going on everywhere, while the C. M. R.'s
were getting down, and they rushed the farm in splendid
style.   Just before dawn one of the guns which had been
brought up the hill with great difficulty fired several
rounds at the ridge behind the farm.

Behind the house was a gorge, through which Col.
Scobell told the " D " Squadron to go and keep the
Boers in touch.   It was a terrible piece of country, and
the squadron came in for a good deal of sniping, and
after going a couple of miles or so found they could go
no further without support.   The best part of the Boers
were within view and making good almost inaccessible
heights.

1901.
JUNE.

Lieut. Durand, with the " A " Squadron, had worked along the hills to the left over very nasty ground and was here opposed by a party of Boers. He managed to do them some damage before they retired. After everything had been collected, prisoners, ponies, etc., we all went back to the plateau, where we made a halt.

The result was 18 prisoners, 163 ponies, 97 saddles, nearly 13,000 rounds ammunition and 25 rifles, and number of blankets, etc., evidently looted from Jamestown. This was all done with one wounded C. M. R., the only casualty.

We started back at noon, and reached the convoy at the drift about 1.30 p.m.

Most of the Boers were Cape Rebels.*

Fri. 7th

The column only moved back some three miles to the small spruit, the C. M. R.'s remaining at Abbots Ann. Patrolling was done all round.

Heard Gorringe's guns to the north.

Sat. 8th

Remained here all day and had to send the wagons back to the ox convoy at Roode Nek, as the poor brutes were too done to come on.

Heard from C. M. R. that four dead Boers had been found at Wildefontein.

Sun. 9th

18 miles.

Started at 6.30 a.m., and went south until we met the main Dordrecht–Barkly East road, when we went on to Spitzkop, getting there at 1 p.m. Finding the transport

---

* Owing to the limited space having been rather encroached on, it is found impossible to give a full description of the country passed through, but the few details given will probably recall their surroundings to those who were present.

could not get up for some time, we were ordered to
bivouac. The C. M. R.'s moved on towards Barkly, on
the west side of river.

Remained here all day, getting information that the
Boers had gone west, and then orders came for us to
·return to Dordrecht.

Started at 6.30 a.m., and made a long march to
Nooitgedacht, which was reached at 4.30 p.m.

Started at 7 a.m., and got to Dordrecht about 10 a.m.
From here a fresh start was made at 2 p.m. towards
Molteno. Bivouacked at Leeuwfontein.

Gen. French has now taken over the command of the
whole of the operations in Cape Colony.

Started at 6 a.m. with the intention of getting to
Molteno, but halted at Buffelsfontein at 10 a.m., and
sent out patrols as the Boers were reported only some
eight or nine miles north of us.

The " C " Squadron was sent out at midnight to work
round the right, viâ Vlakfontein, while the rest of us
started about 3.30 a.m., making for Bamboes Hoek some
seven miles on. By the first streak of dawn we had got
to Morgenzon Farm, a couple of miles short of our
destination. Here we left our cloaks, and Scobell dis-
posing the troops, we galloped down to the farm, but
only to find it unoccupied. Lund's squadron arrived
on the spot at the same time.

At midday Scobell got news that the Boers had all
crossed the line, and so started at 1.30 p.m. for Molteno.
Went into bivouac some five miles short of the place
owing to the transport being a long way behind.

1901.
JUNE.
Sat. 15th
5 miles.
Tues. 18th

Started at 7 a.m., and got into Molteno at 8.30 a.m., and remained here all day.

Have remained here during the last three days, the C. M. R.'s having rejoined yesterday morning. Capt. Lund has been given the command of a column of the new Yeomanry, and takes his own squadron with him, entraining for De Aar.

Wed. 19th

Started at 7 a.m., and marched steadily on until we reached Vlakfontein about 1 p.m., when we went into bivouac and the scouts were sent out.

Thur. 20th

Off at 6.30 a.m., and marched to near Witkop, getting there at 10 a.m. Went on again at 1.30 p.m. and bivouacked near Kraalfontein.

Fully expected another night march, as the Boers were reported only seven miles from us.

A despatch arrived telling us to go back to Burghersdorp and entrain.

Fri. 21st

20 miles.

Started at 7 a.m. for Burghersdorp and marched straight in. Arrived at 1.30 p.m. after a long march in the rain, and met the Connaught Rangers going out, the whole Regiment having been turned into M. I.

Sat. 22nd

After a very wet night, the C. M. R.'s began entraining at 6 a.m., but owing to the scarcity of rolling stock it was 4 p.m. before their second train got away.

At 10.15 p.m. orders came for the Regiment to begin entraining at midnight. "D" Squadron prepared to do this, followed by "A" at 2 a.m., but it was 1.20 a.m. before any trucks turned up.

Sun. 23rd

It had rained all morning and had begun again, and was pitch dark.

After an awful journey, full of delays and difficulties, Graaf Reinet was not reached until midday by the " D " Squadron, who had had to fill their engine cisterns from a spruit by means of nosebags. The men had had nothing to eat for 24 hours, and the horses two days'

SERGT. GENTRY AND " JACK."

forage in three, and great scarcity of water. The " A " Squadron came in later in the day.

After collecting here, and refitting in every way, in- Sun. 30th cluding pack mules, as we shall probably have to take to the mountains, we made a start at 8 a.m. towards Petrusberg, which lies in the centre of a small plain, sur- 24 miles.

1901. rounded by high mountains, with miles of impenetrable prickly pears and acacia trees.

After a midday halt from 1 to 3 p.m. we reached De Plaats, where we went into bivouac at 7 p.m. in a most

JULY.

Mon. 1st uncomfortable place.

Started at 7 a.m. and got to Petrusberg about 11 a.m. Scouts were sent out, but failed to get any information

12 miles. of Kruitzinger.

Tues. 2nd Started at 7 a.m., and after barely covering a mile, rain came on and continued till we reached our midday

22 miles. halt at De Plaats. As the rain cleared off, the hills were seen covered with snow. Moving on again at 2 p.m., we got into bivouac at 5 p.m.

Wed. 3rd Started at 7.30 a.m. and reached camp at Graaf Reinet

14 miles. about midday.

Sat. 6th Have been sitting here the last three days, so the C. M. R. got up sports, open to the column, which was a most successful afternoon's amusement.

Tues. 9th Still here, but rumours were afloat that we may start in the afternoon, which would have been rather annoying, as the Regiment was giving a " skittle " gymkhana, with four events for the men and four for officers, the latter being all ladies' nominations.

Fortunately we were not disturbed, and the afternoon passed off most successfully, quite a number of Graaf Reinet Society turning up, and competing quite keenly for the events. Our old friends the 2nd Batt. Coldstream are in garrison here. Lord D. Compton returned last night.

Wed. 10th Our holiday having come to an end, we started out

this morning at 7 a.m. along the Murraysberg road.
Marching on till 12.30 p.m., we made a halt till 3 p.m.,
and eventually got to bivouac at Houd Constant about
5 p.m.

The Regiment left Houd Constant at 2 p.m., accompanied by about 150 Yeomen, under Capt. St. John
Brodrick, and one C. M. R. field gun. The remainder
of the C. M. R. were to stay here and co-operate later
with us. Taking a path across the hills to Langefontein, our portion of the column with Scobell moved as
far as Zuurpoort, which we reached about 5 p.m. The
idea was for us to move roughly south and parallel with
the C. M. R., but just outside the hills for some 14 miles,
and then turn to left into the hills. Crewe's column
was marching from Murraysberg to the south of us.
Wyndham was coming from the south, and was to be
some 20 miles west-north-west of Aberdeen, and Doran
was coming out from Graaf Reinet by the south side of
hills.

Having taken the transport with us as a blind, this
was all sent back to Houd Constant, and we started at
1 a.m. with pack mules only. Just after starting a shot
was fired close in front of us, which turned out to have
been done by a native scout, evidently in a funk.

As daylight broke we had reached Eland's Poort, and
here two advanced scouts went through the Poort and
disturbed 18 or 20 Boers at a farm close by. Having done
for both horses and slightly wounded Pte. Potter (" D "),
they galloped away. After seeing that the place was
clear we went through the gorge and halted further on

15

at Knofloekfontein. The " A " Squadron had sent on a troop in advance, and had run up against these Boers again and hunted them.

Here got into communication with Col. Crewe, and then turned east into the hills. After going up and down several impossible-looking slopes, the colonel halted for a while by a stream, as we had been going just 24 hours. Lieut. Theobald went on with his troop as a detached post, and here waylaid and collared a Boer carrying despatches to Scheepers. We started on again about 2.30 p.m. and soon came to a plateau, from the far edge of which one looked down on to the Langefontein Farm.

The Colonel sent Lieut. Sadleir-Jackson's troop to the right front, and Lieut. Theobald's was in the centre, and the remainder of " D " Squadron were sent to the left front, where they captured two Boers coming up the kloof. The C. M. R. were now down at the farm, and heavy firing going on on the right. The " A " Squadron had been sent over there and was endeavouring to prevent any more Boers getting up the kloofs. A good many had already got up, and much time was unfortunately wasted on account of a wire fence. Compton and Bell rode at several who were making for a kraal, but they threw down their arms, amongst them being Lieut. Limburger.

The " A " Squadron managed to capture 11 prisoners and 30 ponies, and Lieut. Wynn had a narrow shave of being shot, the bullet going through the brim of his hat. Darkness came on, and it was a very difficult business collecting the men together.

We eventually formed a chain of small posts at 200 yards interval all the way along the top of the kloofs and lit fires, everyone being on outposts throughout the night.

The Colonel's idea was that they had not all come up. It was a nasty cold night, and we had nothing to eat and very little to drink. It was very bad luck, for had we been there half-an-hour sooner, I believe we should have bagged the lot.

At daybreak every troop had to send a party dismounted down the various kloofs to see if there were any stragglers ; this was a long, tiring job after the last 36 hours' work, and it was 11 a.m. before anyone got breakfast. Moved on down the Zwart Valley at 1 p.m., and reached Uitkomst about 6 p.m. The bag of 23 prisoners was fairly satisfactory, though with a little more luck might have been trebled.

Spent most of the morning signalling to Gen. French at Graaff Reinet, and then moved down to the end of the valley to get some grazing for the horses and wait for our convoy.

The convoy turned up late last night, but it was 8 a.m. before we got away and moved back up the valley some seven miles, and then turned off to the left. Halted soon afterwards for a short time and then started climbing once, this time by single file, up a very steep and stony sheep track. After going another seven miles or so we halted to let the pack mules get up, and went into bivouac.

A couple of troops and some C. M. R. were sent out, as

Sat. 13th

15 miles.

Sun. 14th

5 miles.

Mon. 15th

16 miles.

15*

1901.   it was reported that a party of Boers, who had burnt a
JULY   Kaffir kraal just before our arrival, were coming back.
However, it proved a false alarm.

Tues. 16th   " Stood to " at 6.30 a.m., and marched about 8 a.m.
After a terrific climb a halt was made, the plateau on
top reconnoitred, and then passing the scene of our late
scrimmage, we dropped down into the Langefontein
16 miles.   Valley once more, and made a halt at the farm from 1 to
3 p.m., after which the march was continued to Vrede
Farm, where we arrived about 6 p.m., as it was getting
dark, and were not ill-pleased to find the transport and
everything ready and fires blazing.

Wed. 17th   Marched at 8.30 a.m. and bivouacked at a farm some
13 miles.   four miles beyond Uitkomst, near the Aberdeen–Graaff
Reinet road.

Thur. 18th   Marched at 7.30 a.m., and got into Graaff Reinet about
14 miles.   11.30 a.m.

Fri. 19th   Remained here all day.

Capt. Bell leaves us to join Col. Hunter-Weston as staff
officer.

Sat. 20th   Started at 6.30 a.m. and marched to Wellewood,
getting there just before dark, the C. M. R. going on
towards New Bethesda.

20 miles.   Unfortunately we have got to escort a huge ox convoy
with supplies for Richmond.

Sun. 21st   We started towards New Bethesda at 6.30 a.m., having
to negotiate a very long, narrow defile through the
mountains, and by a very steep road in places. Much
to our annoyance we found the ox convoy well blocked
up in the defile, the oxen (in half-starved condition) being

absolutely " done." After much delay, and wedging our
way through the string of carts, it was 10.30 a.m. before
we reached the top. After an hour's rest we went on to
Assvogel Kranz, leaving the Yeomanry with the convoy
as escort, arriving at 1.30 p.m. A further move was
made at 3.15 p.m., and Smith Vale reached at
7.15 p.m.

The C. M. R. went out last night on a rounding-up
game, and surprised the commando, brought in 10
prisoners, including Field Cornet Luys, over 100 ponies,
10 rifles and 1,000 rounds ammunition, besides destroying most of their kit. We left bivouac at 8 a.m., and
got to Dreifontein at 10.30 a.m.

Moved on at 7 a.m., halted from 10.30 a.m. to 1.30
p.m., and finally bivouacked at Klein Tafelberg (Middle
Mount) about 3.30 p.m.

Remained here all day.

Started at 7 a.m., and marched on till 11.15 a.m.,
going on again at 2 p.m. ; bivouac was reached at Groote
Valley about 6.15 p.m. The guide was terribly out in
his reckonings, and we must have covered from 27 to
28 miles.

Started at 8 a.m. and got to Middelburg about noon.

Remained here all day. Very cold indeed. Lieut.
Cavendish went sick with pleurisy.

Gen. French inspected both the Regiment and Cape
Mounted Riflemen, and made very flattering speeches to
both corps. In addressing the Regiment he laid parti-
cular stress on the gallop of the 3rd Cavalry Brigade
(9th and 16th Lancers) from Klip Drift towards Kim-

1901.
JULY.

berley, and said that when he gave the order he was afraid that there was a chance of few getting back. However, it was successfully carried out, and enabled his Cavalry Division to perform the magnificent feat of relieving Kimberley, which was the making of his own reputation.

Tues. 30th

Leitrim went sick and Follett went on leave, so we are brought to a very low ebb as regards officers.

Wed. 31st

23 miles.
AUGUST.

Started at 7 a.m., reaching Tafelberg Station about 11.30 a.m. Halted here till 2.30 p.m., and got to Conway about 5 p.m.

Thur. 1st

20 miles.

Started at 7 a.m., and marched as far as Visch River Station, where we halted and turned the horses out to graze. Orders came for us to go on to Baroda, but Col. Scobell would not move before 7 p.m., and camp was reached at 9 p.m.

Fri. 2nd
10 miles.

Off at 7 a.m., and made a midday halt at Varker's Kop, eventually remaining here all day, as water was scarce further on.

Sat. 3rd

20 miles.

In consequence of reports received yesterday evening the Regiment was sent out at 4.15 a.m. to endeavour to get round the Boers supposed to be at a farm called Groenfontein. The remainder of the column were to march direct at 4.30 a.m. However, no Boers were to be found, and the others coming up, we all went on to Doorn River Farm. Patrols could find out nothing, so we moved over to Rietfontein, and went into bivouac about 2 p.m.

Sun. 4th

Remained here all day patrolling, while the ox convoy are collecting families.

Still here, but the C. M. R. have moved over to Doorn Hoek.

Started at 7 a.m., and marched to Varker's Kop. In the afternoon the " A " Squadron and one gun were sent west to Post Chalmers to take up a position there, the " D " Squadron remaining on the Cradock road, while the Yeomanry covered the northern road, and the C. M. R. moved up to Marlow Station.

Kruitzinger, Botha and Lotter were reported north-east of Cradock, and it was feared they might attempt to break south.

All troops marched this morning and concentrated at Visch River Station. The advance guard saw a commando a long way off moving north and at a fast pace.

We were warned at 11 o'clock last night that we might have to turn out at any moment, and sure enough at 1.45 a.m. we did, thanks to an explosion and the armoured train in action to the north of us.

Got away at 2.30 a.m., and had covered some 10 or 12 miles by dawn, but could see no signs of Boers. Moved on some miles further, and then saw a cloud of dust and horseman some seven or eight miles off, making south behind a long ridge. We were making for a farm so as to water and feed, when on topping a stiff climb the advance was fired on from a ridge in front.

The Colonel sent two troops to the left front, and then gave the " D " Squadron orders to send two troops round this flank, and supporting with the other two, endeavoured to turn the flank. Lieut. Theobald was with the leading troops and, finding Lieut. Durand round this corner with some of his men, tried to push on a bit to some rocks. Here it was that he was badly wounded, shot sideways through the abdomen. The " A " Squadron at this point also had a very severe time of it and had several casualties, but held on till the Boers went back.

The rest of " D " Squadron had moved still further to the left front, owing to a commanding ridge being there. Soon after this, the C. M. R. having come up on the right, the Boers all fell back to a high kopje in front. No advantage could be obtained by moving further forward, our chief object being to prevent their breaking east again, and Hunter-Weston's column ought to have been coming up from the south, so the Boers ought to run into them. We spent a long time trying to get into communication with what we took to be Hunter-Weston's whereabouts. It was 3.45 p.m. before we all got back to the farm, and we started back at 4.30 p.m.

Theobald was left at the farm Wolverfontein, in charge of Surg.-Capt. Forrest, R.A.M.C.

It was a horrible march back by a very dusty road, and camp was not reached till 12.30 p.m., something like 25 miles without a stop.

We had been going exactly 22 hours with a rest of only 45 minutes, and the majority of the Regiment covered fully 50 miles. The casualties in the Regiment were, in addition to Lieut. Theobald :

Killed : Pte. G. Cooper (" A ").

Wounded : Lance-Corpl. H. Hilliard ; Pte. H. Howse.

Remained stationary all day.

Started off at 8 a.m., and marched up the line as far as

Cypress Grove Siding, when we turned west and bivouacked at Wildehoenderberg.   Received a not too satisfactory note from Forrest last night.

It seems that it was Smith's commando, and not
Hunter-Weston's, whose dust we saw on the afternoon
of the fight.

We got news this morning from Capt. Forrest that Mon. 12th
poor Theobald had died at 5.30 a.m., and as our camp
was only some five or six miles off, he intended bringing
the body over for burial.   The sad ceremony took place
at 10.30 a.m., and in the afternoon we moved on some 8 miles.
seven or eight miles towards Roode Hoogte, where we
were to fill up our supply wagons.

Received orders to march straight into Middelburg. Tues. 13th
                                                     22 miles.

Got orders during the night that the Regiment was Wed. 14th
to start at 8 a.m. and proceed along the Richmond road
to Vinkfontein.   The rest of the column were to come on 15 miles.
in the afternoon.

Our column was one of several which were to endea- Thur. 15th
vour to encircle the Boers, who were at Uitzigt, and had
to make for Klip Krans in a northerly direction.   Did
not get away till 9 a.m., owing to having to transfer our
supplies from wagons to pack mules.

" D " Squadron was in advance and was told to push
on well ahead so as to reconnoitre and make good the
hills up into which we had to climb.   After going a few
miles a column was seen coming off the hills, which were
very naturally taken for Boers.   However, after a longish
gallop to try and make good a ridge from which to intercept them we found they were Kavanagh's column,

1901.
AUGUST.

which had been sent out from Middelburg during the night, and had reached Uitzigt only to find the Boers gone. He was now following their track.

18 miles.

After this we turned and moved towards Rhenoster-berg, halting to wait for orders soon after recrossing the main road.

These came at 5 p.m., and we moved on as far as Twist Kraal, which was reached at 7.30 p.m. after a cruelly cold ride.

Fri. 16th

Started at 6.30 a.m. and reached Zunsfontein, where we went into camp.

12 miles.

Stayed here the rest of the day, but could get hold of no intelligence.

Sat. 17th

Left this morning at 7 a.m., and after a march over a very rough road got to Blaauw Water Siding about 11 a.m.

Gen. French turned up in the afternoon in his armoured train, and then we moved on another eight miles or so to Bethesda Road Station.

20 miles.

Sun. 18th

Left camp at 7 a.m., taking the Cradock road, which crosses a range of hills some eight miles on by the Hoogte Pass. At the far end of the pass we halted, and there ascertained that the Boers were south of us at Paarde Kraal.

14 miles.

Scobell decided to send all wheeled traffic, except two guns, on to Lange Kloof, thence into Cradock under escort of the I. Y., while the rest of us loaded up the pack mules and climbing down the hills retired behind a small ridge, in order that our fires should not be seen.

Mon. 19th

Marched at 12.30 a.m. and reached Paarde Kraal

about 5.30 a.m., only to find the Boers had gone on last
night. After a short halt we pushed on to Zuurfontein,
which was reached about 8.30 a.m., and here we learnt
that the Boers had gone in the direction of Zuurkop and
Quagga Hoek. Going on once more at 12.30 p.m. to
Klip Plaats at the foot of the hills, we found the Boers
only four hours ahead of us, so that there was every
chance of their stopping on top. The climb now began,
the C. M. R. being in front, and very stiff it was.

After getting up, the C. M. R. went on across the com- 38 miles.
paratively flat plateau and ran into the Boers, but by
the time we had all got up, the majority of them had
gone, and so no harm was done them, unfortunately.

After this we had a terrible time wandering along the
rocky top to where there was a certain amount of water,
and did not get to bivouac till 8 p.m.

Left the hills about 8 a.m., and halted at 9.30 a.m. Tues. 20th
for breakfast, as there was a chance of getting nothing
more all day. Moving on again at 1 p.m., we halted
just beyond Modder Farm, and from here the " A "
Squadron was sent off to climb the hills again and get
at the back of Hoeksfontein.

Kavanagh's column was also seen up on top of the
hills. After this we trotted on through a very long and 10 miles
nasty defile till nearing Hoeksfontein, when we bivouacked just beyond at another farm.

The " A " Squadron did not turn up till about 8 p.m.

Although we did not manage to get at the Boers themselves, we got some 30 of their ponies.

Started at 6.30 a.m., and marched north through Wed. 21st

1901.
AUGUST.
18 miles.

Tweefontein and on to Colonie Plaats Siding, which was reached soon after 9.30 a.m. Here we halted till 3 p.m., and then went on to Bethesda Road Station, getting there at 5.30 p.m.

Thur. 22nd   Remained here all day.

Fri. 23rd   After "standing to" all morning, we started eastwards at 1.15 p.m. along the Cradock road. It was wet
20 miles. and cold, and we were not looking forward to bivouacking on Hoogte Pass. Fortunately the convoy was spotted on the other side at Lange Kloof, so we made for it and got there at 7 p.m.

Sat. 24th   Last night was a terror, for at 8 o'clock it began to rain, and the morning found us in the middle of a snowstorm and everything in a horrible condition. It is scarcely to be wondered at that we were unable to make a move till 9 a.m. Lieut. Jackson with his troop had been sent out as a patrol to work to Fish River Station, via Wolve Vlei and Cypress Grove.

The column marched straight on for some 10 miles
18 miles. along the Cradock road and there halted, while the remainder of "D" Squadron were sent on towards camp via Poortje and Elandsfontein.

The rest of the column halted for the night some seven miles out, as the roads were found to be too heavy for further travelling.

Sun. 25th
7 miles.   The remainder of the column got in about 9 a.m.

Mon. 26th   Marched to Cradock.
23 miles.
Tues. 27th   After numerous orders during the morning, we eventually marched at 2 p.m. in a southerly direction and bivou-
15 miles   acked at Driefontein.

There strong reconnoitring parties were sent out eastwards from camp at 8 a.m. The " D " Squadron formed
the one from the Regiment, and was in the centre with
Wilge Kloof, right in the heart of the hills, as its objective.

The Boers were supposed to be split up, collecting 30 miles.
ponies, and Doran's column was also to be looked for.
Not a sign of a Boer was seen, and, although Doran's
camp was located, no answering signal could be got, so
a move home was made and camp reached at 9 p.m.
Doran's guns could be heard in action.

Marched at 1 p.m. and got to Cradock about 5.30 p.m. Thur. 29th
15 miles.

Remained here all day. Gen. French came down to Fri. 30th
have a talk with Col. Scobell.

Marched at 7 a.m. along the Bethesda road, halting at Sat. 31st
midday at Varken's Kop, and bivouacking at Uitkyk 25 miles.
(Antrobus' Farm). SEPT.

Remained here all morning and at 2.30 p.m. moved on Sun. 1st
six miles to Fish River. We were to work south towards
Waterval Valley, the southern slopes of which were held
by the Midlands M. R., and Doran was to come out from 6 miles.
Cradock, viâ Garstland's Kloof.

The transport, two guns, and a portion of the I. Y. Mon. 2nd
went back to Varken's Kop this morning, the fighting
portion of the column having started last night at 11 p.m.
By 3 a.m. we had got to the head of the Upper Doorn
River Valley, and then began a stiff climb. After a time
the guns had to be sent back. Leading in single file had
then to be resorted to until we got to another ridge which
overlooked the Waterval Valley. At daybreak there

were no signs of Boers, but the M. M. R. were visible along the southern heights.

After searching the place thoroughly, we went down the valley till close to Rietfontein, where Doran's column was.

Patrols were sent out by both columns, but to no effect, and it was not till late in the evening that Scobell's black scouts brought in information.

Started at 4 a.m., and reached Paarde Kraal at day-break, Doran keeping on up Waterval Valley. At the next farm it was discovered that the Boers had been there at 10 a.m. yesterday, so after a halt for breakfast and watering and feeding, we moved on again at 9 a.m., and after going about one and a half miles, had a stiff climb and nasty walk along the side of a hill, when we got on to the plateau beyond. Crossing this, we found the face edge almost a precipice. It was a terrible climb down, and took an individual just an hour. After going on a few more miles an intelligence scout galloped back to say that the Boers were at a farm only a few miles on. On we all went, and when we caught the C. M. R.'s up found the valley very narrow with a farm just in front. Half a mile further on it opened out again. Col. Scobell sent a troop of " D " Squadron (Jackson's) dismounted down a donga to try and get beyond the farm, and when this had been done, the rest of the squadron were to go on as far as they could. The Boers were amongst the bushes near Paarde Kraal Farm, where it was necessary to halt and return their fire.

Just as Col. Scobell came up a cloud of dust appeared

a couple of miles or so on amongst the trees, so he told " D " Squadron to mount and hunt the Boers hard, while he would bring on the rest.   The advance troop got up within 500 or 600 yards of their tail, but was brought up short by a hot fire from a neck in the hills for which they had been making.   It was necessary to move to the left and get under cover in a donga.

CAPT. E. R. GORDON, 9TH LANCERS ; CAPT. J. V. FORREST, R.A.M.C.

The men were able to work up this donga, and keep down the Boer fire a bit, helped by the " A " Squadron, 23 miles. which had come up in support.   The Boers cleared off just before dark, leaving several saddled ponies and kit.

Got into camp at Middel Water at 7.30 p.m.

Pte. H. Thorp (" D ") was wounded.

Paraded at 4 a.m., but did not march till 5 a.m., and Wed. 4th soon afterwards pulled up to feed the horses on oat hay. We went back on our tracks for a few miles, and then turned up to the west and were very soon making the stiffest climb most of us had done. It was wet, too, so that we were lumbered up with cloaks or mackintoshes.

A halt was called at Vlakfontein, and in clouds and drizzling rain we moved on at midday, and soon after had " the " bit of the climb to negotiate, and judging by the remarks that were heard the climb will not easily be forgotten. Eventually the track (?) we were to descend by into the Petrusberg Valley was reached. We were not sorry to get to the bottom of it and go into bivouac. Both men and horses were hungry and soak-
15 miles.
ing wet. Fortunately the climbing kept one warm.

" D " Squadron had to send a troop to the village for the night to prevent anyone leaving it. Col. Scobell here got information that the Boers were on top of the hills on the south side of the valley—some nine miles off—and so made an appeal to the column to make a final effort, as to-morrow we must go in to Graaff Reinet, being out of all food.

Thur. 5th
The column marched at 1 a.m. in pouring rain, and just before reaching Groene Kraal Farm turned to the left through the prickly pears and reached the foot of the kloof. Up this we struggled and stumbled, sliding away in the wet mud until the top was at last reached. The Colonel here explained his plans to C.O.'s and squadron leaders. The farm, where the Boers were supposed to be, was behind a ridge, which could be seen near the far end of the plateau, and a donga ran from it,

passing pretty close to the left edge of the rise and then into a steep kloof. The " A " Squadron was told off to get round this flank, the C. M. R. were to go direct for the ridge, while the " D " Squadron were sent round the right flank and rear.

There was just a suspicion of dawn when the Colonel sent us on our way. The " A " Squadron were restricted in their movements to the flank by the donga, and on getting to the corner of the ridge came upon some kraals, in one of which (covered at one end) the Boers were.

Thinking those he saw only an outpost, Lord D. Compton called to Lieut. Wynn in front, who was commanding the advance party of half-a-dozen men, to gallop on. This he did with his party.

Lord D. Compton himself had a narrow escape, for dropping his pistol at the gate of the kraal he dismounted, picked it up, mounted, and galloped on after the advance party unscathed, but several other unfortunate men who then tried to get past the kraal were knocked over. However, a certain number of the squadron managed to get to the kraal walls and others behind some sort of cover. While this was going on the C. M. R. had made good the ridge, so that the Boers, cooped up in the kraal, were having a bad time of it, but like fools kept on firing. Wynn's party had got on beyond the farm, from which only five Boers came out, and they were all subsequently shot in the donga. The unfortunate " D " Squadron were out of it, having a longer round to make on the right and several wire fences to cut, and had the poor satisfaction of rounding up most of the ponies, though

16

1901.

had the Boers been on the alert this squadron would have been in an important position. The Boers thought they were so safe that they had no outposts out, and had only sent out one patrol to look for forage. The work was most complete, for the whole of Lotter's commando, with everything it possessed, with the exception of the patrol that had been sent out during the night, had fallen into Scobell's hands. He well deserved his success for the dogged way in which he had stuck to his game. The real hard week's work was soon forgotten.

But this success had not been achieved for nothing, it had cost the Regiment seven killed and five wounded, and the C. M. R. two men killed, one officer and two men wounded.

16 miles.

Of the Boers 13 were killed, and some 120 taken prisoners, out of whom about 50 were wounded. After the wounded had all been dressed and the dead buried, the awful business of getting the wounded and prisoners down off the hill to bivouac was begun about 1 p.m., and everything at peace by dark.

The casualties here (Bouwer's Hoek) were :—

Killed : Sergt. J. B. Mercer.

Lance-Corpl. W. J. Priest.

Ptes. W. Vipond, H. Clifford, W. Kennedy, V. Ward, A. Dodge.

Wounded : Lance-Corpl. W. Perkins.

Ptes. W. Norbron, F. King, W. Ginn, J. Power.

All these men belonged to the " A " Squadron.

The following column order was published this evening :

" The O.C. column cannot adequately express his thanks to all ranks for the way in which they have worked for the past four days, culminating this morning in a very important capture of Lotter and practically the whole of his commando. Col. Scobell is perfectly sure no other column operating in the Colony could have done what the 9th Lancers and C. M. R. have done, and he is sure that Gen. French will be more than pleased at what they have accomplished.

" Col. Scobell's thanks are particularly due to Capt. Lord D. Compton and the " A " Squadron 9th Lancers for the splendid dash and bravery they showed to-day, and he has already brought the names of the officers of this squadron to the notice of the G.O.C., and also the name of Capt. Purcell, C.M.R., for the fine work he and his men did."

Started at 8 a.m., and on reaching Slegtoenoeg found a small convoy waiting for us, so needless to say a halt was called and man and beast fed. After a rest a forward move was made, and bivouac at McNaughton's Farm, reached about 5 p.m. **Fri. 6th**

21 miles.

The " A " Squadron had had the pleasant job of bringing the prisoners along through the prickly pear region.

The " D " Squadron had to do escort to-day, and in order not to waste too much time, three ox wagons were commandeered and the other prisoners piled into these. These were, however, to be unloaded before reaching **Sat. 7th**

14 miles.

16*

1901.
SEPT.
Graaff Reinet, and a ceremonious procession formed of the two mule wagons and the prisoners on foot.

They were safely lodged in jail by 12.30 p.m.

Fri. 13th
Have had a six days' rest here, and it was much wanted ; besides, a quantity of equipment was required, especially boots. This climbing is cruel work on them.

Sat. 14th
22 miles.
Started off once more towards Cradock at 8.30 a.m., and halted for the night at Wellwood, Col. Lukin, C.M.R., in temporary command, as Col. Scobell gone on short leave.

Sun. 15th

15 miles.
A terrible storm came on during the night, and it poured nearly all day. After struggling along to a farm three miles beyond Bethesda Road Station, we went into bivouac, as it would have been impossible for the transport to have got any further.

Mon. 16th

9 miles.
Rained nearly all night, consequently the going was made very heavy. Started off in rain at 7 a.m., but after going from two to two and a half miles, found the transport was hopelessly behind, and it had not all got up when we moved on again at 11 a.m. The troops moved on as far as Dassies Hoogte Pass, where we bivouacked. Another bad storm came up soon after we had got into camp, and the whole place was soon turned into a quagmire.

Tues. 17th
It rained the whole of last night and was bitterly cold, thanks to the biting wind. On account of the transport it was found necessary to stay here all day, and their difficulties may be somewhat realized from the fact that the last wagons did not get in till 3 p.m., having only

covered nine miles since 7 a.m. yesterday. The climb
up the hills is very severe on draught animals.

A cruelly cold night and freezing hard, so we were
not sorry to be away by 6 a.m. and walk down the hill
to warm ourselves.

Made a midday halt at Fish River, after doing some

BOER PRISONERS.
[Reproduced by permission of *The King* and *Navy and Army Illustrated*.]

14 miles. Col. Lukin wanted to make good Varken's
Kop that night, as he expected supplies there, so we
moved on again at 3 p.m., but on reaching Antrobus'
Farm were ordered to go to whichever place was nearest,
Cradock or Visch River Station. Went on till nearly
dark and then bivouacked at Alleman's Kraal. Lieut.
Nelson had been sent out at 2.30 a.m. with his troop to

try and capture two Boers reported at Henning's Farm.

Our men completely surprised them, finding them both in bed. These were two of Lotter's patrol that had escaped capture on September 5th.

Thur. 19th
10 miles.
Started at 6 a.m., and marched into Visch River Station, a terrible battle against an unfortunate herd of buck taking place most of the morning.

Fri. 20th
Remained here all day. Heard of the disaster to a squadron of the 17th Lancers at the hands of Smuts near Tarkastad.

Sat. 21st
23 miles.
Started at 10 a.m. for Cradock, which we reached at 7 p.m.

Sun. 22nd.
10 miles.
Started at 1 p.m., and marched eastwards as far as Virsch Gewaagd, where we bivouacked.

Gorringe's column is following Smuts, and several others are moving into position to combine.

Mon. 23rd
20 miles.
Marched at 7 a.m., halted at Eland's Drift, and bivouacked near Paling Kloof in the afternoon.

Tues. 24th
Started at 7 a.m. and followed on after Gorringe's column. Halted between Rondable and Beeste Kraal; went on again at 2 p.m., and went into bivouac at 5 p.m.
23 miles.
at Spitzkop. The road was a cruel one for wheeled transport; several very bad drifts also had to be crossed.

Wed 25th
Started at 8 a.m. in a southerly direction and made a midday halt at Kelkoen Kranz, going on again at 4 p.m.,
19 miles.
and reaching Emerald Vale about 5.30 p.m. Here we bivouacked. The supply wagons had to be sent back to Tarkastad to fill up.

Thur. 26th
Marched at 6.30 a.m. and kept down the Fort Beaufort

road, halting at Koonap Drift for instructions from Col. 1901.
Haig, who is running this show. Eventually remained SEPT.
here and heard that Smuts was half-way between Bedford and Fort Beaufort, and that Doran's column, the 10 miles.
17th Lancers, and Major Officers men were after him.

Gorringe's column has kept him on the run.

Marched at 6.30 a.m., making a midday halt at the Fri. 27th
foot of Bush Nek and reaching Adelade at 5 p.m., where 20 miles.
we bivouacked. Quite a pretty march for a change,
down a long, wooded valley.

Started at 8.30 a.m. and arrived at Bedford at noon. Sat. 28th
Halted here for the rest of the day. 12 miles

Started for Cookhouse Station at 6.30 a.m., and on Sun. 29th
arrival found part of Doran's column entraining. Smuts
had crossed the line below Middelton, and Gorringe was 19 miles.
once more on his heels.

The Regiment got orders to march down the line to Mon. 30th
Middelton and entrain there, so made a start at 6.30
a.m. The C. M. R. were to stop and entrain at Cookhouse.

Having done about six miles, a helio message was
received telling us to remain where we were, but this
was cancelled about noon, and we reached Middelton 15 miles.
about 4.30 p.m. Here we found Doran's Yeomanry
entraining. OCTOBER.

The " A " Squadron commenced their entraining at Tues. 1st
7 a.m., but owing to inefficient railway arrangements it
was noon before they finished, and 3.30 p.m. before the
" D " Squadron could begin.

The " A " Squadron did not get away till 9 p.m., and Wed. 2nd
it was 2 a.m. before the " D " Squadron started.

1901.
OCTOBER.

We had to go down to Uitenhage and then up the Graaff Reinet line to Klipplaat.

It was a cruel journey. The trains were continually being split up, delays were frequent, and unaccustomed to heavy trains the water-supply for the engines was most inefficient. It was 8.30 a m. on October 5th before the last train of the " D " Squadron turned up. Col. Scobell has once more taken over command. Lord Roberts' despatches with names of those " mentioned " arrived to-day. The list will be found at the end of the book, under " Mentioned in Despatches."

Sat. 5th

Sun. 6th
18 miles.

The column started south at 7 a.m. for Barroe, and after a long midday halt at Mount Stewart, arrived about 5 p.m.

Mon. 7th

Moved out this morning at 7 a.m. for Jansenville, and after halting at Dassies Rand, got in about 5 p.m. Col. Haig came out as far as this with us.

23 miles.

This is an awful piece of country, the whole of the flat part, as far as one can see in every direction, being one mass of cactus bush.

Tues. 8th
7 miles.

Started at 1.30 p.m., and moved out seven miles, as there was no camping-ground at the town, we having had to dump down in the market square.

Wed. 9th

Col. Scobell had got news yesterday evening of some 100 Boers supposed to be fairly near, so he started at 3 a.m. on the chance of picking them up. We marched on until Uitkyk was reached about 8.30 a.m., and here we halted till 10.30 a.m. Stanford Farm was reached at 12.45 p.m., and after an hour's rest we pushed on to Marais Siding, getting in at 7.15 p.m., and only to learn

38 miles.

that all Smuts' commando had crossed quite close last
night.

It was a very long ride of some 38 miles.

Remained here all morning, while the Intelligence
scouts went out.   At 2 p.m. orders came for us to be
ready to move at 3 o'clock with pack mules only, the

BOER FAMILY BROUGHT IN ON SUSPICION OF DISLOYALTY.

transport to go to Aberdeen.   We only marched eight 8 miles.
miles, to a place a few miles short of Glendenning Farm.

We have once more been made an independent column,
so Col. Scobell evidently means hunting down Smuts,
if possible, single-handed.

Started this morning at 4.30 a.m., and soon afterwards
had to work our way in single file through a nasty defile

28 miles.

some three miles long. Zeekoe Gat was reached about 9 a.m., and here a halt was made till 11.30 a.m.

After going a few miles a great deal of dust was seen on ahead, so we pushed on fast for four or five miles, only to find it "wind-blown." Zeekoe River was reached at 3 p.m., and here we bivouacked.

Sat. 12th

The scouts brought in information that the Boers had been at a farm only some 10 miles on, and had decamped into the hills somewhat hurriedly, making, it was supposed, for Oorlogs Poort.

7 miles.

The supplies were expected in the middle of the night, but did not turn up till nearly 7 a.m. However, we were off by 7.15 a.m., and made no delay during the march, trotting a very considerable part of the way, and only made one short halt. Sneew was reached about 1.30 p.m., when the Intelligence scouts were sent out.

Sun. 13th

It was reported late yesterday that the Boers were, or had been, at a farm (Voster's) some five miles off and up in the hills, so the fighting part of the column paraded at 1 a.m., and then had a very stiff climb. However, nothing came of it, as the Boers had not stopped, though they returned in the evening, and, having evidently seen us, scrambled down an awful place in rear of us. While the scouts were getting this information they cap-

21 miles.

tured a Boer who had lost his way in the mist. He was dressed almost entirely in clothes taken from the 17th Lancers.

About 10 a.m. we returned to our mules, and then went back to Lotter's Uitvlugt, where we found the transport.

According to the orders, the Boer—Baxter—was tried
by court-martial and shot as we left camp at 4 p.m. for a
farm about four miles to the west, where we bivouacked.

Having got on the spoor of the Boers, we pushed on in a
south-westerly direction, until the Aberdeen–Beaufort
West road was met, along which we went for a few miles,
and then turned south-west again, making a midday halt
at Ganna Leegte.   Here it was ascertained that the
Boers were only some seven miles ahead.   Pushing on
for another four or five miles, reports came back to say
they were only two miles on amongst the bushes on the
Kariega River.   On nearing the m,the C. M. R. and a
gun were sent over a drift to try and get round their
flank, and the Yeomen and a gun had the same order,
and soon afterwards the " A " Squadron were sent on
down the left bank to try and head them off, while
" D " Squadron were ordered to cross another drift,
spread out and draw the bushes—prickly mimosa—
amongst which the bivouac was found and one man
captured.

The C. M. R. had their part spoilt owing to the difficulty in getting across the drift, and the Boers were
enabled to make good their retreat owing to darkness
coming on.   The pack mules went on some seven miles,
and owing to darkness coming on before the work was
finished, it was getting on for midnight before everyone
got into camp.

The " A " Squadron went out this morning at 4.50 a.m.
to make a further search of the bushes, but without effect.

The column moved on at 6.30 a.m., and followed the

river down as far as Karree Leegte, where we went into bivouac about 5 p.m.

Started at midnight in a westerly direction for Vallei Kuil Farm with only pack mules, the transport having orders to move off early up the Beaufort West road.

It was a pitch-dark night, and finding our way across country was no easy task. At dawn a small picquet was disturbed by the advanced scouts and bolted, and it was found that the Boers had not stopped here after
all, but had gone south-east. After waiting till 10.30 a.m. to let the mules come up, we followed on, and then found the direction changed to south. After a longish march through hills and bush country, Slabbert's Poort Farm was reached about 5 p.m., and here we went into bivouac.

The Boers were here reported to be only nine miles ahead, so Col. Scobell decided to risk a good deal and push after them hard. The mules were left under an escort mounted on the weakest horses, and were to make their way towards Prince Albert, supposed to be 48 miles off.

The horses were pretty well sewn up, and had had their last feed, and the men only had one day's rations left. Still it was worth the attempt.

Having got as far as Strydam's Vlei, we found Crabbe's convoy in camp. This was evidently what our scouts had seen. We learnt from the escort that Smuts was still travelling fast, and would now be making good the Hex River Mountains. Crabbe's column was following them. Under these circumstances it was useless our attempting to go on, and, what was worse, it was discovered that Prince Albert was not 48 miles on, but 72.

There was nothing left for us but to make for the town, so we pushed on and reached Rondavel about 5 p.m., and 24 miles. here bivouacked, the Colonel sending on to have food sent out to meet us. The men were fast getting dismounted, owing to their horses giving out, and the inhospitable "Karroo" afforded no grazing, while nearly all the water was abominably brackish.

An early start was made and we completed 28 miles Fri. 18th by evening, and were 20 miles from Prince Albert, where we found a welcome feed for the horses in the form of oat- 28 miles. hay.

Marched in to Prince Albert, getting to camp about Sat. 19th 1.15 p.m. 20 miles.

Started at 6 a.m., and got to Prince Albert Road Sun. 20th Station in the late afternoon. 28 miles.

Since leaving Graaff Reinet on September 14th, the marching record has been a pretty good one, especially when the country travelled over is taken into consideration, as well as unavoidable scarcity of food and bad water.

From September 14th to Sept. 30th   ..   251 miles
From October 1st to Oct. 5th (in train)..
From October 6th to October 20th   ..   343 miles

         Total   ..   ..   ..   594 miles

Began entraining at 5 a.m., and throughout the after- Mon. 21st noon the different portions of the column arrived at Beaufort West.

The transport marched out at 5 p.m. *en route* for Victoria. Wed. 23rd

West Road, but the fighting portion of the column "stood fast," awaiting further orders from Gen. French.

Thur. 24th Orders were received for us to begin entraining at 7 a.m. The C. M. R. and " A " Squadron got away first and went on to Victoria West Road, while the " D " Squadron was stopped at Beestje Poort and told to detrain, but later on were told to re-entrain and come on to Victoria West first thing in the morning.

Fri. 25th The same sort of thing happened to the rest of the column, who went out to Brak Kraal and had to return. However, the whole column assembled in camp during the morning.

The " Honours " Gazette came out by this mail, the details of which will be found at the end of the book.

Sat. 26th We started soon after midnight for Beestje Poort, as it was reported that the Boers intended crossing to the west of this place. As we arrived we heard firing going on, which turned out to be the convoy outposts engaging the Boers, who had marched up quite close, evidently innocent of any of our people being there.

The Yeomanry, who were in front, supported by the " D " Squadron, were sent direct towards them, while the " A " Squadron and C. M. R. went forward on the right. The Boers, however, soon fell back, and on reaching the last kopjes they had held, we could see some of them still on the plain below, but going away south pretty fast.

Col. Scobell had to go back to the convoy, so sent the " D " Squadron after the Boers as a contact squadron, intending to follow on with the remainder.

The Boers were followed viâ Phisante to near Tyger Poort, and were located there by Du Plessis and his natives. It was impossible to attack them, owing to weakness of numbers, and as there were no signs of reinforcements, the squadron started for the line, soon afterwards getting a message from the Colonel to rejoin at Three Sisters Station. After a very rough journey across the hills a bad thunderstorm came on, and camp was not reached till 8.45 p.m., everyone being soaked to the skin. Some 30 of the Boer distressed ponies were destroyed.

Started at 7 a.m., and marched down the line to Krom River Station, where we bivouacked.

Did not leave camp till midday, when we marched to Nelspoort, getting there about 4.30 p.m. After an hour's halt we went on towards Poortje, and had an uncomfortable and cold ride, made worse by our guide going wrong. It was midnight before we halted a few miles short of the place and lay down as we were.

Marched at 6 a.m., but only went on to Poortje, when the Intelligence scouts were sent out.

Started at 6 a.m., and marched as far as Spitzkop, where we bivouacked, and were threatened with another night march. A most uncomfortable day.

Moved out of camp at 3 a.m., and going back, bivouacked at Stellenbosch Vlei.

Orders arrived for us to go into Beaufort West. The transport started to cross the drift at 4.30 a.m., and the troops moved off at 5.45 a.m. Camped at Salt River Vlei. Van der Venter and his men had crossed near

1901. Nov.	Victoria West, evidently having turned back after being followed to Tyger Poort.
Sat. 2nd	Marched at 5.30 a.m., and went solemnly on till 11.30 a.m.; after a halt we pushed on to Beaufort West and got in to
28 miles.	camp shortly before dark, after a very tiring, sultry march.
Mon. 4th	Lieut. Wood joined the Regiment.
Tues. 5th	Last night it was given out that we were probably going west, and in consequence transport was cut down to its lowest minimum. However, at 4 p.m. orders came for us to begin entraining at 6 o'clock.
Fri. 8th	The column has been arriving here—Stormberg— during the last two days.
Sat. 9th	2nd Lieut. the Hon. R. B. Cole joined to-day.
Thur. 14th	At 6 p.m. orders were issued for us to march at 9 p.m., the transport and an ox convoy to start to-morrow morning, going direct to Jamestown.
Fri. 15th	We started at 9 o'clock last night, going down the line for a bit and then turning roughly north-east, until Tabaks Kloof was reached about 4 p.m. It was a very dark night, and keeping in touch was most difficult.
17 miles.	We remained saddled up till daylight, and then stayed here all day more or less in hiding, as it was probable that we should march during the night.
Sat. 16th	We moved out at 8 p.m. last night, the force being divided up. Maj. Follett took the Regiment and the remains of Gorringe's flying column, with orders to move viâ Plaatje Kraal, Kapokfontein to Kalkfontein, while Col. Scobell, with the remainder, moved viâ Klein Hoek
30 miles.	to Kalkfontein. At 2 p.m. we all moved on to Dank-fontein, getting in about 6 p.m.

Started at 6 a.m., and marched to Modder Poort, when it was reported that the Boers were not very far off, and in the afternoon we heard guns, which turned out to be Col. Moore's and Lovat's Scouts.

These have also come under Col. Scobell's orders, as well as a squadron of 17th Lancers and a Tasmanian contingent.

The C. M. R. and ourselves marched at 2 a.m. in an easterly direction to Laf Krans, while Scobell with the remainder kept more to the north to Uitkyk.

We got to our destination about 6.30 a.m., and eventually everyone collected at Kleinfontein. The Boers are now reported to have crossed the Kraai River and to be at Bosje's Laagte.

The C. M. R. and ourselves, with Col. Scobell, set out as 8.30 last night, and traversing our old road, reached Abbot's Ann about 4 a.m. Here we crossed the river to the right bank and remained in hiding all day. Late in the evening it was reported that the Boers were at a farm only some six or seven miles on, so we were ordered to saddle up and once more started at 9 p.m.

After going up the river a few miles, we crossed over to left bank, and had some pretty stiff climbing to do. On arrival at Ventnor, we saw lights ahead, which proved to be Munro's column. We moved on to Zuur Vlakte, where we rested during the morning.

Saddled up again at 2 p.m., the Regiment working round the right of the high hills in front of us into the Honeynest Kloof Valley. The remainder went round by the left. Our Intelligence scouts had seen some Boers on

17

1901.
Nov.
34 miles.crossing the pass, so we hurried along, passed Clifford, and soon afterwards saw them going through a poort some four or five miles on. We pushed on as far as Waai Kraal, when Scobell ordered us to return, as it was too late to tackle such a place.

We fell back on Clifford, getting in about 7.30 p.m.

Thur. 21st It rained and blew hard all last night and was a horrible day. The Boers were reported to have gone north-east after going through the poort at Driefontein last night, and late in the afternoon the Colonel sent the squadron of 17th Lancers and Lovat's Scouts out to follow them

18 miles. up, while he took the remainder on to Barkly East. We left Clifford at 6 p.m., and got to Barkly East at 11 p.m.

Fri. 22nd Remained here all day, but marched at 8.30 p.m., and
18 miles. got to Doon Farm at 1.30 a.m. next morning.

Sat. 23rd Marched at 11 a.m. for Siberia, which was reached between 3.30 and 4 p.m. A party of G. F. C.'s captured
12 miles. Bester and six other Boers yesterday.

Sun. 24th Bester was tried yesterday evening for being in khaki as well as being a deserter from the Cape Police. He was shot this morning.

The transport was sent back to Dordrecht, but the 9th, I. Y., and Tasmanians remained with Col. Scobell, and started at 9 a.m. for Wasch Bank, which was reached
14 miles. about 1.30 p.m.

We were to have gone on to Roode Nek at 4 p.m., but a scout came in to say that Fouchee and 60 men were in a kloof a few miles off, and it was thought meant to cross the Kraai River at Abbots Ann.

The Colonel decided to try and ambush them with the

two squadrons, and a magnificent position was taken up
for the purpose. .

We remained in position until 2 a.m., getting frozen
to the marrow, and then went back to Wasch Bank, as it
was evident that the Boers did not mean crossing here.

SERGT.-MAJOR CASEBOW.

We got back to bivouac at 3.30 a.m.   It was now settled
that the " A " Squadron should remain here and then try
and get on to Fouchee's track. The rest of us started about
9 a.m. for Roode Nek, which we reached at 1.30 p.m.

Orders were later issued for a night march at 8.30 p.m.
We all went on as far as Uitkyk together, and about

17*

1901.
Nov.

midnight split up. Maj. Follett, with the " D " Squadron and I. Y., was sent in a northerly direction with orders to swing round to the west and then south to Zuur Vlakte, searching all farms *en route*. We reached this farm about 5.30 a.m., having travelled pretty fast most of the way.

About 35 miles.

The Kaffrarian Rifles had patrols out on the hills west of us, and about 9 a.m. sent us a message, saying they wanted reinforcements. Consequently, we had to saddle up and move over to Morgenzon, but to no purpose, and finally arrived at Nek about 1.30 p.m., everyone dead beat.

Wed. 27th

Remained here all day while arrangements were being made for supplies, and none regretted the whole night and day's rest.

A synopsis of the actual marching hours since leaving Stormberg may prove of interest, so it is here given.

Date	Night.	Day.
Nov. 14th—15th	9 p.m.—4 a.m.	—
,, 15th 16th	8 p.m.—4 a.m.	2 p.m. —6 p.m.
,, 16th—17th	—	6 a.m. —10 p.m.
,, 17th—18th	2 a.m.—6.30 a.m.	12 (noon)—4.30 p.m.
,, 18th—19th	8 p.m.—4 a.m.	—
,, 19th—20th	9 p.m.—6 a.m.	2 p.m. —7.30 p.m.
,, 20th—21st	—	—
,, 21st —22nd	6 p.m.—11 p.m.	—
,, 22nd—23rd	8.30 p.m.—1.30 a.m	11 a.m. —3.30 p.m.
,, 23rd—24th	—	6 a.m. —1.30 p.m.
,, 24th—25th	7 p.m.—3.30 a.m. ambush	8.30 a.m.—1.30 p.m.
,, 25th—26th	8.30 p.m.—5.30 a.m.	10.30 a.m.—1.30 p.m.

and the total distance covered was some 235 miles.

Fri. 29th

Moved out at 4.30 a.m. to Smiling Valley, and here Col·

Scobell split up the column, sending Maj. Follett with the " D " Squadron and C. M. R., to work south-west and then north to Poortje, he taking the remainder by the east and north.

We had made a short halt at Kraaifontein, when a message arrived to say that the Boers had left Klipfontein at 11 a.m. and were moving slowly south.

We moved off at 12.45 p.m., and trotted to near Paarde Verlies, when the Boers were viewed. Galloping on after them past Kalkfontein, they made for a gorge leading to some high hills. The going was very bad, and having left a party to check us, they carried on at best pace, dropping a considerable amount of stuff *en route*. They made good the hills and the neck over which one had to pass with the loss of only one prisoner, and as turning them was by no means easy, it took us most of the afternoon to dislodge them, and by the time we got to the neck, they had scattered to the four winds, not a sign of them being visible.

Bivouacked at Sterkfontein, and spent a very cold night without kit or food, except for sheep which we managed to secure.

This party was under Odendall.

Marched to Klein Buffels Vlei, where a halt was made, and then on viâ Strypoort to Lelie Kloof, about five miles short of Jamestown.

Marched at 6.30 a.m., and after a three hours' halt at Jamestown, getting supplies and loading up pack mules, we went on to Modder Poort, where we bivouacked in soaking rain, which continued most of the night.

1901.
DEC.

The " A " Squadron, under Maj. Lord D. Compton, rejoined, having been detached since November 25th. They had captured four prisoners with their arms, horses and mules at Holywood, on November 26th, while they were trying to locate Fouchee.

Mon. 2nd

After giving things a chance to dry, a start was made at 10.30 a.m., when Maj. Follett was sent out with the two squadrons and the C. M. R. with orders to work the country south-east to Toom Nek and then north-east to Roode Nek.

Got to Driefontein about 3 p.m., where Compton's squadron, augmented by a strong troop from " D " Squadron, remained for the night, with orders to go direct to Roode Nek.

24 miles.

The remainder moved on at 5.45 p.m., and although we only had to march some seven miles, it was 9.30 p.m. before we reached our destination, owing to a very severe storm coming up, and its being pitch dark.

Tues. 3rd

Starting at 7 a.m., we travelled viâ Tekenfontein to Winter's Hoek, which was reached at 2 p.m. Compton sent us a message to say that Fouchee and 50 men had

16 miles.

gone on towards Willow Kloof, so we climbed down to Riet Poort and waited for positive information from the Intelligence scouts.

Had to do a lot of stiff climbing to-day.

Wed 4th

It was ascertained that the Boers had gone on in the direction of Bonte Hoek, so we started at 2 a.m. and had a march through very nasty country, including a long river defile, getting to Smoorfontein at 11 a.m. Compton had gone to Frauxhe Hoek.

Both parties moved on in the afternoon and met at
Bonte Hoek, the " A " Squadron scouts coming into
contact with a Boer picquet just before dark.

It was 10 p.m. before the others got in.

" Stood to " at 3.30 a.m., but did not march till 8.30
a.m. After a very stiff climb, a long descent brought us
into the valley which runs north to Clifford Farm. This
was followed by another severe climb to Schilde Kras,
and a drop down to Bamboes Hoek, where the advance
guard had come in contact with the Boers' rear. Before
descending we had seen the Boers going over the neck
near Spitzkop.

After a short halt we moved on at 4.30 p.m.

The Boers lay very " doggo," and allowed the advance
troop (Jackson's) and the Intelligence scouts to get well
up the hill before firing a shot. It was a nasty steep
place, necessitating leading the horses up, and three unfortunate scouts were shot just as they were nearing the
top, two of them being killed. The Boers having done
this much damage, cleared off as fast as possible before
support could get up. Pursuit for a few miles was
carried on by the " A " Squadron and C. M. R. until
darkness put a stop to further progress, and after collecting the scattered troops, we moved into bivouac at
Botha's Vale, but did not get anything to eat till about
11.30 p.m.

Started at 8.30 a.m., and after a long downward climb,
made a midday halt at Jollystone.

Heard that the Boers had gone on, and crossing the
Barkly Pass, were on the Sterk Spruit.

1901.
DEC.

As the horses had had practically nothing for the last three days except grass, Maj. Follett decided to let them graze during the afternoon and then make a night march into Barkly East for supplies.

Sat. 7th

24 miles.

Moved off last night up Long Kloof, which is a defile of some 18 or 19 miles in length, to Barkly East, which was reached at 4.15 a.m. Found Barkly East cleaned out, but fortunately got a few carts in from the convoy. A missing scout had found Col. Scobell, and told him a wonderful yarn about yesterday's affair. Consequently, the rest of the force moved out to our succour !

Sun. 8th

Maj. Follett moved out to Ashton at 7.30 p.m.

Mon. 9th

27 miles.

Col. Scobell turned up just as we were starting, and decided to move on at midnight with his lot, keeping between us and the 17th Lancers, whom he had left on the right.

We arrived at Ashton at 12.30 a.m., and at 4 p.m. went on to Eagle's Nest.

Tues. 10th

18 miles.

Marched at 5 a.m., and got to Holder Ness Farm at 7.15 a.m. ; here we remained till 3 p.m., when a helio message from Col. Scobell told us to move on at once, so getting away at 3.30 p.m., we were at Bidstone by 7 p.m.

Wed. 11th

22 miles.

Started at midnight, and spent the night in severe climbing. It was 4 a.m. before we reached the top, and we went on till 7 a.m., when a halt was made till 11 a.m. Our route then lay by Table Hill, Goat Fell and Traguadir, after which a very steep descent was made down into the valley leading to Rhodes. Bivouacked at Eli Bank about 4 p.m.

Maj. Follett, hearing that fighting was going on on the Basuto border, started at 11 p.m. last night, and after a very stiff march of some 18 miles, we halted near Lebana's Pass at 6 a.m., and found that it was Scobell's party we had seen in the distance yesterday. A very large number of horses gave out, and had to be destroyed, this being the second day the poor brutes have gone without any corn. Another move was made at 2.30 p.m., and after a stiff climb and descent Killowen was reached about 7 p.m., when a terrific storm came on, making everything most uncomfortable.

1901.
DEC.
Thur. 12th

About 32 miles.

Started this morning at 8 a.m. for Barkly East, but when *en route* got orders from Col. Scobell to join him at Hillbury, which was done about 1 p.m. Here we waited for the transport to come out. This is the third day without corn, consequently, with this continual climbing, the horses are pretty beat.

Fri. 13th

14 miles.

Remained here all day, and did not get our forage till the evening.

Sat. 14th

Marched at 10.15 a.m., the force being again split up. We were with Col. Scobell's portion in the centre, and had rather a stiff journey by Knock Warren, Lion Lair, Fairlie to Cold Brook, which was reached at 6 p.m. At the farm we learned that the Boers had gone over Bottel Nek yesterday, and had a considerable number of their men dismounted. We are also terribly short of horses, the squadrons being only between 60 and 70 strong.

Suɳ. 15th

18 miles.

Started at 4 a.m., and reached Raven's Feld about 8 a.m., going on again at 2.30 p.m., and getting to Kapok Kraal about 6.30 p.m. Here we bivouacked, and heard

Mon. 16th

23 miles.

1901.
DEC.

that we had done a certain amount of damage to the Boers at Spitzkop on December 5th.

Tues. 17th

9 miles.

Preparations were made for a dash at the Boers during the night by a portion of the force. It was rumoured that they were close by, but this turned out to be false.

Moved on at 4.30 a.m., and halted at Bamboes Hoek, and here heard that Munro had got on to the Boers and captured 12.

At 2.30 p.m. Col. Scobell sent the " D " Squadron on to Knoppjes to hold the place, in case Fouchee should " break back."

Wed. 18th

14 miles.

Patrols were sent out before daybreak and ascertained that the Boers had gone on. At 6.30 a.m. the " A " Squadron and C. M. R. passed on their way to Bonte Hoek, where we all bivouacked.

Thur. 19th

10 miles.

A strong patrol was sent out to Wasch Bank, and in the afternoon (2 p.m.) the remainder started for Siberia, where we arrived at 5.30 p.m., having had a march in pouring rain. Here we found the convoy and the rest of the troops.

Fri. 20th

25 miles.

After preparations had been made for a forced march, a general move was made for Dordrecht. Started at 10.30 a.m., made a halt from 2.30 p.m. to 4 p.m., and got into camp at 7.30 p.m.

It has been a very trying time on the horses lately, as our pack mules are limited, and much corn cannot be carried. The climbing about these mountains has also been very severe on them, and many of the men are almost without boots.

Paraded dismounted at 9 a.m., and marched down to the far side of the town for inspection by Gen. French. His train was late, and it was 1 p.m. before we got back to camp. 1901.
DEC.
Sun. 22nd

Xmas Day not much of a holiday, as Col. Long, Insp.- Wed. 25th

CAPT. E. BELL (ADJT.), COL. M. O. LITTLE, MAJ. W. FOLLETT.

Gen. of Remounts, had the whole column out, and made a long and minute inspection of the horses, which lasted till past 1 p.m.

Numerous " sing-songs " in the evening.

Everyone was sorry to hear that Col. Scobell was very seedy, and was forced to give up command and go home. . Fri. 27th

Maj. Follett is to take over his troops, with the exception of the Tasmanians.

1901.
Dec.
Sat. 28th
25 miles.

After our much-needed week's rest, a start was made at 5 a.m. Halting at Gelegenfontein, a forward move was made at 2.30 p.m. and Siberia reached just before 5 p.m.

Sun. 29th

19 miles.

Nickalls with the squadron of the 17th Lancers and I. Y. went eastwards, viâ Bonte Hoek and Ravensfeld, while the rest of us started at 4.30 a.m. and marched straight to Clifford, getting in shortly after 10 a.m., but the transport did not arrive till after 3 p.m., most of the way being very steep and no water to be got.

Mon. 30th

16 miles.

Moved off at 4.30 a.m., and reached Barkly East soon after 9 a.m., when we went into camp.

Tues. 31st

20 miles.

Off once more at 4.30 a.m., and after rather a stiff journey, made Raven's Craig about 10 a.m. Here we heard from Nickalls that he had come in contact with the Boers and had followed them up until 3 a.m., when he lost trace of them.

We then pushed on to Mostyn, getting in at 5.30 p.m.

1902.

WE moved up a very steep kloof to Jer Point, and found Nickalls only a few miles off, he having been fighting the Boers near Cherry Vale and Lion Lair most of the morning. After which they went westwards and climbed down to Raven's Craig, and thus getting behind us once more. Nickalls was now sent to Willowleigh, while we went to Rosneath, and Lord Leitrim took a strong patrol viâ Raven's Craig.

About 6.30 p.m. a native brought in a report to say that a party of some 70 Boers intended having a " bean-feast " at a farm up Rifle Spruit, so Maj. Follett thought he would endeavour to get round them.

The force was again split up, the two squadrons starting last night at 11 p.m., and soon afterwards had about the worst climb we have yet had, it being 3 a.m. before everyone got up.

We had our climb for nothing, as the Boers had been alarmed and had made off during the evening. After scouring the top of the hills, we dropped down to Moss-dell, finding the Boers' spoor going up. At 11 a.m. we moved on to Hillbury, getting in at 2 p.m. Nickalls

1902.
JANUARY.

got on the Boers' spoor and thought they were making for the Maclear district, but after a while he came in, as his horses were beat.

Maj. Follett in the evening gave orders for the 9th Lancers and C. M. R. to move out in the morning, under Capt. Gordon, to reconnoitre towards Pondo Pass, and follow the Boers should they have gone over the border.

Fri. 3rd

Started at 6 a.m. for Willow Leigh, getting in at 8 a.m. From here the Intelligence scouts, under Lieut. Maasdorp, and a party of the C. M. R. were sent on to the pass.

7 miles.

After a long day they returned at 5.30 p.m., having seen nothing of the Boers, but positive that they had not crossed or gone south.

Sat. 4th

Yesterday's information was sent back to Maj. Follett, and at midnight orders were received to reconnoitre the pass again with a squadron, the remainder to go to Marino.

15 miles.

Started at 4.30 a.m., and reached Groogh Patrick at 8 a.m. Here we off-saddled till 11 a.m., as it was the only convenient place from which the helio could communicate with Durand, who had taken out the " A " Squadron.

Bivouacked at Castle Mahon, a few miles beyond Marino. Durand could not get back, but sent in a message to say that they had the same negative news as yesterday.

Sun. 5th
15 miles.

Left Castle Mahon about 6.30 a.m., and halted at Rose Hill about 9.30 a.m. Durand did not reach this place till

midday, so remained for the night. The rest went on at 1902.
12.30 p.m. and got to Raven's Feld about 1.45 p.m. JANUARY.

Orders arrived at 11.30 last night for us to come in to Mon. 6th
Barkly East.

As soon as the " A " Squadron had rejoined, we all
moved off at 5.30 a.m., made a halt at Rypfontein, and 18 miles.
got into Barkly East about noon.

Col. Munro is now in command of the operations in
these parts.

Maj. Follett moved out at 4.30 a.m. with the 9th Tues. 7th
Lancers and C. M. R., and went to Zuur Vlakte. Two 17 miles.
troops " D " Squadron left with convoy.

Remained here all day. An extended drive is to be Wed. 8th
undertaken in a westerly direction during the next two
days.

Started at noon for Ricksu Hill, the remaining two Thur. 9th
troops of " D " Squadron, under Lieut. Jackson, being
sent to Abbots Ann. After struggling through Honeynest Kloof, we bivouacked at 4.30 p.m. near Ricksu
Hill.

Moved off about 7 a.m., and meeting the convoy at Fri. 10th
Wasche Bank, loaded up the supply mules and went on
again about 10 a.m. ; and after a rough and hot journey 11 miles.
got to Damfontein about 1 p.m. Several Boers were
picked up by the various parties.

Started at 6 a.m., and reached Plaatfontein about Sat. 11th
8.30 a.m., where we halted till 2 p.m., and then went on
and bivouacked at Marshall's Kraal. 13 miles.

A troop had to go to Zwartfontein and another to
Plaat Kop Drift for the night.

1902.
JANUARY.
Sun. 12th

Remained here all day. The M. M. R. ran into a party, under Van de Wolt, and captured some 70 of their ponies, etc. Part of these approached Leitrim's troop in the evening, and were hunted, but they all made good their escape except one.

Mon. 13th

14 miles.

Marched at 10 a.m. for Bloemfontein, meeting our convoy at Rietfontein. Here the two troops of " D " Squadron rejoined, and the C. M. R. remained as escort. Got to bivouac at 3 p.m.

Wessels passed here a few days ago.

Tues. 14th

9 miles.

Marched at 6 a.m., and reached Modderfontein at 8.45 a.m. After halting here for awhile, we went into bivouac and awaited orders.

Wed. 15th

Last night detailed orders arrived for the various columns under Munro, and our old friends the C. M. R. left us for defence purposes.

13 miles.

Marched at 8 a.m., and got to Zuur Vlagte about noon, the " A " Squadron having gone into Jamestown to bring out the convoy.

Thur. 16th

19 miles.

Started at 6 a.m., and off-saddled at Plaat Kop Drift at 9.15 a.m. Moved on again at 3 p.m., and bivouacked at Bosjes Laagte about 5.30 p.m.

Fri. 17th

20 miles.

Marched at 6 a m., halting at Nooitgedacht, on the Karnmelk Spruit, about 9 a.m. Moving on in the afternoon, we passed Myburg's Farm, and soon afterwards, hearing that a party of dismounted Boers were in the hills to the north, the Intelligence scouts and Lieut. Wynn's troop were sent out to try and get hold of them.

There being no water at Drizzly Hill, we had to move

on some three miles to Wepener Outspan, where we   1902.
bivouacked.   JANUARY.

Started at 7 a.m. for Barkly East, making a midday Sat. 18th
halt at Glen Almond, where Lieut. Wynn rejoined us, 27 miles.
having been unsuccessful.

Orders to march at 8 p.m. for Spitz Kopje, viâ Ravens- Sun. 19th

WATERING HORSES AT BETHLEHEM.

feld, as Fouchee was reported to be still there.   It is a
long march.

Started at 9 p.m. last night, and reached Ravensfeld Mon. 20th
about 1 a.m.   After a short halt, the march was resumed,
and we got to the neck near Spitz Kopje about 7.30 a.m.,
going over and off-saddling at the farm below.

The Boers had cleared out.

18

1902.   At 2 p.m. we went on down the valley to Bamboes
JANUARY. Hoek, and had not been in camp more than half-an-hour
when firing was heard towards Naauwpoort.

45 miles.   In consequence of this we saddled-up again, and
climbed up the steep hill to Knoppies, the " A " Squadron
going viâ Stop Poort.   Met some of Munro's people, who
had been engaged, and saw the " A " Squadron active.
Climbed down and went on in pursuit to Klipplaats,
where we went into bivouac about 7.30 p.m., it being
pitch dark.

It was a very long and trying march.

Tues. 21st   Started at midnight for Greenlands, and a very bad
journey we had across the hills, as there was no moon,
and keeping in touch was most difficult.   Smoorfontein
was reached at 8.30 a.m.

26 miles.   Moved on again at 12.30 a.m., ostensibly for Schilder
Kranz, but on meeting the main road to Dordrecht,
heard that the Boers had turned north-west.   Maj.
Follett accordingly moved up the road as far as Strypoort and went into bivouac, awaiting orders.

Wed. 22nd   Received orders to go to Toom Nek, so loaded up from
the supply wagons and moved off at 8.30 a.m., reaching
the nek at 1.30 p.m.   Receiving fresh orders here, a
27 miles.   move was made at 3 p.m., and Oorlogs Poort reached
at 7.30 p.m.

Thur. 23rd   Started for Alleman's Poort at 1 p.m., and got in at
15 miles.   5.30 p.m.   Here we have to await our convoy.

Fri. 24th   Remained here all day, and got our wagons at 4.30
p.m., but got orders to march at 8 p.m.

Sat. 25th   Moved out at 8 o'clock last night, and got to Vlak-

fontein about midnight, when Bowers and his scouts
went on and ran up against the Boers near Klein Buffels
Vley about 3 a.m.   Two troops went out to their support, but the rest of the column remained in camp.

Started at 1 p.m. towards Stormberg.   The column Sun. 26th
halted some five or six miles short of the town, but " D "
Squadron was sent on.   Found Capt. Lord D. Compton,
Lieut. Trower, and Lieut. Gordon Stirling awaiting us
here, having returned from short leave.

The rest of the column came in this morning. Mon. 27th

Orders arrived in the middle of the night for us to Tues. 28th
entrain at dawn.

On reaching Middelburg, our destination—Bethesda
Road Station—was made known.

The " D " Squadron got in at 11.30 p.m. last night, Wed. 29th
but the " A " Squadron did not till 8 a.m. this morning.

Capt. Lawson, our staff officer, left us at Middelburg to
join Sir John French's Staff.

Remained here all day awaiting orders and the arrival 30th & 31st
of remainder of column. FEB.

Our next move was to get across to Cradock as quickly Sat. 1st
as possible, so the wagons with the " A " Squadron
started at 3 a.m. and the rest of us at 6 a.m.

Spitzkop was reached about 11.30 a.m., and the march 25 miles.
resumed at 3 p.m., and we went on until Fish River
Farm was reached, when we went into bivouac.   The
Boers under Wessels were reported to have crossed the
Cradock line from the east.

Moved on to Groen Valley, picking up Antrobus and Sun. 2nd
Whitney at the former's farm, and got in about 11.30

18*

1902.
FEB.

18 miles.

a.m. Continued the march at 2 p.m., and got to Varken's Kop 3.45 p.m. Here the fighting portion of the
column went into bivouac, while the transport went on
to Cradock. We had learned that the Boers under
Wessels were in the hills at Doorn Hoek, with Vaughan's
column watching them from the south, so a night march
was ordered.

Mon. 3rd

24 miles.

Started at 9.30 last night and marched steadily on till
nearly 4 a.m., by which time we had got to Karre Bosch,
where it was intended to start the climb into the hills.
But on arrival it was found that the Boers had passed
through during the evening on their way towards Garstland's Kloof. Started back to Kaal Plaats at 2 p.m.,
Antrobus and Whitney going out to try and locate the
Boers, which they did near Mist Kraal.

Tues. 4th

15 miles.

Started last night at 8.30 and reached Groote Vallei
about 3.15 a.m. Halted here till 1 p.m., when we followed up the spoor, which led up to the hills. Information received from native sources pointed to the Boers
having gone over the hills and dropped down into Sneeuw-
berg Kloof, but we found that they had turned to the
right and gone down to Paarde Kraal. It was late in the
evening (7 o'clock) before the head of the column began
its descent in single file by a ghastly path to the farm,
and 8.30 p.m. before it was reached, the rear-guard not
getting in till 10 p.m.

A great sell here awaited us, for only a few Boers had
come down by this rough path, the remainder continuing
their march along the top of the hills and their tracks
were lost in the long grass.

Started at 7 a.m. to once more climb the hill by a path that led round the heads of Paarde and Waterval Kloofs, but seeing no signs of anyone, the march was continued till midday, when we halted at Riet Poort. At 2 p.m. we moved on towards Zuur Kop, whither the Boers were reported to have gone.

On reaching Klipplaats, where we made a short halt, the Boers observed us and saddled up and climbed up to Zuur Kop, but by the time we had done the same, they were once more ahead of us.

We were told that the Boers had split up on the mountains, and not being able to find their spoor, we dropped down on the other side by a nasty stony path to Poplar Grove Farm, it being 8 p.m. before the head of the column got in. A day full of disappointments.

We were out of all supplies, so started at 7.30 a.m. for the line, and got to Let's Kraal at 9.15 a.m. Here we learnt that Wessels had descended last evening and gone on to near Bethesda Road Station. Antrobus had unfortunately to leave us here.

Moved off at 4.30 a.m., and passed Vaughan's column at Colonie Plaats Siding, and made for Karee Leegte Farm, and then on to Patrysfontein, where we off-saddled about 10.30 a.m. Moving on at 3 p.m., we soon afterwards met some Yeomanry, who said that the Boers were at Kriegar's Baken, so Follett pushed on, and just before dark our scouts observed the Boers at the farm. Their observation post had seen us, so that by the time those in rear were able to get over the nasty rocky ground, they were beginning to gallop away at

1902.
FEB.

best pace, offering only a feeble resistance.   The ground on our side prevented haste, and darkness soon put a stop to a long, hard day of at least 36 miles.

Sat. 8th

Started at 6 a.m., taking the Yeomen, who had come on with us, and marched as far as Dassiefontein, where we halted from 1 p.m. to 4 p.m.   A fair number o wounded and exhausted ponies were found.   About 6 p.m. we heard that the Boers were at a farm only some

32 miles.

six or seven miles on.   Maj. Follett ordered us to gallop on, which we did the whole way, but only to find the Boers gone, having seen us arrive at the last farm.

We remained here—Georgiafontein—all night.

Sun. 9th

Although warned that we should probably march on during the night, a start was not made till 5 a.m. and Klipplaats reached at 9 a.m.

Here we learnt that the Boers had split up, and as a message was received from Gen. French, saying that we were to take over our transport, which was coming out

28 miles.

with Doran's column, the " A " Squadron was sent to meet it, while the Yeomanry went back, and Maj. Follett went on with the " D " Squadron and Maxim, leaving at 3 p.m.   Oude Plaats was made good about 7 p.m. after a good deal of trotting in consequence of a cloud of dust having been seen.

Mon. 10th

Had to send into Richmond for supplies, so remained here all day, while Maasdorp and his scouts went out to try and locate the Boers.   They found one lot, and caught their commandant at the farm, but were then seen and had to beat a hasty retreat without their prisoner.   This   was   the   farm—Leeuwfontein—whe

Lieut. Chadwick was severely wounded in attempting
to surround Malan at night.

Having waited till 12.30 p.m. without any signs of the
Boers turning up, the order was given to saddle up, and
a start was made at 12.50 p.m.

A very heavy storm came up during the afternoon,

COMMANDEERING FORAGE NEAR BETHLEHEM.

making the going very heavy.   On nearing Onderplaats
Farm, the scouts ran into the Boers, but they were off
by the time the column got up.   As nothing was to be
got at this farm, it was decided to go to the next, some
six miles on.   This was reached about 9.30 p.m.

Seeing lights ahead we pushed on, and on arrival
caught seven or eight saddled horses at the farm, and 24 miles.

1902.
FEB.

were told that the Boers had only arrived 10 or 15 minutes before us, so they slipped away without firing a shot, evidently fearing being surrounded. It was a hard march, ending in disappointment. Drenched to the skin, and with only 2 lbs. of corn for the horses, we got into bivouac at 10 p.m. !

Wed. 12th

The intelligence went on at 3.30 a.m., the rest starting at 5 a.m., and pushed on to Los Kop, getting there soon after 9 a.m. Here we found the spoor going west, when a report came in to say Boers were approaching from the east. Making for a large kopje, and sending a troop round each side, only a few Boers were seen going away with led horses. These Lord Rocksavage, on the right,

25 miles.

hunted for several miles. Halted here from 10 a.m. till 12 noon, when we pushed on to Drie Hoeksfontein, getting in at 4 p.m. Learning from Doran's convoy, which we met, that he had come across our Boers and had sent a couple of squadrons after them, Maj. Follett decided to wait here for our transport.

Thur. 13th

The transport did not turn up till nearly 1 p.m., and as it had only sufficient corn to give the horses a small

11 miles.

feed, a move towards the line was made at 3 p.m., and Tyger Poort reached about 6.30 p.m.

Fri. 14th

Started at 5 a.m., and reached Three Sisters about noon. A wire was soon afterwards received from Gen. French telling us to go on to Krom River Station. Leaving at 2 p.m. we got in at 4.30 p.m., and here

18 miles.

we were told we had to hand over 200 horses to the 5th Lancers with Doran's column. This was to save time, as they were about to start on a big drive. We

also heard that we should be sent back to India next
month.

Paraded all the horses for the 5th Lancers, but their
C.O. decided to keep their own.   Ours really wanted a
rest as much as theirs.

Have been resting here since February 14th, but have
had to put up with very hot weather, which is trying
when without tents.

Late in the afternoon orders came for us to send out
two strong patrols of 20 men each north and north-west,
as it was thought the Boers might attempt to cross the
line.   " D " Squadron found these under Lieuts. Jackson and Trower.   Besides these patrols the " A " Squadron had to send 50 men up the line to strengthen the
block-houses.

A party of the Boers got across the line early yesterday
morning near Beestje Poort.   We got orders from Gen.
French this morning for the two squadrons and the
pom-pom to move out, under Lord D. Compton, in conjunction with Wormald from Victoria West, after these
Boers.

Started at 10.30 a.m., getting to Three Sisters about
1 p.m.   Patrols were sent out in the afternoon, but
could obtain no information.

Had to remain here for our supplies.

Did not get away till 1 p.m., delay being caused by
late arrival of the transport mules.   Got to Tyger Poort
at 5 p.m., where Wormald passed us and went further on.

Started at 5 a.m., and crossed Buffalo river about
9 a.m., where we made a halt, and then went on about

midday, reaching Toversfontein at 4 p.m. As Wormald
was pushing on towards Murraysberg, he wanted rein-
forcing, so Maj. Lord D. Compton went on with the " A "
Squadron, leaving the " D " Squadron and pom-pom to
bring on the transport in the morning.

Tues. 25th The " D " Squadron and transport caught the others
up about 7.45 a.m., and all moved on at 9.30 a.m., getting
to Riet Valley at 11.30 a.m. Soon after arriving, Wormald sent back for reinforcements, as he was held up
at Voetpads, having his flanks threatened as well. It
was a very nasty place and a strong one also. Lord D.
Compton took the " D " Squadron and Maxim on, and
getting a guide from Wormald, worked south across the
mountains and came round on the Boers' left rear. It
was a complete surprise, but the ground was very nasty,
and although two troops were at once dismounted and
two others under Jackson and Trower made their way
up a donga leading past the farm, the Boers made good
their escape at best pace along the high ground north.
On Wormald's troops appearing they cleared out alto-
gether. We then returned and bivouacked at the farm
—Hout Kraal. Pte. Ede (" D ") was wounded.

Wed. 26th The whole force moved on at 5.15 a.m. and made for
Kleinfontein. The Boers being reported at the farm,
Wormald went on and then sent back for a squadron and
pom-pom.

However, the Boers did not wait, so we off-saddled at
the farm.

In the afternoon we moved on finding that the Boers
had gone north over a nasty pass. However, this was

only held by an observation post, and from the top the 1902.
Boers could be seen at Nooitgedacht Farm, a few miles FEB.
on. The intermediate ground was a succession of ridges,
which were carried one after the other by the two
squadrons, the remainder of the column being practically
inactive. It was 7.30 p.m. before we got into bivouac.

Left camp at 5.15 a.m., going viâ Georgefontein to Thur. 27th
Schietfontein. Here our scouts came into contact with
the Boer rear-guard. The supply wagons going in to
Richmond to fill up, the remainder went on after a
heavy thunderstorm towards Geelbekfontein, and when
a few miles short of it found ourselves opposed in front
and on the right flank from a long high kopje running
parallel to the road. The 12th Lancers advance guard
was allowed to get close up to a cross ridge, and then
came under hot fire. The pom-poms and Maxim got
to work, but the Boers stuck to their position till dark,
it being just on 6 p.m. when the first shot was fired.
The 12th Lancers had several casualties, but we got off
with one man wounded—Pte. Pyke (" A "). We had
to retire about one and a half miles to get near water,
and it was very late before we all got settled down.

" Stood to " at 5 a.m. and marched about 6 a.m., Fri. 28th
getting to Geelbekfontein about 8 a.m., where we waited
for the convoy. Went on again at midday and reached
Scheurfontein at 4 p.m. On arrival saw the Boers
starting off from Grootfontein, some five miles on.
Camped here for the night MARCH.

Left at 5.15 a.m. for Wildman's Kloof. The Boers Sat. 1st
being reported at Wortelfontein, " D " Squadron was

detached to demonstrate on the right to prevent their breaking east. All eventually collected at Wildman's Kloof, and after a halt moved on at 2 p.m. to Wortel-fontein, which was found to be unoccupied.

A few miles further on the Boers were found in position. Some of the 12th Lancers were sent to the left front, while the pom-poms got into action, and then " D " Squadron was sent to the right, had to cross a nasty hill and descend on the plain on the Boers' left. This had the desired effect of making them quit their position, but their rear-guard made it pretty hot for the " D " Squadron for a time. While this was going on the " A " Squadron was getting up on to the kopjes in front. Went into bivouac near Elandsfontein Farm.

Pte. Johnson (" D ") was wounded here.

Sun. 2nd

Left Elandsfontein at 6.30 a.m. for another farm of the same name. The Intelligence scouts had gone on ahead, and were led into a trap at the farm, two being killed at a few yards range, and a third wounded, Maasdorp being the only one to get off. There were some dozen Boers here, who had gone east last night and so missed the others.

Our course was now turned westwards to Hartebeeste-fontein, thence on to Jagtpoort, which was reached about 3.30 p.m. Later in the evening scouts reported the Boers at Mesfontein.

Mon. 3rd

A start was made about 5.45 a.m., but we crawled along, partly on account of the difficulties for the transport and partly because Mesfontein and its surroundings formed a very *ugly* place from a fighting point of view.

However, Mesfontein was not held, and getting into
rather more open country we went on to Knoffelfontein,
off-saddling about 10 a.m.   On starting again at 1 p.m.
we kept along the high ground and then dropping down
on to the plain, swung round to the right.   A couple of
miles or so further on some shots were fired, and then
up spurted an enormous column of smoke—the Boer
signal of danger—which told us they were there.

Across the front ran a ridge, behind which were the
farms, so Wormald sent the 12th Lancers to the left
front and " A " Squadron to the high ground on the
right, while what remained of " D " Squadron stayed in
the centre with the pom-poms.

Judging by the dust, their spare ponies were evidently
being galloped away to the left rear, past Tafelberg,
while fairly heavy firing was going on to the left front.
Wormald was now keen on getting hold of some small
kopjes in the centre of the ridge in front, but only had
some 35 men of the " D " Squadron available.

However, this party opened out and galloped for the
ridge, coming under fire from front and left-front at from
800 to 900 yards.   This was kept up till within about 300
yards, when a wire fence loomed in front.   Fortunately
it did not extend across the whole front, and so Lieut.
Sadleir-Jackson's troop was able to incline and avoid it.
The Boers then took to their heels.   It was a very fine
piece of straight riding in the face of fairly heavy
firing.   The ridge being thus carried, a wire fence was
found on the other side, and on this being cut our only
casualty occurred—Pte. Scott being mortally wounded.

1902.   Jackson went on down to the farm, and we all peppered
MARCH.   the retreating Boers well, and then some men followed
up a couple of dismounted Boers, who, however, made
good the hills beyond.

Malan himself went away with those in front of the
12th Lancers, whose advance got rather severely handled.

After a while everyone was ordered to concentrate at
Visser's Farm, pursuit being useless, as the Boers had
scattered to the four winds.

This proved to be the Regiment's last day of active
work in the field.

Tues. 4th   Wormald wanted to go in to the line for orders and
supplies, so we started for Deelfontein at 5.30 a.m., and
reached Droogfontein about 9.30 a.m. Here we off-
saddled, and a message came out in the afternoon to say
that the Regiment was to make for Victoria Road and
there demobilize. Scott died last night, so the body
was brought on and buried here.

Wed. 5th   The column marched to Blaauwbank at 6.30 a.m.,
getting in about 9 a.m., and in the afternoon the Regiment bade farewell and went on to Richmond Road,
where we went into bivouac about 5.30 p.m.

Thur. 6th   Marched as far as Brakpoort.

18 miles.   Started at 5.30 a.m. and got to Victoria Road at
Fri. 7th   11.30 a.m.

8th to 10th   Busy squaring up and handing over horses, equipment,
transport, etc. The " C " Squadron rejoined.

Tues. 11th   The Regiment entrained for Cape Town.

Thur. 13th   Arrived Cape Town at 5.30 a.m., and went into camp
at Green Point.

The Regiment embarked on board the *Mohawk*, and
sailed about midday for Durban, where we take on the
5th Dragoon Guards.

Before leaving Cape Town the following telegram was
received from Sir John French :—

" I deeply regret that operations which require my

FAREWELL TO THE VELDT, 9TH LANCERS ENTRAINING AT
VICTORIA WEST.

instant attention prevent my going personally to say
good-bye to the 9th Lancers, and to congratulate them
upon all the splendid work they have done during the
past two and a half years.

" During the greater part of that time it has been my
good fortune to be associated with you and to have wit-

1902.   nessed on many occasions how splendidly all have maintained the traditions of your magnificent Regiment
throughout the war.

" I deeply mourn the exceptionally heavy losses you
have sustained, and my earnest and heartfelt good wishes
will go with you, as also my grateful thanks for your
valuable help on many trying occasions."

Account of the ceremony of unveiling tablets at Graaff
Reinet on March 16th, 1902 :—

" The Honoured Dead."

The ceremony of unveiling tablets to the memory of
soldiers who have fallen in the war in defence of their
country and at the call of duty was performed in St.
James' Church yesterday morning.

Gen. French, who kindly and thoughtfully responded
to the invitation to be present and take part in the ceremony, arrived here on Saturday afternoon.   Long before
the time for the commencement of the special service
yesterday morning St. James' Church was crowded,
and a large number of spectators witnessed the arrival of
Gen. French and Staff from coigns of vantage in the
vicinity of the church.   The service was opened by the
singing of the hymn " Fight the good fight " ; this was
followed by the chanting of a psalm and the singing of
another appropriate hymn.   The Rev. J. H. Carter,
the rector, then offered up a special prayer, at the conclusion of which Gen. French unveiled the two tablets,
one of which is placed in the south wall of the church
and the other opposite it in the north wall.   Gen. French

then delivered the following address : " We are met here 1902. to-day to perpetuate the memory of gallant men of the 2nd Battalion of the Coldstream Guards, 9th Lancers, and Cape Mounted Rifles, who have given their lives for their country. The gallantry they have displayed is fresh in your memory, and it is not necessary for me to refer to or recapitulate their brave deeds, for they are being repeated and emulated day by day in the field of battle. I wish to call attention to a custom which prevailed in the Napoleonic Wars. It was the custom to call out on parade the names of the men who had fallen in action, and to proclaim they had died on the field of honour. I think that that idea was present in the minds of all when the tablets were unveiled to-day. You know how many rolls of honour there are, but there is no roll of honour which appeals so strongly to the mind as the roll of honour which records the names and the deeds of men who have fallen in the path of duty and in defence of our great Empire. And we can imagine no more powerful aid and incentive to the living soldiers in times of trouble and anxiety and danger than the fact that they are giving their lives in the service of their country. You all know of the battles of Graspan and Belmont, and you remember the capture of Lotter's Commando. They all afford examples of gallant deeds, and the names of some of the men who performed them are recorded on the tablets unveiled to-day. I wish to express our deep and heartfelt gratitude to the Rev. Carter and the congregation and to the inhabitants of Graaff Reinet, who have shown such generosity and heart-

19

felt sympathy for the men whose memory we commemorate to-day. I am told that many railway men have subscribed to the tablets. Their action is much appreciated since they, in their sphere, have gone through many dangers in this war and done splendid service. My gratitude I must express, too, to the members of the Loyal Women's Guild for what they have done in this matter."

The brass tablets are finished pieces of artistic work. The lettering is in black and red, and shows up distinctly on the brass ground. The tablet in the southern wall contains the following :—

" Dulce et decorum est pro patria mori."

To the Glory of God and in memory of the 9th Lancers.

> Sergt. John Brighton Mercer.
> Lance-Corpl. William John Priest.
> Pte. William Vipond.
> Pte. Henry Lionel Clifford.
> Pte. William Kennedy.
> Pte. Victor Ward.
> Pte. Augustus Dodge.

Cape Mounted Rifles.

Corpl. Waldemar Reder.
Pte. Ronald Rudstone Garthorne.

Who fell at the capture of Lotter's Commando by the column under Lieut.-Col. H. J. Scobell, Sep. 5th, 1901.

This tablet has in the corners in silver relief the badges of the 9th Lancers and the C. M. R.

2nd Battalion Coldstream Guards.

The tablet in the opposite wall has been raised by their comrades in the memory of those of the 2nd Battalion Coldstream Guards, who fell during the year 1901, and contains the following names :

Capt. T. H. E. Lloyd.

Killed in action at Brakenlaagte :

Lance-Sergt. J. Oates.
Pte. C. Powell.
Pte. H. Frogley.
Pte. A. Kilian.
Pte. E. Parkes.
Pte. J. Kemp.
Pte. B. Goodwin.
Pte. J. Emery.
Pte. R. Richardson.

On the sides of the tablet are given the battles in which the Regiment has taken part since the days of Dettingen, Talavera, and Malplaquet. The crest of the Regiment, " Nulli Secundus," ornaments the head of the tablet.

Arrived at Durban about daybreak. Wed. 19th

The 5th Dragoon Guards arrived yesterday afternoon, Sat. 22nd and we were to have sailed to-day, but a storm prevented our getting out of the harbour.

The following wire was received from Lord Kitchener :

" Please tell all ranks how sorry I am to lose their valuable services, but after close on two and a half years' active operations in South Africa I feel that you have

19*

well deserved a change.   In wishing you good-bye and good luck I feel I am only giving expression to the wishes of the Army in South Africa."

Sun. 23rd   The *Mohawk* left Durban at 2 p.m., and after an un-
APRIL.   eventful though good voyage landed us at Bombay at
Sat. 5th   dawn on the morning of April 5th.

Wed. 9th   Entrained in the late afternoon and arrived at Sialkote on the afternoon of April 9th.

The following is a list of the officers who returned to India with the Regiment :

Majs. Follett, Lund, Lord D. Compton.

Capts. Gordon and Bell.

Lieuts. Stirling, Durand, Cavendish, Sadleir-Jackson, Wynn, Trower, Tooth, Neilson, Brocklebank, Wood, Earl of Rocksavage, Hon. R. Cole, Laing.

The following remained in Africa on Staff employ :

Col. Little.

Bt.-Lieut.-Col. Colvin.

Capts. Campbell and Brooke.

Lieuts. Kincaid-Smith and Abadie.

CASUALTY LIST.

N.C.O.'S AND MEN.

DATE.	PLACE.		RANK.	NAME.	SQUAD-RON.
10/11/99	Belmont (reconnaissance)	wounded	S.S.M.	R. Gidden ..	C
23/11/99	Belmont	,, ...	L.-Corp.	P. Featherstone	A
,,	,, ...	,, ...	Private	G. Lockett ...	C
,,	,, ...	,, ...	,,	R. Morgan ...	C
,,	,, ...	,, ...	,,	— Lazenby ...	C
25/11/99	Enslin	killed	,,	W. Wilkins ...	D
,,	,, ...	wounded	,,	J. Hobbs ..	A
,,	,, ...	,, ...	Sergeant	G. Grupie ..	A
,,	,, ...	,, ...	Private	T. Smith ...	C
,,	,, ...	,, ...	,,	A. James ...	C
,,	,, ...	missing (prisoner)	Corporal	J. Marriott ...	A
,,	,, ...	,, ,,	Private	— Pierce ...	C
26/11/99	near Enslin ..	wounded	,,	F. Young ...	C
28/11/99	Modder River	,, ...	,,	E. Lloyd ...	A
11/12/99	Magersfontein ...	killed	,,	R. Rae ...	C
,,	,, ...	died of wounds ...	,,	J. Moore ...	A
,,	,, ...	wounded	Sergeant	C. Ambrose ...	C
,,	,, ...	,, ...	L.-Corp.	W. Burton ..	C
,,	,, ...	,, ...	Private	W. Gilchrist ...	C
,,	,, ..	,, ...	,,	J. Clarkson ...	C
,,	,, ..	,, ...	,,	J. Lee...	C
,,	,, ...	,, ...	,,	A. Reeve ...	C
,,	,, ...	,, ...	,,	H. Whitehead	C
,,	,, ...	,, ...	,,	J. Newman ...	C
,,	,, ...	,, ...	,,	A. Fenn ...	C
5/2/00	Koodoosberg Drift	killed	,,	E. McNicol ...	C
,,	,, ,,	wounded	,,	A. Frost ...	D
,,	,, ,,	,, ...	,,	J. Huxham ..	D
,,	,, ,,	,, ...	,,	J. Bayley ...	D
,,	,, ,,	,, ...	,,	J. Kelly ...	D

CASUALTY LIST—N.C.O.'S AND MEN—*continued*.

DATE.	PLACE.		RANK.	NAME.	SQUAD-RON.
12/2/00	Relief of Kimberley	wounded	Private	J. Prescott ...	D
15/2/00	,, ,,	died of wounds ...	,,	G. Golding ...	C
,,	,, ,,	wounded	,,	A. Bacon ...	C
,,	,, ,,	,, ...	,,	G. Dormer ...	D
16/2/00	Dronfield	,, ...	Sergeant	J. Blatchley ...	A
,,	,, ...	,, ...	Private	S. Moxon ...	C
,,	,, ...	,, ...	,,	C. Turnbull ...	C
,,	,, ...	,, ...	,,	J. Jeffers ...	A
,,	,, ...	,, ...	,,	J. Price ...	A
,,	,, ...	,, ...	,,	T. Caister ...	D
,,	,, ...	,, ...	Corporal	J. Foord ...	A
21/2/00	Paardeberg	,, ...	Private	A. Rowley ...	A
,,	,, ...	killed	,,	L. Turner ...	C
7/3/00	Poplar Grove ..	,, ...	L.-Corp.	J. Johns ...	C
,,	,, ,, ...	died of wounds ...	Private	H. Pyke ...	A
,,	,, ,,	wounded	Sergeant	F. Draper ...	D
,,	,, ,, ..	,, ...	Private	J. Reid ...	A
,,	,, ,, ...	,, ...	,,	A. Turner ...	C
,,	,, ,, ...	,, ...	,,	F. Clarke ...	C
,,	,, ,, ...	,, ...	Sergeant	G. Herrick ...	C
,,	,, ,, ...	,, ...	Private	J. Lavender ...	C
,,	,, ,, ...	,, ...	,,	G. Holben ...	C
,,	,, ,, ...	,, ...	,,	R. Morgan ...	C
,,	,. ,, ..	,, ...	,,	R. Thickpenny	C
,,	,, ,, ...	,, ...	,,	J. Ottley ...	C
,,	,, ,, ..	,, ...	,,	F. Ridewood ...	C
,,	,, ,, ...	,, ...	,,	A. Malthouse ...	C
10/3/00	Petrusberg	,, ...	,,	J. Ehus ...	A
25/3/00	Brandfort	,, ...	Sergeant	F. Andrews ...	C
,,	,, ...	,, ...	Private	— Brownrigg...	C
,,	,, ...	,, ...	L.-Corp.	T. Allin ...	C
,,	,, ...	,, ...	Private	J. Jones ...	C
,,	,, ...	missing (wounded and prisoner)	,,	J. Dawson ...	C
,,	,, ...	missing (prisoner)	,,	J. Warren ...	C
,,	,, ...	,, ,,	,,	F. Stevens ...	C
26/3/00	Klipfontein ...	wounded	,,	G. Hill ...	A
28/3/00	,, ...	missing (prisoner)	L.-Corp.	T. Lapworth ...	C
,,	,, ...	,, ,,	Private	G. Charlton ...	C
24/4/00	Rooi Kop	killed	,,	W. MacDonald	D
,,	,, ,, ...	,, ...	,,	H. Underwood	D
,,	,, ,, ...	d. of wounds, 27th	Sergeant	J. Gratton ...	D
,,	,, ,, ...	,, ,, 24th	Private	W. Lacey ...	D
,,	,, ,, ...	,, ,, 24th	,,	G. Hemming ...	D
,,	,, ,, ...	,, ,, 24th	,,	J. Scully ...	D

CASUALTY LIST—N.C.O.'S AND MEN—*continued.*

DATE.	PLACE.		RANK.	NAME.	SQUAD-RON.
24/4/00	Rooi Kop	d. of wounds, 26th	Private	A. Kerr ...	D
,,	,, ,, ...	wounded	Corporal	A. Holmes ...	D
,,	,, ,, ...	,, ...	Private	G. Twyford ...	D
,,	,, ,, ...	,, ...	,,	S. Taylor ...	D
,,	,, ,, ...	,, ...	,,	J. Kerr ...	D
,,	,, ,, ...	,, ...	,,	A. Hay ...	D
,,	,, ,, ...	,, ...	,,	W. Webber ...	D
,,	,, ,, ...	,, ...	,,	J. Elliott ...	D
,,	,, ,, ...	,, ...	,,	J. McCrea ...	D
,,	,, ,, ...	,, ...	,,	J. King ...	D
28/4/00	near Thaba'Nchu..	,, ...	R.S.M.	W. Grant ...	
,,	,, ,,	d. of wounds, 30th	Private	T. Crabtree ...	A
,,	,, ,,	prisonr. (wounded)	L.-Corp.	C. Henty ...	D
,,	,, ,,	prisoner	Private	P. Swaffer ...	D
,,	,, ,, ...	,, ...	,,	H. Hinchcliffe	D
,,	,, ,, ...	,, ...	,,	T. Griffiths ...	C
,,	,, ,, ...	,, ...	,,	P. Keon ...	A
,,	,, ,,	wounded	,,	A. Clegg ...	C
28/5/00	Viljoen's Drift ...	prisoner	,,	J. Greig ...	C
30/5/00	Elandsfontein ...	wounded	,,	J. Nixon ...	C
2/6/00	Orange Grove ...	killed	,,	T. Merryman ...	C
,,	,, ,, ...	wounded	Sergeant	J. Mercer ...	A
,,	,, ,, ...	,, ...	L.-Corp.	W. Joyce ...	C
,,	,, ,, ...	,, ...	Private	G. Lloyd ...	C
,,	,, ,, ...	,, ...	,,	H. Letts ...	D
,,	,, ,, ...	prisoner	,,	T. Leybourne...	C
3/6/00	near Pretoria ...	killed	,,	J. Briggs ...	C
28/6/00	Paarde Kraal ...	prisoner	,,	W. Loe ...	A
19/7/00	near Lindley ...	wounded	,,	J. Scully ...	C
,,	,, ,, ...	,, ...	,,	P. Martin ...	C
,,	,, ,, ...	,, ...	,,	S. Albert ...	C
,,	,, ,, ...	,, ...	,,	H. Sullivan ...	D
31/7/00	Kopje Aileen ...	prisoner	,,	W. Lanham ...	A
31/8/00	Quaggafontein ...	wounded	Sergeant	T. Atkins ...	D
,,	,, ...	,, ...	L.-Corp.	H. Cook ...	A
16/10/00	near Boschrand ...	,, ...	Private	G. Williams ...	A
17/10/00	Bethel	,, ...	,,	E. Brindle ...	A
18/10/00	Tweefontein ...	,, (by Brit-ish sentry)	,,	E. Stolle ...	C
22/10/00	Phillipolis ...	prisoner	,,	C. Cook ...	A*
,,	,, ...	,, ...	,,	L. FitzGerald...	A*
,,	,, ..	,, ...	,,	G. Scott ...	A*
,,	Johannesburg ...	wounded	,,	H. Webster ...	
30/10/00	Ventersberg ...	died of wounds ...	,,	S. Chapple ...	D
2/12/00	Slick Spruit ...	wounded	L.-Corp.	J. McCrea ...	D

* Detached.

CASUALTY LIST—N.C.O.'S AND MEN—*continuea.*

DATE.	PLACE.		RANK.	NAME.	SQUAD-RON.
2/12/00	Slick Spruit ...	wounded	Private	G. Pickford ...	D
3/12/00	,, ,, ...	,, ...	,,	H. Frisby ...	A
,,	,, ,, ...	,, ...	,,	A. Sear ...	A
,,	,, ,, ...	,, ...	L.-Sergt.	A. Creighton ...	C
,,	,, ,, ...	,, ...	Private	T. Heights ...	C
24/12/00	Gelegenfontein ..	,, ...	,,	C. Sarsfield ...	C
,,	,, ...	,, ...	Sergeant	W. Odell ...	C
,,	,, ...	,, ...	L.-Corp.	J. Burton ...	C
,,	,, ...	,, ...	Private	W. Armstrong	C
,,	,, ...	,, ...	,,	H. Bastine ...	C
1/1/01	near Lindley ...	,, ...	,,	H. Wilkinson	D
8/1/01	Doornkloof ...	,, ...	,,	W. White ...	A
27/1/01	Odendaalstroom ...	killed	,,	T. Griffiths ...	C
30/1/01	Thaba'Nchu ..	wounded	,,	H. Jeffries ...	D
17/3/01	Driefontein ...	,, ...	,,	J. Greig ...	C
17/4/01	Vaal Kop	killed	Sergeant	W. Hart ...	C
,,	,, ,, ...	,, ...	L.-Corp.	R. Heanes ...	C
,,	,, ,, ...	,, ...	Private	A. Banks ...	C
,,	,, ,, ...	,, ...	,,	E. Lavers ...	C
,,	,, ,, ...	d. of wounds, 19th	,,	P. Moody ...	C
,,	,, ,, ...	,, ,, 20th	,,	J. Cook ...	C
,,	,, ,, ...	wounded	,,	P. Botling ...	C
,,	,, ,, ...	,, ...	,,	A. Prior ...	C
,,	,, ,, ...	,, ...	,,	G. Elliott ...	C
,,	,, ,, ...	,, ...	,,	W. Philp ...	C
18/4/01	Edenburg	,, ...	,,	M. Donnelly ...	D
27/5/01	Ospoort	killed	,,	R. Winn ...	C
,,	,, ...	d. of wounds, 28th	,,	J. Ridge ...	C
,,	,, ...	,, ,, 28th	,,	C. Baker ...	C
,,	,, ...	,, ,, 9th J.	,,	C. Ward ...	C
,,	,, ...	,, ,, 29th	,,	T. Allen ...	C
,,	,, ...	wounded ... { Shoeing Smith	{ A. Hersey ...	C
,,	,, ...	,, ..	L.-Corp.	W. Murrant ...	C
,,	,, ...	,, ...	Private	J. Powers ...	C
28/6/01	Spytfontein ...	,, ...	L.-Corp.	W. Ferguson ...	C
,,	,, ...	,, ...	Private	F. Clinton ...	C
12/7/01	Camdeboo Mounts	,, ...	,,	— Potter ...	D
9/8/01	Wolverlei	killed	,,	G. Cooper ...	A
,,	,, ...	wounded	L.-Corp.	H. Hilliard ...	A
,,	,, ...	,, ...	Private	H. Howse ...	A
3/9/01	Low's Farm ...	,, ...	,,	H. Thorp ...	D
5/9/01	Bower's Hoek ...	killed	Sergeant	J. B. Mercer ...	A
,,	,, ,, ...	,, ...	L.-Corp.	W. J. Priest ...	A
,,	,, ,, ...	,, ...	Private	W. Vipond ...	A

DATE.	PLACE.		RANK.	NAME.	SQUAD-RON.
5/9/01	Bower's Hoek ...	killed	Private	H. Clifford ...	A
,,	,, ,, ...	,, ...	,,	W. Kennedy ...	A
,,	,, ,, ...	,, ...	,,	V. Ward ...	A
,,	,, ,, ...	,, ...	,,	A. Dodge ...	A
,,	,, ,, ...	wounded	,, .	W. Norbron ...	A
,,	,, ,, ...	,, ...	,,	F. King ...	A
,,	,, ,, ...	,, ...	,,	W. Ginn ...	A
,,	,, ,, ...	,, ...	,.	J. Power ...	A
,,	,, ,, ...	,, ...	L.-Corp.	W. Perkins ...	A
27/9/01	Leeuwfontein ...	killed	,,	W. Guy ...	C
25/2/02	Voetpads	wounded	Private	T. Ede ...	D
27/2/02	Geelbekfontein ...	,, ...	,,	— Pyke ...	A
1/3/02	Elandsfontein ...	,, ...	,,	G. Johnson ...	D
3/3/02	Visser's Farm ...	died of wounds ...	,,	A. Scott ...	D

TOTALS.

	Killed or Died of Wounds.	Wounded.	Prisoners.	Died of Disease or from Accident.
Officers	5	15	1	1
N.C.O.'s and Men ...	40	115	23	25

PERCENTAGES.

	Killed and Wounded.	Other Deaths.
Officers	52·5	2·5
N.C.O.'s and Men	19·7	2·7

COMPLETE LIST OF OFFICERS WHO SERVED WITH THE
REGIMENT DURING THE CAMPAIGN.

Lieut.-Col. B. Gough.
  ,,   ,,   M. O. Little.
Maj. S. W. Follett.
  ,,   F. F. Colvin.
  ,,   Hon. C. H. Willoughby.
  ,,   F. T. Lund.
Capt. Lord D. Compton.
  ,,   H. W. Stanley.
  ,,   H. E. Fiennes.
  ,,   R. Ellison.
  ,,   E. R. Gordon.
  ,,   D. G. M. Campbell.
  ,,   F. H. Allhusen.
Capt. and Adjt. E. F. Bell.
Capt. V. R. Brooke.
  ,,   G. H. Skeffington Smyth.
Lieut. T. M. Kincaid-Smith.
  ,,   J. G. Stirling.
  ,,   H. M. Durand.
  ,,   Hon. D. M. P. Carleton.

Lieut. E. H. Abadie.
  ,,   Lord F. Blackwood.
  ,,   F. S. H. Cavendish.
  ,,   S. R. Theobald.
  ,,   J. S. Duckett.
  ,,   J. F. Pollok.
  ,,   L. Sadleir-Jackson.
  ,,   P. Brassey.
  ,,   R. V. Wynn.
  ,,   A. S. Trower.
  ,,   Earl of Leitrim.
  ,,   Hon. A. Macdonald.
2nd Lieut. R. S. Chadwick.
  ,,   ,,   D. K. Lucas-Tooth.
  ,,   ,,   G. M. Neilson.
  ,,   ,,   R. H. Brocklebank.
  ,,   ,,   H. F. Wood.
  ,,   ,,   Earl of Rocksavage.
  ,,   ,,   Hon. R. B. Cole.
Lieut. and Quar.-Master D. Laing.

Capts. Lord Charles Bentinck and D. J. E. Beale-Browne also served
during the campaign with other commands.

Capt. J. V. Forrest, R.A.M.C., and Civil Vet.-Surg. H. Phelan were
attached to the Regiment throughout the campaign.

CASUALTY LIST.

OFFICERS.

Killed :—

2nd Lieut. P. Brassey	....	Dronfield	Feb. 16th, 1900.
,, ,, The Hon. A. Macdonald.		Vaalkop........	April 17th, 1901.

Died of Wounds :—

Capt. H. W. Stanley..........	.....	Rooikop	April 28th, 1900.
Lieut. S. R. Theobald	....	Wolve Vlei	Aug. 12th, 1901.
2nd Lieut. J. F. Pollok	....	Orange Grove	June 3rd, 1900.

Died of Disease :—

Capt. R. Ellison	....	Kroonstad............	June 6th, 1900.

Wounded :—

Lieut.-Col. M. O. Little	....	Zeerust	Aug. 24th, 1900.
Capt. E. R. Gordon	....	Dronfield	Feb. 16th, 1900.
,, D. G. M. Campbell	....	Paardeberg	Feb. 21st, 1900.
,, Lord C. Bentinck	....	Mafeking (Siege) ..	April 24th, 1900.

CASUALTY LIST—OFFICERS—*continued.*

Wounded :—

Lieut. V. R. Brooke ...	....	Rooikop	April 24th, 1900.
,, G. H. Skeffington Smyth	......	Quaggafontein	Aug. 31st, 1900.
,, J. G. Stirling .... }		Enslin	Nov. 26th, 1899.
,, ,, ,, ... }		Slick Spruit.........	Dec. 2nd, 1900.
,, H. M. Durand .... }		Dronfield	Feb. 16th, 1900.
,, ,, ,, ... }		Orange Grove	June 2nd, 1900.
,, Lord F. Blackwood		Near Burghersdorp	Dec. 24th, 1900.
,, F. Cavendish		Koodoosberg Drift	Feb. 5th, 1900.
2nd Lieut. S. R. Theobald		Slick Spruit	Dec. 2nd, 1900.
,, ,, L. Sadleir-Jackson		Orange Grove	June 2nd, 1900.
,, ,, R. S. Chadwick		Leeuwfontein	Sept. 27th, 1900.

Taken Prisoner :—

2nd Lieut. S. R. Theobald .... Thaba'Nchu......... April 28th, 1900.

DIED OF DISEASE.

Date.	Place.	Rank.	Name.	Squadron.
	Durban	Pte.	Stewart	C
	Cape Town......	,, ...	Board	A
	Modder River	,, ...	Donoghue	D
	Wynberg	,, ...	Watson	C
	,, ...	,, ...	Charlton	D
	Orange River...	Corp.......... ..	Wilkins	C
	Wynberg	Lance-Corp. ...	Winterbottom...	C
	Kimberley	Pte.	Richardson	A
	Bloemfontein...	Lance-Corp....	Bence	A
	Pretoria	Pte.	Norman	C
	Bloemfontein...	,, ...	Knight............	D
	,, ...	,, ...	Innis	D
	Kroonstadt	,, ...	Bacon	C
	Johannesburg...	Lance-Corp....	Gower............	A
	Mafeking	Pte.	Wilson*	D
	Bloemfontein...	Pte.	Dever	D
	Aliwal North ..	,, ...	Brown	C
	Thaba'Nchu ...	,, ...	Pentlow	C
	Cradock	,, ...	Bathgate	D
	Naauwpoort ...	,, ...	Stone	C
	Aberdeen	,, ...	Burrowes	D
	O.R. Colony...	,, ...	Dale†	A
	Springfontein	Pte.	Randoll	A
	Mooi River ...	,, ...	Buckley	A
	Kimberley	,, ...	Clarke...	C

* Accidentally killed in storm.

† Killed in railway accident.

RECORD OF SERVICE OF THE REGIMENT.

The 9th Lancers served in the South African War from 1899—1902, and were present at—

The Advance on Kimberley, including actions at BELMONT (Nov. 23rd, 1899), ENSLIN (Nov. 25th, 1899), MODDER RIVER (Nov. 28th, 1899), and MAGERSFONTEIN (Dec. 11th, 1899).

The Relief of KIMBERLEY.

Operations in the Orange Free State (Feb. to May, 1900), including operations at PAARDEBERG (Feb. 17th to 26th), actions at POPLAR GROVE (March 7th), KAREE SIDING (March 29th), HOUTNEK (Thaba'Nchu) (May 1st), and ZAND RIVER (May 10th).

Operations in the Transvaal in May and June, including actions near JOHANNESBURG (May 29th), PRETORIA (June 4th), and DIAMOND HILL (June 11th and 12th).

Operations in the Transvaal, West of Pretoria (July to Nov. 29th, 1900), including action at ELAND'S RIVER.

Operations in Orange River Colony (May to Nov. 29th, 1900), including actions at WITTEBERGEN (July 1st to 8th), CALEDON RIVER (Nov. 27th to 29th, 1900).

———

CLASPS gained by the Regiment as a whole :—

Queen's Medal :—

> BELMONT.
> MODDER RIVER.
> RELIEF OF KIMBERLEY.
> PAARDEBERG.
> JOHANNESBURG.
> DIAMOND HILL.
> WITTEBERGEN.

King's Medal :—

> " 1901."
> " 1902."

MENTIONED IN DESPATCHES.

Lord Methuen's despatch, February 15th, 1900.

MAGERSFONTEIN—

> Major Little, in the firing line, did good work all day.
> Lieut. Allhusen did good work with Maxim.

Lord Roberts' recommendations in despatch, March 31st, 1900.

3rd Cavalry Brigade .... 9th Lancers.

> Major (local Lieut.-Colonel) M. O. Little.
> Lieut Lord F. Blackwood.
> 2nd Lieut. L. Sadleir-Jackson.
> Corpl. C. Wilson.
> „   C. Green.
> „   T. Mitchell.
> Ptes. C. Stanford and T. Holman.

From despatch of Major-General Baden-Powell, June 6th, 1900.

> Lieut. Lord C. Bentinck, good service in action.

Lord Roberts' despatch, April 2nd, 1901. For Meritorious Services.

Lieutenants—

> Lieut. V. R. Brooke, 9th Lancers.
> „   D. K. Tooth, N.S.W.M.R. (now 2nd Lieut. 9th Lancers).

Lord Roberts' despatch, September 4th, 1901.

Staff—

> Lieut. E. H. Abadie (9th Lancers).
> „   L. Sadleir-Jackson (9th Lancers).

9th Lancers—

> Majors F. F. Colvin, Hon. C. H. Willoughby.
> Captains F. T. Lund, Lord D. Compton, E. R. Gordon, D. G. M. Campbell.
> Lieuts. G. Skeffington Smyth, H. M. Durand, Lord F. Blackwood.
> Regt. Sergt.-Major (now Q.M. and Hon. Lieut.) W. Grant.

MENTIONED IN DESPATCHES—*continued.*

S.S.M. C. Wardell, R. Gidden.

S.Q.M.S. D. Ankers, L. C. Bell.

Sergts. J. Mercer, R. J. Mason, F. Andrews, T. M. Smith, G. Casebow.

Ptes. S. Albert, S. Taylor.

Lord Kitchener's despatch, March 8th, 1901.

  9th Lancers—

Ptes. W. Leutchford, S. Vincent.

Despatch, July 28th, 1901.

  9th Lancers—

Lieut. J. G. Stirling, at Twyfelfontein, O.R.C., May 27th, for coolness in action and for returning to fetch a dismounted man; has lost one arm and been wounded in the other during campaign.

Despatch, October 8th, 1901.

  9th Lancers—

Capt. Lord D. Compton.

Lieuts. R. V. Wynn, G. M. Neilson. For marked gallantry in capture of Lotter's commando near Petrusberg, Cape Colony, Sept. 5th.

Also—

Sergts. Cook, Beckett, Mason.

Corpl. Pearson.

Ptes. Willcox, Capon.

Despatch, December 8th, 1901.

  9th Lancers—

Lieut. S. R. Theobald (died of wounds), for exceedingly gallant conduct on several occasions with Col. Scobell's Column in Cape Colony.

Lieut. L. Sadleir-Jackson, D.S.O., gallantry on several occasions.

Pte. J. Bradfield, for several instances of gallantry whilst with Col. Scobell's Column.

Pte. R. Belsey, for very good work with Maxim gun with same Column.

Lord Roberts' final despatch, March 1st, 1902.

9th *Lancers—*

Lieut. J. G. Stirling (since deceased).

Lord Kitchener's final despatch, June 23rd, 1902.

Brevet-Colonel (local Brig.-Gen.) M. O. Little has twice held command of British Cavalry Brigades, and has proved himself a capable leader of mounted troops in the field.

9th *Lancers—*

Bt.-Lieut.-Col. F. F. Colvin.

Major S. W. Follett.

Capts. E. F. Bell, V. R. Brooke, D.S.O.

S.S.M. G. Drury.

Trumpeter J. W. Pelter.

Ptes. J. Whitton, S. Vincent.

Sergt. Andrews (local R.S.M., 2nd Battn. I.Y.)

HONOURS AND PROMOTIONS.

OFFICERS.

Awarded Distinguished Service Order :—

Lieut. Lord F. Blackwood.

   ,,   V. R. Brooke.

   ,,   L. Sadleir-Jackson.

   ,,   H. E. Abadie.

   ,,   G. Skeffington Smyth.

   .,   J. G. Stirling (since deceased).

Promotions :—

Lieut.-Colonel M. O. Little to be Brevet-Colonel.			
Major F. F. Colvin	,,	,,	Lieut.-Colonel.
Capt. F. T. Lund	,,	,,	Major.
,, Lord C Bentinck	,,	,,	,,
,, ,, D. Compton	,,	,,	,,
Bt.-Major F. T. Lund	,,	,,	Lieut.-Colonel.
Major S. W. Follett	,,	,,	,,
Capt. D. G. M. Campbell	,,	,,	Major.

HONOURS AND PROMOTIONS—*continued.*
N.C O.'S AND MEN.

Awarded Distinguished Conduct Medal :—
  Regt. Sergt.-Major W. Grant.
  S.S.-M.s R. Gidden, G. Drury.
  Sergts. F. Andrews, F. Beckett, H. C. Cook, R. J. Mason, J. Mercer.
  Pte. S. Albert.
Clasp to D. C. Medal :—
  Sergt. F. Andrews.
Promoted by the Commander-in-Chief :—
  Corporal Pearson to be Sergeant.
  Pte. Willcox   „   Corporal.
   „ Capon   ,,   ,,

DISTANCES COVERED DURING THE CAMPAIGN.

	1899.	1900.	1901.	1902.
January	—	118	388	389
February	—	194	397	428
March	—	178	277	128
April	—	152	393	
May	—	313	275	
June	—	201	248	
July	—	343	310	
August	—	363	481	
September	—	159	366	
October	—	303	464	
November	141	314	347	
December	—	427	433	
Totals........	141	3,065	4,379	945

Grand total, 8,530 miles.

Where not accurately known, most of the daily distances have, if anything, been underestimated. No account has been taken of ground covered during fighting, farm clearing, independent reconnaissances, etc., except that covered by the transport from camp to camp.

www.ingramcontent.com/pod-product-compliance
Lightning Source LLC
Chambersburg PA
CBHW030935150426
42812CB00064B/2879/J